NEW ACCENTS

General editor: TERENCE HAWKES

Criticism in
Society

IN THE SAME SERIES

Criticism in Society

Interviews with Jacques Derrida, Northrop Frye,
Harold Bloom, Geoffrey Hartman, Frank Kermode,
Edward Said, Barbara Johnson, Frank Lentricchia,
and J. Hillis Miller

IMRE SALUSINSZKY

METHUEN
New York and London

First published in 1987 by
Methuen, Inc.
29 West 35th Street, New York
NY 10001

Published in Great Britain by
Methuen & Co. Ltd
11 New Fetter Lane, London
EC4P 4EE

Filmset by Mayhew Typesetting,
Bristol, England
Printed in Great Britain by
Richard Clay Ltd, Bungay, Suffolk

*Library of Congress Cataloging in
Publication Data*
Criticism in society.
  (New accents)
  Bibliography: p.
  1. Criticism. 2. Literature and
society. 3. Critics – Interviews. I.
Derrida, Jacques. II. Salusinszky,
Imre, 1955– . III. Series:
New accents (Methuen & Co.)
PN98.S6S7 1987   801'.95   86-32641
ISBN 0 416 92270 8
    0 416 92280 5 (pbk.)

*British Library Cataloguing in Publication
Data*
Salusinszky, Imre
  Criticism in society: interviews with
  Jacques Derrida, Northrop Frye,
  Harold Bloom, Geoffrey Hartman,
  Frank Kermode, Edward Said,
  Barbara Johnson, Frank Lentricchia,
  J. Hillis Miller. – (New accents)
  1. Criticism
  801'.95   PN81
  ISBN 0 416 92270 8
      0 416 92280 5 (pbk.)

For Karen

Contents

General editor's preface

It is easy to see that we are living in a time of rapid and radical social change. It is much less easy to grasp the fact that such change will inevitably affect the nature of those disciplines that both reflect our society and help to shape it.

Yet this is nowhere more apparent than in the central field of what may, in general terms, be called literary studies. Here, among large numbers of students at all levels of education, the erosion of the assumptions and presuppositions that support the literary disciplines in their conventional form has proved fundamental. Modes and categories inherited from the past no longer seem to fit the reality experienced by a new generation.

New Accents is intended as a positive response to the initiative offered by such a situation. Each volume in the series will seek to encourage rather than resist the process of change; to stretch rather than reinforce the boundaries that currently define literature and its academic study.

Some important areas of interest immediately present themselves. In various parts of the world, new methods of analysis have been developed whose conclusions reveal the limitations of the Anglo-American outlook we inherit. New concepts of literary forms and modes have been proposed; new notions of the nature of literature itself and of how it communicates are current; new views of literature's role in relation to society flourish. *New Accents* will aim to expound and comment upon the most notable of these.

In the broad field of the study of human communication, more and more emphasis has been placed upon the nature and function of the new electronic media. *New Accents* will try to identify and discuss the challenge these offer to our traditional modes of critical response.

The same interest in communication suggests that the series should also concern itself with those wider anthropological and sociological areas of investigation which have begun to involve scrutiny of the nature of art itself and its relation to our whole way of life. And this will ultimately require attention to be focused on some of those activities which in our society have hitherto been excluded from the prestigious realms of Culture. The disturbing realignment of values involved and the disconcerting nature of the pressures that work to bring it about both constitute areas that *New Accents* will seek to explore.

Finally, as its title suggests, one aspect of *New Accents* will be firmly located in contemporary approaches to language, and a continuing concern of the series will be to examine the extent to which relevant branches of linguistic studies can illuminate specific literary areas. The volumes with this particular interest will nevertheless presume no prior technical knowledge on the part of their readers, and will aim to rehearse the linguistics appropriate to the matter in hand, rather than to embark on general theoretical matters.

Each volume in the series will attempt an objective exposition of significant developments in its field up to the present as well as an account of its author's views of the matter. Each will culminate in an informative bibliography as a guide to further study. And, while each will be primarily concerned with matters relevant to its own specific interests, we can hope that a kind of conversation will be heard to develop between them; one whose accents may perhaps suggest the distinctive discourse of the future.

TERENCE HAWKES

Acknowledgments

The interview with Jacques Derrida was first published in *Southern Review* (Adelaide); the interview with Harold Bloom was first published in *Scripsi* (Melbourne).

"Not Ideas about the Thing but the Thing Itself," copyright 1954, by Wallace Stevens is reprinted from *The Collected Poems of Wallace Stevens* by permission of Alfred A. Knopf, Inc. and Faber and Faber Ltd.

I would like to thank the Australian–American Educational Foundation for a Fulbright Fellowship, which allowed me to study and teach at Yale for eighteen months, and without which none of these interviews could have been recorded.

Not Ideas about the Thing but the Thing Itself

At the earliest ending of winter,
In March, a scrawny cry from outside
Seemed like a sound in his mind.

He knew that he heard it,
A bird's cry, at daylight or before,
In the early March wind.

The sun was rising at six,
No longer a battered panache above snow . . .
It would have been outside.

It was not from the vast ventriloquism
Of sleep's faded papier-mâché . . .
The sun was coming from outside.

That scrawny cry – it was
A chorister whose c preceded the choir.
It was part of the colossal sun,

Surrounded by its choral rings,
Still far away. It was like
A new knowledge of reality.

Wallace Stevens

Introduction

Literary criticism, if it is a discipline, is surely that discipline which
has been most exclusively concerned with the question of its own
function. The main subject within criticism seems always to have
been "The Function of Criticism," and one could construct a brief
history of the field simply by tracing the sequence of major essays
bearing that title. Such a study would suggest that the sense, within
criticism, of its own importance has, up to a certain point, risen in
direct proportion to the cultural marginalization – or professionalization – of criticism as a whole.

The early history of these essays is the attempt to separate criticism
off from the art that it deals with, generally with unhappy consequences for criticism. In Matthew Arnold's "Function of Criticism
at the Present Time," published in 1864, criticism turns out to be
a rather furtive and secondary activity, for all of the grand language
associated with it. The function of criticism is "simply to know the
best that is known and thought in the world": in other words, it is
a kind of eavesdropping, knowing what other people *already* know and
think. This, of course, separates critics from those who do the
properly original thinking, the artists themselves. Everybody would
admit, says Arnold, "that the critical faculty is lower than the inventive," and that the "critical power is of lower rank than the
creative." It is true that criticism is invested by Arnold with vague
powers of cultural renovation, but these powers are so indirect as
almost to comprise a series of absences or reservations; they are a
curious combination of foreword and afterword. In relation to art
itself, criticism is preparatory: it cultivates the right atmosphere for
epochs of real creative achievement, those epochs comprising "the
promised land, towards which criticism can only beckon." The true

calling of the critic lies "in preparing for it, in rendering it possible."
But while, in relation to art, criticism is defined as pre-creative, in
relation to wider cultural and historical forces it is defined as a kind
of afterbirth. Towards these forces, criticism must remain "disinterested," which is why it does its work best during low-fronts of
political pressure. Criticism can only occur *after* what Arnold calls
"epochs of concentration," when "all danger of hostile forcible
pressure of foreign ideas upon our practice has long disappeared,"
and when we have already achieved "our railways, our business, and
our fortune-making." So the moment of criticism is always *between*
epochs; a transitory moment. At such times, "like the traveller in the
fable . . . we begin to wear our cloak a little more loosely."[1]
Criticism is presumably what occurs in the folds and flappings of that
cultural cloak.

Writing more than half a century later, T.S. Eliot takes strong
exception to Arnold's distinction between criticism and art, but more
with a view towards deconstructing the opposition than towards
elevating criticism. Arnold, says Eliot in *his* "Function of Criticism,"
"distinguishes far too bluntly . . . between the two activities: he
overlooks the capital importance of criticism in the work of creation
itself." This criticism *within* literature is the artist's secondary work,
that "frightful toil" of "sifting, combining, constructing, expung-
ing, correcting, testing." Although frightful, the toil is crucial, since
it turns out that criticism is precisely that *preventative* quality which,
within literature, saves it from collapsing into the indulgences of
romanticism. For this reason, Eliot believes that "the criticism
employed by a trained and skilled writer on his own work is the most
vital, the highest kind of criticism." What morsel, then, is left to the
critic proper? The sado-masochistic imagery which pervades Eliot's
poetry is not absent from his essays: he says that the monuments of
literature form an "ideal order," that the problem of criticism is thus
"a problem of order," and that the critic's task is "quite clearly cut
out for him" in "the elucidation of works of art and the correction
of taste." Arnold was the school inspector, but it is Eliot who wants
to turn criticism into a kind of inspectorate, complaining that it is not
yet "a simple and orderly field of beneficent activity, from which
imposters can be readily ejected" but simply "a Sunday park of
contending and contentious orators." Critics would be best advised
to concern themselves with *facts*, since "a fact even of the lowest order
about a work of art is a better piece of work than nine-tenths of the
most pretentious critical journalism, in journals or in books."

---

1 "The Function of Criticism at the Present Time," in R.H. Super (ed.), *Lectures and Essays in
Criticism* (Ann Arbor: University of Michigan Press, 1962), pp. 270, 259, 260, 285, 269.

Goethe and Coleridge are among those ticked off by Eliot for ignoring this fact about facts, and for thus helping to create "a vicious taste for reading about works of art instead of reading the works themselves."[2]

Eliot says that criticism is a problem of order, but he doesn't say much *about* that order. The pre-history of modern literary criticism draws to a close in 1949 with Northrop Frye's essay "The Function of Criticism at the Present Time." For Frye, the critic is not a fact-gatherer, but ideally "the pioneer of education and the shaper of cultural tradition." Eliot was among the last "men of letters"; with Frye, we enter the critical modern age, the era of the total professionalization of literary criticism in the university. Frye declares openly that criticism – the field to which the pioneer and shaper contributes – is "clearly a social science." Against Eliot, he claims that critics have been too concerned with individual facts about literature, leaving criticism in a state of what he calls "naive induction," like those primitive sciences which "come immediately in contact with phenomena and take the things to be explained as their immediate data." Criticism should instead take an "inductive leap" and move towards the "total comprehension" of literature by seeing its masterpieces as "phenomena to be explained in terms of a conceptual framework which criticism alone possesses." Literature, from this new perspective, comes to be seen as a "verbal universe, as forms integrated within a total form." The investigation of these forms, within the university, can proceed in an orderly, objective and progressive manner: Frye views most earlier critical arguments as mere pseudo-debates, and both Eliot and Arnold are, for him, among the contentious Sunday orators. Once criticism has embarked upon its proper work of investigating the generic forms and categories of the verbal universe, specific projects within criticism will lose their arbitrary quality. Frye complains about the set-up in 1949:

> Asked what he is working on, the critic will invariably say that he is working on Donne, or Shelley's thought, or the period from 1640 to 1660, or give some other answer which implies that history, or philosophy, or literature itself, constitutes the structural basis of criticism. It would never occur to any critic to say, for instance, "I am working on the theory of genres."[3]

Asked what he was working on today, a critic would be more likely to say "the theory of genres" than "the period from 1640 to 1660,"

2 "The Function of Criticism," in *Selected Essays* (London: Faber & Faber, 1951), pp. 30, 23, 24, 25, 33.
3 "The Function of Criticism at the Present Time," *University of Toronto Quarterly*, 19 (1949), 1, 6, 8, 16, 9.

which only shows how much things have changed since 1949: and they have changed largely because of Frye.

But, just at the point when criticism seems finally to have established itself as an independent study with its own "conceptual framework," Terry Eagleton and others want to turn the wheelbarrow over, and seem to have good reasons for doing so. Criticism today, according to Eagleton, "lacks all substantive social function," and in *The Function of Criticism*, published in 1984, he views the entire movement from Arnold to Frye, not as the growth of an independent criticism, but as the final episode in its "effective demise as a socially active force." Eagleton takes a different sort of leap from Frye's, a leap backwards, beyond Arnold, to the days of the *Tatler* and *Spectator*. He looks back nostalgically to the pre-institutional infancy of criticism, in the "public sphere" of the eighteenth century:

> Literary criticism as a whole, at this point, is not yet an autonomous specialist discourse, even though more technical forms of it exist; it is rather one sector of a general ethical humanism, indissociable from moral, cultural and religious reflection. The *Tatler* and *Spectator* are projects of a bourgeois cultural politics whose capacious, blandly homogenizing language is able to encompass art, ethics, religion, philosophy, and everyday life; there is here no question of a "literary critical" response which is not wholly determined by an entire social and cultural ideology.

According to Eagleton, Arnold's myth of "disinterestedness" represents nothing but the withdrawal of criticism from the public sphere, and hence its voluntary demise as a social force of any consequence. Arnold's "disinterestedness" is still going strong in Frye's transcendentalism, and reaches its height, according to Eagleton, in the total withdrawal of literary criticism into the universities:

> The academicization of criticism provided it with an institutional basis and professional structure; but by the same token it signalled its final sequestration from the public realm. Criticism achieved security by committing political suicide.

The university, according to Eagleton, is "an institution which permits the critic's voice to be 'disinterested' to the precise extent that it is effectively inaudible to society as a whole."[4]

Eagleton's attack upon the myth of disinterestedness, as a mere tacit support for bourgeois hegemony, contains a certain irony, of course,

4 *The Function of Criticism* (London: Verso, 1984), pp. 7, 65, 18, 66.

in that it is precisely the myth of the university's ideological immunity which has allowed it to become much more widely and genuinely politically representative than any other state institution. If the myth of disinterestedness ever crumbles, those who agree with Eagleton may well be among the first to suffer, since in terms of allowing a voice to Marxism our universities would soon achieve parity with our parliaments.

Nevertheless, with Marxists and Foucauldians telling us that the perpetual ideological virginity of criticism is a dangerous myth, with deconstructors returning to an Eliotic sense of criticism as continuous with or contained by literature, and with more pragmatic voices claiming that an overall theory of criticism is philosophically untenable anyway, it has been easy lately to become obsessed, all over again, with the whole question of the function of criticism and its social and institutional contexts. And, since the best thing to do with one's obsessions is always to foist them upon unwilling strangers, it seemed a good time to go around and put questions about the function of criticism to people who might be expected to provide some interesting answers. Of course, no critic thinks about the function of criticism without thinking about the function of his or her *own* criticism, so the questions soon broadened into discussions of how each critic's own ideas had developed and been formed.

As well as being largely about the function of criticism, these interviews are themselves a set of critical functions, in the sense of "social or festive meetings conducted with ceremony" (*Oxford English Dictionary*). And as well as being about "criticism in society," the interviews are *examples* of criticism in society: that is, criticism performed as a group. This effect has been achieved in two ways. First, all of the critics (with the exception of Derrida) have been asked to comment on the same poem, Wallace Stevens's "Not Ideas about the Thing but the Thing Itself" (the epigraph to the book), with a view to showing up some of the practical consequences of different theoretical positions. Second, and more importantly, each interviewee was shown all of the previous interviews in the series, and invited to insert his or her own voice into dialogue with them (hence, logically, the interviews are printed in the order in which they were conducted). This device has, I hope, helped to make this a book of interviews, rather than simply a set of interviews thrown together as a book.

Since I cannot emulate John Haffenden's skills as an interviewer, I will simply plagiarize something he says in his Introduction to *Novelists in Interview* (London, Methuen, 1985): no "critical inference" should be drawn either from the different lengths of the interviews, or from the fact that some highly influential North

American critics are not included at all. These things are the mere accidents of time and circumstance. In addition, the device mentioned a moment ago – of inviting each critic to read and comment upon the earlier texts – has created a natural "snowball" effect in the length of the later pieces.

In order for a project like this one to succeed, it was necessary for the interviewer to possess two important and stringent qualifications. First, since the purview of the book is North American, the interviewer had *not* to be an American, so as to avoid any suggestion of an investment in local professional disputes. Second, the interviewer had to be a complete unknown, in order to be able to become a transparent cipher for the thoughts of the famous interviewees.

Stringent as these qualifications are, I must in all modesty claim them for myself. Tough as they are, though, anybody would have greatly enjoyed doing the job. I am grateful to *Criticism in Society* on many scores, not least because it has brought me the friendship and counsel of Janice Price and Terry Hawkes. Above all, I am grateful to the book because it has served as a convenient excuse to talk to these nine writers. Regarding my deeper thoughts on that subject, I will leave the final words to my friend Gerald Murnane, from his extraordinary novel, *The Plains* (Harmondsworth, Penguin, 1984):

> But one of the townsmen who followed the publisher into the inner lounge had come back whispering that his future was assured. He was a young man previously unable to earn a living from his specialized interests. He had studied the history of furnishings, fabrics and interior design in the great homes of the plains. Most of his research has been done in museums and libraries but he had recently arrived at a theory that he could test only by visiting some mansion where the tastes and preferences of several generations were all evident under the one roof. . . . The young man explained his theory to the landowners soon after midnight. He had proposed it hesitantly and reminded them that it could only be verified after months of research in great homes of every district of the plains. But the landowners were delighted with it. . . . All but one of the landowners sent for supplies of paper and pencils and sat down among the ashtrays and glasses and empty bottles to plot the coloured lines that might reveal unguessed-at harmonies beneath the seeming confusion of a century and a half of impulsiveness and eccentricity. They soon agreed that each colour should denote the same cultural vector in each of their charts. And they referred all doubtful points to the young man for his ruling. But even so, the variety of patterns that appeared was remarkable. . . . The next hours, so the young man told me afterwards, were the most rewarding of his life.

Jacques Derrida

1
Jacques Derrida

"I would say that deconstruction is affirmation rather than questioning, in a sense which is not positive: I would distinguish between the positive, or positions, and affirmations. I think that deconstruction is affirmative rather than questioning; this affirmation goes *through* some radical questioning, but is not questioning in the final analysis."

Jacques Derrida teaches philosophy at the Ecole Normale Supérieure, in Paris, as well as a course each spring in the Department of Comparative Literature at Yale. He was born in Algiers in 1930, and first went to France for military service. Derrida's enormous influence on the course of literary studies in the United States began to be felt in the early and middle 1970s, with the appearance in English of three books which had been published in French in 1968: *Speech and Phenomena, Writing and Difference*, and *Of Grammatology*.

In 1966, Derrida had been invited to a now-famous conference at Johns Hopkins University, in Baltimore, which was intended to introduce structuralism to the American university intelligentsia. In fact, and primarily in the person of Derrida himself, the conference was announcing not the advent of structuralism, but its demise. Derrida's impact on literary studies – we cannot even begin to summarize here his broader *philosophical* contribution – has been through a mode of reading he inaugurated as "deconstruction," which has become the major strand in the wider intellectual movement referred to as "*post*structuralism." Derrida's paper at the Johns Hopkins conference was a critique of the notion of "structure" in the structuralist anthropology of Claude Lévi-Strauss. The paper depicts structuralism as the latest moment in a long succession of philosophical structuralities, and as the latest one willingly to "neutralize" or "reduce" itself by referring its entire structure to a point of presence, or fixed origin, or center:

> The function of this center was not only to orient, balance, and organize the structure – one cannot in fact conceive of an unorganized structure – but above all to make sure that the organizing principle of the structure would limit what we might call the *play* of the structure. By orienting and organizing the coherence of the system, the center of a structure permits the play of its elements inside the total form. And even today the notion of a structure lacking any center represents the unthinkable itself.
>
> (*Writing and Difference*, pp. 278–9)[1]

Derrida reads the history of philosophy as the genealogy of such stabilizing centers or godly "transcendental signifieds," and he calls this history the "metaphysics of presence," or "logocentrism."

Thinking the "unthinkable itself" involves thinking through and beyond dialectic, and this gesture is amply illustrated in Derrida's treatment of the other cardinal concept of structuralism, that of the sign. In structuralist or Saussurean linguistic theory, language is a synchronic system of signs, these signs being constituted out of the unity of a signifier (the sensible, audible, or material aspect) and a signified (the intelligible concept or meaning). Signs are arbitrary and conventional, in that they are defined by relation rather than essence – so that the sign "dog," for example, is constituted not out of any direct connection with a canine quadruped, but rather by virtue of its *not* being "log" or "hog" or "bog." Derrida takes this notion of a differential relation *between* signs and reinscribes it *within* them. The stability of the opposition between signifier and signified, which serves to unite the sign, cannot be maintained unless we are willing once again to accede to some version of a theological or philosophical "transcendental signified" which would arrest the *play* of significations. Derrida's critique forces us to recognize that every signified is also in the position of a signifier, and so does not function to anchor the sign securely in any extra-linguistic reality. How, after all, are we supposed to gain access to a pure, pre-linguistic signified? We cannot explain what any sign or text "means" without producing another text – that is, a parallel set of signifiers. Signs differ not only from each other, but also from themselves, and their nature consists neither in essence *nor* in relational difference, but in displacement or *trace* – the trace left by a chain of infinite and

1 Where references are given in parentheses, a full citation may be found in the selected bibliography.

unstable re-signification. The notion of the trace marks the presence of the sign with an absence in the form of internal difference and deferral – the infinite deferral of any final meaning. This has led Derrida to his famous neologism: *différance*, or the effect by which an opposition reproduces itself inside each of its constituent terms. The word, in French, is suspended between "to differ" and "to defer," and involves the idea that meaning is *always* deferred, as there is always one more supplement to be assimilated into it.

Wherever Derrida comes across a binary opposition, he treats it in much the same way as he treats the signifier/signified opposition. The most famous and important example is his treatment in the *Grammatology* of the traditional opposition between speech and writing – an opposition which, since the *Phaedrus*, has been consistently used to privilege speech *over* writing. Once again, Derrida undoes the opposition, not by reversing or abolishing it, but by showing that it cannot be sustained *as an opposition*. Writing, in its exteriority and secondarity, is in precisely the position of the signifier in the signifier/signified pair. But we will find speech constantly turning into an aspect or species of writing, in the same way as every signified becomes another signifier the moment we turn our backs on it; and the relaxation of surveillance which permits this reversal to occur takes place constantly *in those very texts* which most want to privilege speech over writing.

If we are looking for parallels to this skeptical side of Derrida's work in recent British thought, we need look no further than – strange as it may sound – the work of A. J. Ayer. Ayer's analysis of metaphysical statements *as* statements, and his eventual conclusion that they are in fact non-statements about nothing – containing an absence in place of an object – is strictly proto-deconstructive. Ayer proceeds to distinguish stringently between empirical or verifiable knowledge and metaphysics. The properly deconstructive extension of his point might be to ask questions about the status of a system of knowledge founded upon its opposition to an absence, and to ask whether that absence might not infect the entire opposition, rather than simply one of its terms.

The fascination of Derrida's texts is in large measure a function of the fact that he is himself a product of the deductive-analytical philosophic tradition of which his work is such a powerful critique. In this affiliation – and in this alone – he may be compared with Northrop Frye. The greatest texts of this tradition always fascinate and influence, because they hold out to us the promise that we may discover really important things about the world by meditating on the meaning of very simple words. In Plato, these are words like "piety" and "good"; in Frye, they tend to be the traditional terms of literary criticism – words like "comedy," "symbol" and "image"; in Derrida, they are words as simple as "writing," "supplement" and "difference." Derrida has himself remarked on the fact that those who seek to destroy metaphysics, like Nietzsche and Heidegger, are "trapped in a kind of circle," which describes the "form of the relation between the history of metaphysics and the history of the destruction of metaphysics" (*Writing and Difference*, p. 280). In the difference between wanting to "destroy" metaphysics and wanting to "deconstruct" it there is inscribed one's *awareness*, at least, of borrowing all of one's resources from that which one seeks to undo. But I still don't know that Derrida would want to deny being inside that "circle," or being the latest – though not the last – "last Platonist."

Whatever the source of Derrida's influence, it has affected literary studies in countless ways. For example, there has been an increased interest in all of those things which a text seems *not* to want to say, or to say only quickly or marginally: these are often the points from which a "deconstruction" of the text can proceed. But Derrida's way of showing how hopelessly the two sides of a binary opposition will always cross-infect each other has been especially influential – which is why I have stressed that aspect here. Criticism, after all, has been an obsessively dualistic enterprise. It has taught us to read works of literature in terms of their carefully balanced thematic, imagistic and linguistic oppositions. One level of generality up, it has distinguished works of literature from each other on the basis of such distinctions as comedy and tragedy, poetry and prose, romanticism and classicism. Then it has distinguished literary language from other kinds of verbal discourse on the basis of its radical metaphoricity, immediately breaking that metaphoricity down into vehicle and tenor (an opposition which comes apart very much along the lines of signifier/signified, and which Derrida himself deconstructs in the essay "White Mythology"). All of these favorite oppositions of criticism are open to deconstruction, but none more so than the really big, heavily invested ones that criticism has sought to establish between literature *as a whole* and all the things that it *isn't*: literature against philosophy, literature against history, literature against reason. And not forgetting, lastly, the daddy of them all, the distinction made *inside* criticism *between* criticism and its own object. I mean, of course, the inaugurating distinction between criticism and literature itself, made at criticism's degree-zero, only to be muddied at critical zero-plus-one by all those speculations about the "literary" element in criticism, and the "critical" element in literature.

The following interview – the first which Derrida has ever given in

English – was recorded at Yale University in April, 1985. After struggling for so long with the difficult rigour of his texts, one is intimidated at the prospect of actually meeting Jacques Derrida – so of course he turns out to be the most genial and easygoing of men. There is a great sense of liveliness about him: he fidgets constantly with his pipe, and there is always a smile playing about his lips. He seems to enjoy having questions – even stupid ones – thrown at him; he visibly savors those which are less stupid. The whole sense is of a man whose pleasure is in *communicating* whatever is obscure, illuminating whatever is dark.

Imre Salusinszky: I'd like to talk, today, about the university, and the place of the university in society. First, I want to ask you a question about teaching.

The sorts of discourses that occur in the university are supposed, eventually, to have a "trickle down" effect whereby, if they meet with a certain success, they come to affect educational practices in schools, and other institutions. I hope it isn't too trivial a question, but I was wondering whether it's possible for us to imagine what grammatology or deconstruction would look like at the school level. I suppose I'm asking. what would a school be like, in which the teachers were conscious of such concepts as trace, *différance*, logocentrism, and phonocentrism? Have you ever considered how your own ideas might eventually apply in the educational system, outside the university?

Jacques Derrida: In high schools?

IS: That's right.

JD: I have no clear answer to that. Of course, I've been anxious about this, about clarifying these questions, especially in France – I'm not very familiar with the high schools in this country, or in other countries. But in France, in fact, with friends or colleagues or students of mine, I was involved in trying to make a topic, a thematic problem, of this. We founded a group, in 1975, which is called "Groupe de Recherche sur l'Enseignements Philosophique," dealing not only with the teaching of philosophy in high schools – as you know, in France we have philosophy in the last grade of high school. At the time, this teaching of philosophy was threatened by the government, which intended more or less to suppress philosophy in the high schools. So we had to fight against this policy, but at the same time to analyze what this teaching of philosophy in the high schools was, or should be. We advocated the teaching of philosophy *before* the last grade of high school, beginning at the age of 10 or 11, which implied not exactly the transportation of the existing teaching, but a general transformation of teaching in the high school, in all disciplines: a new structure of teaching, which was not, for us, a matter of political decisions coming from the top and being applied, but, as I say, a transformation in the minds of the teachers, of the families, of the children, and so on. We thought that it was just a prejudice to think that philosophy could be taught only at a certain age. We tried to analyze what this prejudice was, on what grounds it was founded – on what grounds, or non-grounds, or fantasies, or fears. Which implied, at the same time, the study of the structure of the institutions, especially in France, but not only in France.

So: it implied that we analyze the institutions, but also philosophy itself, getting to the roots of this prejudice within the history of philosophy: for what social or sexual reasons it has been believed, since Plato, that having an access to philosophy before, let's say, 17 or 18, was impossible or dangerous. We think it's not. We've made experimental teachings of philosophy in what in France we call *sixième et septième*, which means at the age of 10 or 11, and it was quite a success. Those young boys and girls were not only interested, but were demanding and enjoying philosophy, and having access to what we would call difficult texts. This move, of course, won't be possible for a long time, but our idea has made some progress. It implies a general transformation of everything: not only in schools, but the family, the state, the city, and so on.

This doesn't mean that I have the precise idea of what *they* could call an application of deconstruction or grammatology in teaching. I was the founder of this group, and wrote the preamble, but I didn't want to transform it into my own group, or into a doctrine, so I refrained from imposing my views. But, all the time, I was asking myself the question you are asking me, and I have no clear answer in terms of methods or institutions. I cannot say that there could be a deconstructionist teaching, even in the university. I think that deconstruction, to the extent that it's of some interest, must first insinuate itself everywhere, but not become a method or a school. So I've no firm answer to such a question – especially improvising in English! But I'm sure it's an important question and, if deconstruction *is* of some interest, it must have effects on teaching at all levels. I would say this without hesitation. But from this point to another step, a constructing step, I couldn't really speculate.

IS: Following on from that, those who have been reading your work in English have heard you mention the new International College of Philosophy, which you have been involved with in Paris. I'd be fascinated to hear a little of what is envisaged in this project.

JD: It's not only a project, it's already a reality. We submitted a project to the French government, who agreed in principle to support the thing. They asked me and three other colleagues to write a report, before creating the institution, and the report was accepted. The institution was created, on a provisional basis, in October 1983, and it has worked since. Now it's in the process of becoming a public establishment. At the moment it could still be called a private association with public support – but that's a fiction: in fact, it's a public institution.

Well, what is the general structure of this institution? First, it wants to be international, which means not only open to foreign scholars, in the form of invitation and so on, but *really* international. Which means that we want non-French people to share the responsibilities in the decisions. Already, there are some non-French people who are associate members, but we hope that they will be full members. So: really international in its administration. Also, international to the extent that the themes that will be privileged here will have do do mainly with the problems of differences of culture, with translation, with the problem *of* the institution in its international problematic, and so on. So the substance of the research – it will be a research institution – should have to do with internationality, in a new mode. That's what we hope.

IS: It's not a teaching institution?

JD: It's not *simply* a teaching institution. The regulating principle of this institution could be formulated in the following manner (it's easy to formulate, not so easy to practice): it would be an institution which would give priority to problematics, topics, research, which are not legitimized or accepted in the given institutions in France and in the other countries. Wherever a topic, even if it's necessary, is already received and practiced in other institutions, it's not of interest for the International College. We are interested, in a privileged manner, in new objects, in new disciplines – not only in interdisciplinary things, but in objects which are not already determined as disciplines, in departments. As soon as something appears as such – something not well received in other institutions but which to us looks necessary, well, we open the college to at least an attempt to constitute this as a real object of research.

The college will be, and is already, open to anybody, without consideration of academic title. Everybody can apply to be a student, or to run a program in this college. The only thing that has to be done is to send a project, according to the lines I was just defining. Titles don't matter; age, nationality and, of course, sex don't matter. There will be no tenured positions, no Chairs, only contracts for a rather short period, be it a lecture or a seminar for some months, or a long-range program, which means three or four years. That's all; no stability from that point of view, no occupied Chair for life.

Then we want to be as free as possible as to the state. Of course, there is a paradox in being supported by the French state and wanting to be free, but we know that it can be managed; it's not impossible. We have to be vigilant, we have to be careful, but it's not impossible. And, as you know, private institutions are not freer. So that's what we want to do.

IS: Will your professional responsibilities shift to the International College to any extent?

JD: No, no: I've been, first, responsible for this report, and then the college was founded. I've been Director, but at the beginning I said that I wanted to be Director for one year and no more, and that I would resign exactly one year later, which I did. So I resigned in November. I'm still a member of the staff, but I'm no longer Director. I've been replaced by Jean-François Lyotard. Of course, I belong to another institution – this venture of the college has been something extra for me.

IS: In an essay called "The Principle of Reason: The University in the Eyes of its Pupils," you talk about the college in connection with the words "the basic, the fundamental" (p. 16). Is there any sense in which the impetus for the International College of Philosophy has come from a desire to found an institution which will somehow be free of the compromises that the teaching of philosophy has entered into, probably since Plato's Academy?

JD: As free as possible. Of course, we know the difficulties.

IS: Could Plato's Academy be re-created?

JD: I don't know whether Plato's Academy could be a model. That's a difficult question, because the idea of the Academy implied some kind of link between philosophy and the state, which we're not sure we want to reproduce. It is a difficult problem; I cannot improvise on it. Of course, we would like to avoid those compromises, if possible.

You were referring to fundamental research, and in the essay you were quoting I was suspicious as to the possibility, today, of distinguishing between what we call "fundamental" research and "applied" or "oriented" research. Even this *concept*, of fundamental research, has a history. Sometimes you may find that fundamental research is end-oriented research, only with a detour. We want to pose this problem, as such, without knowing where we are going. The problem of the relationship between the research – fundamental or end-oriented research – and the state, the military and industrial structure of the state, is one of our main concerns, I would say. I think that this is the responsibility of the teacher or scholar today.

IS: I wanted to take up precisely that question, again from "The Principle of Reason." As you just explained, that essay suggests to us the complicity of all university work in state power or ideology, and the suspension, in this complicity, of any distinction between pure and applied research. So what kind of independence could the university hope to recover? How can the university be simultaneously careful, as you suggest in your essay (p. 19), about totally opening itself to external power, or totally closing in upon itself?

JD: I would say that there is no general answer to this question. (I wouldn't say that there are *only* empirical evaluations of the situation. When you say there is no general answer you are saying, well, we have to analyze each situation in each country at every moment – the situation in the United States is different from the situation in France, in France it's different after 1981, and so on.) Nevertheless, even if you have a clear principle as to the necessary autonomy of the university, starting from this principle you have to take into account, strategically, a given situation, and to make compromises: you cannot avoid these compromises.

The answer couldn't be homogeneous. I'm sure the corporation, the university, cannot always react the same way. The university is a heterogeneous body. There are different levels – different stages of development, a Marxist would say – according to the individuals, according to different departments, different groups. So everybody, in his place, should react according to this place. And even the concept of autonomy, which is a very classical concept, has to be re-analyzed or re-elaborated. I tried to show in another text, on Kant's *Conflict of the Faculties*, how this concept of autonomy was equivocal, ambiguous, subject to some ruses.[2]

For me, now, I'm in a difficult situation. I've no clear view of what has to be done. I behave – well, it depends on the moment, on the place – with this guiding principle: that we should question, that we shouldn't sleep, that we shouldn't take any concept for granted. Of course, we shouldn't take for granted any end-oriented program, but no principle of autonomy either. Because I wouldn't advocate a university that would be cut off from society. We know that we have to train people towards a profession. I'm against some sorts of professionalization, but it would be silly to think that the university should have nothing to do with any profession. You have to train people to become doctors or engineers or professors, and at the same time to train them in questioning all that – not only

2 See "Mochlos ou le Conflit des Facultés," *Philosophie*, no. 2 (1984), 21–53.

in a critical way, but I would say in a deconstructive way. This is a
double responsibility: two responsibilities which sometimes are not
compatible. In my own teaching, in my own responsibilities, I think
I have to make two gestures simultaneously: to train people, to teach
them, to give them a content, to be a good pedagogue, to train
teachers, to give them a profession; and at the same time to make
them as conscious as possible of the problems of professionalization.
 You'll have to rewrite all this.

IS: I wonder if you'd comment on some national differences – institutional and intellectual – in this regard, being so uniquely involved
in university teaching both in the United States and France. In the
United States, more than in Britain or France, the humanities,
within the academy, seem to be isolated in a rather special way from
their cultural context – from popular culture and from politics. In
Britain, on the one hand, the academy itself seems very resistant
to theoretical discourses; in France, on the other hand, it seems that
even outside the academy there is a large audience for philosophy,
and for theoretical discourses.

JD: To some extent. Of course the situation is very different. I
wouldn't say "outside the academy" but "outside the university,"
because in France there are many institutions which are outside the
university, but which are academic. People outside France often have
the feeling that the French people they know are within the university, which is not true. The people you know outside France, the
most famous people, are not in the university: they are in other
institutions, marginal to the university. The academy in France is
a very heterogeneous body. You have the university proper, and
institutions such as Collège de France, L'Institut de Science Sociale,
Le Collège Internationale Philosophique, L'Ecole Normale
Supérieure. Sometimes such an institution is very conservative, and
on the margin of it there is something else. So it is difficult to speak
of "the French academy."

IS: I guess I was really asking whether the notion of an "amateur
philosopher" is possible in France, but impossible to conceive of
in the United States. Or, rather, an amateur *audience* which connects
the philosopher to his social background.

JD: That's true, there is this difference. But an amateur in France,
even if he or she is not inside the university, is not simply an auto-
didactic person. He or she belongs to a milieu in which people from
the academy are present, to some extent. They are not totally cut
off from the academy.
 Of course, in the United States, culture or intellectual life is
confined to the university, more or less. In France, this is not the
case, especially in Paris. This is, for me, an important difference.

Here, the people I know, the people to whom I speak, are on the faculties. In France, it's almost the contrary: I've very few relations with colleagues or with professors in the university. Well, this is an advantage and a disadvantage too, because those people in France who are not in the academy, and who have an access to philosophy, sometimes are not relevant or competent. They write in the newspapers, they prophetize and so on, sometimes not very seriously, and this might be dangerous too. Both systems have their dangers.

IS: Still on the same essay, "The Principle of Reason," you talk about a possibility: the idea that, standing where we do in the university, there is some hope that we can learn to "view viewing" and "hear hearing" (p. 19). Is that some kind of transcendental position to stand in?

JD: I hope not. That's a formula: out of its context, I would not countersign it. It was a way of saying that the problem of seeing and hearing *is* a problem, and that we should meditate on this, but not simply in the reflexive way of seeing sight or hearing hearing.

IS: You also talk there about the university's "precious freedom of play" (p. 19). Those who have studied your work know that when you use the word "play" you are talking neither about non-seriousness, nor about some kind of obscurantist free-for-all. Could you talk a little about the university's "precious freedom of play"?

JD: The university is not simply a place to play, a playground. But in at least some places within the university – the university is not a homogeneous field – the problems, the constraints, the end-oriented research, are looser. So you can study without waiting for any efficient or immediate result. You may search, just for the sake of searching, and try for the sake of trying. So there is a possibility of what I would call playing. It's perhaps the only place within society where play is possible to such an extent. I'm sure it's not totally free: you cannot do what you want in the university, and sometimes the constraints are rigid, are forceful. But in the humanities, in philosophy, we are freer, so to speak, than in other disciplines. So this measure, this proportion of freedom, is precious, because it's the place where we can try and think *what* the university *is*. The consciousness, so to speak, of the university, may be located here. It's not always the case, because sometimes people who are in philosophy departments, or the humanities, don't care for this concept of the university, for using this possibility of play.

Nevertheless, this is not impossible. Certain societies, when they accept the idea of having, for instance, philosophy departments –

which is not the case with all societies – give themselves the possibility of thinking not only the essence of the university, but the essence of society. That's the place where thought can be free: that's what I call "free play." Play, not in the sense of gambling or playing games, but what in French we call *jouer*, which means that the structure of the machine, or the springs, are not so tight, so that you can just try to dislocate: that's what I meant by play. Of course, this place is getting narrower now, more and more, for reasons of money: the money given to the humanities, to philosophy, is always diminishing.

IS: Following on from that, Socrates – for some reason I still have Socrates in mind – was supposedly rejected by society, not because of a propositional style in philosophy but, according to his own account before the tribunal, for an interrogative style: for asking the wrong questions. I wouldn't be the first to remark that, as a philosophical style, deconstruction is an interrogative style, rather than a propositional one . . .

JD: It's not a propositional one, but I wouldn't say that it's totally interrogative. Of course it's more interrogative than propositional, OK, but the form of the questions, the questioning syntax, is not taken for granted, not taken for the first and last form of thinking. So we have to question the form of questioning. I would say that deconstruction is affirmation rather than questioning, in a sense which is not positive: I would distinguish between the positive, or positions, and affirmations. I think that deconstruction is affirmative rather than questioning; this affirmation goes *through* some radical questioning, but is not questioning in the final analysis.

IS: If we accept, then, that in *one* of its gestures deconstruction is a questioning mode, it seems that, at least in the West, the questioning philosopher is tolerated now, to a very great degree. In fact, the questioning philosopher is rewarded and has a settled place in society. This, of course, isn't the case everywhere: one finds it hard to imagine an interrogative philosophy surviving for very long in most of Europe, especially in Eastern Europe. I wonder whether you have any comments on the limits to the toleration of your type of work. Both the geographical limits, the sense in which you couldn't do what you do everywhere, and also the possible final limits within the West to its toleration of questioning.

JD: You were saying, just at the beginning of this question, that a questioning philosopher was not only accepted but rewarded, in France. It's not so simple. Even if an individual, as a questioning philosopher, was accepted or indeed rewarded, this wouldn't mean that his questions were supported. Tolerating, or rewarding, is not simply giving a Chair or handing a microphone to somebody.

Sometimes even this is not done, but even if it is, it's not enough, if his questions are not embodied in institutions, if he has not the means, if he – not only he, but the group of people – have no possibilities of teaching, of questioning programs, of publishing. The question of publication is very important. Of course, what is possible in France is more than what is possible in the Eastern countries, perhaps more than what is possible in some other Western countries, but it is not totally open, totally tolerated. You have to analyze all the forms of intolerance, which are sometimes very hypocritical, going through money, going through publishing power, going through the media, and so on.

Without denying that, for instance in France, a philosopher may be recognized in a better manner than in some other countries, nevertheless there are limitations, there are constraints, there are – I wouldn't say censorship – but ways of limiting the propagation of these questions. That's what interests me: the ways in which liberal industrial societies do not censor in the literal sense, but through many mechanisms – institutional mechanisms, or commercial mechanisms, or technical mechanisms – limit this questioning activity.

IS: In the United States?

JD: First, there's the fact that these questions remain within the academy. And then, within the academy, there are so many counter-forces, even among the philosophers. So the limitations are very complex and very numerous.

IS: Could I ask you a couple of questions about a theme of your recent work, the theme of "the apocalyptic tone," and its possible application to the nuclear arms debate? In an essay called "No Apocalypse, Not Now," you say, of the apocalypse: "Literature and criticism cannot speak of anything else, they can have no other ultimate referent, they can only multiply their strategic maneuvers in order to assimilate that unassimilable wholly other. . . . Capable of speaking only of that, literature cannot help but speak of other things as well, and invent strategies for speaking of other things, for putting off the encounter with the wholly other" (p. 28). That fascinated me, and made me wonder whether the final social role or relevance of literature and criticism is, somehow, its function of keeping us talking about other things.

JD: Well, to keep us talking is better than to stop us talking and let us use these terrible toys. The only thing I'm sure of is a very trivial thing: that it's better to negotiate and to speak and to postpone the use of these weapons, and to analyze what these discourses – the political discourses – are, and to try to mobilize the people against what is threatening in this. What is the rhetoric of the politicians, the rhetoric of the military, of the scientists who work on this? You cannot separate, any more, some scientists, some politicians, some military decision-makers. One of the responsibilities of the university today is not to let those people do everything by themselves. This is *our* problem. We are competent. And if we are not, we should become competent on these questions and speak aloud. To make the conservation last.

IS: Is criticism like the hero of some movie who, while the villain has his hands on the detonator, keeps the villain talking until the police, who never arrive, arrive?

JD: OK. That would be a good emblem.

IS: In an essay called "Of An Apocalyptic Tone Recently Adopted in Philosophy," you say that "as soon as one no longer knows who speaks or writes, the text becomes apocalyptic" (p. 27). I want to take that sentence as a cheap excuse to ask you a couple of biographical questions, questions about where your texts come from. I wonder what, looking back, you see as the main events in your intellectual life, from the biographical point of view.

JD: First – I don't say this to avoid your question – when you ask me what are the major events in my intellectual life, I would say I don't know what my "intellectual life" is. How could I separate my intellectual life from my life? That would be my first answer.

   I'm not an intellectual. I've not the feeling of being an intellectual in the sense of a man of the profession, who has an intellectual life aside from his private life. So the events in my life are not intellectual events. Even the books I have written: they have origins, perhaps in some events, which are not simply intellectual.

   If I try to answer your question in a more classical way: my reading of Rousseau, Heidegger, Joyce, Mallarmé, Artaud. Then, since I've always been interested in literature – my deepest desire being to write literature, to write fictions – I've the feeling that philosophy has been a detour for me to come back to literature. Perhaps I'll never reach this point, but that was my desire even when I was very young. So, the problematics of writing, the philosophical problematics of writing, was a detour to ask the question, "What is literature?" But even this question – "What is literature?" – was a mediation towards writing literature. So when I tried to think what writing was, especially in *Of Grammatology*, I had the feeling that I was approaching something. Of course, the moment when I wrote *Of Grammatology* was the moment when I felt that something became, not clear for me, but something began to give me an access to what a dominant interpretation of writing had been in Western culture and philosophy. That's an event for me, in my intellectual history: when all the texts I had been reading, which I mentioned – I forgot, of course, Freud and Nietzsche – helped me to have, to some extent, a coherent vision of Western culture and its relation to writing and speaking.

And then I had the feeling that I could write differently. Which I did, to some extent, in writing *Glas* or *La Carte postale*. But right now I have the feeling that I'm always in that preliminary stage or moment, and I would like to write differently again. Differently: that would mean in a more fictional, and a more (so to speak, in quotation marks, many quotation marks) "autobiographical" way. I don't know whether I'll be able to do so, but that's what I would like to do, without giving up teaching and reading philosophy in the classical sense.

Of course, there are many other events in my life, but well . . .

IS: I'm not going to ask you to summarize all of them, but one experience that you've had as a philosopher, an intellectual, a writer, that is very unusual, has been your great fame. I suppose this is partly a voyeuristic question, but I ask it on behalf of all those who will read this interview: do you think your work is affected by the reality of going about everywhere and seeing your work, your name, in discussion? Does it make it in any sense more difficult to work?

JD: It's difficult for me to really take the measure of this. I'm sure it has some effects, especially in this country, where my work is better received, I would say, than in France.

Of course, it helps me to some extent, but at the same time it makes things heavier. You have to deal with this image, with this reception, as if you were bound to what you have already said. To try to free myself from it is sometimes difficult. You are caught in a network of discourses. Even if people are well disposed, even if they welcome you, it's sometimes good and bad at the same time. It's gratifying, so to speak, and at the same time it's threatening, because you become a prisoner of this reception.

That's why I sometimes fight against this reception – "it's not me, it's not what I intend to say." And as you know, this reception is very conflictual in the United States. Not only because it's controversial, because there are some people who react very violently to what I'm saying, but because even among those who are interested in what I'm doing there are many conflicts. It's difficult for me, first, to understand what's going on, because I'm not very familiar with the tradition of English-speaking literature. Sometimes, in the appropriation or the domestication or the adaptation of what I'm saying to other corpora, which I don't know very well – for instance, the main tradition of English literature, of which I have some knowledge, of course, but not a sure knowledge – it's difficult for me to understand what's going on (for instance, when I see such a reading of Wordsworth or Coleridge). I try, but it's not really easy. So sometimes, being interested in what happens, I'm not sure I understand.

Of course, it's a fascinating experience, but it's a dangerous experience, because it distracts me from my "own" (so to speak) "path." At the same time I'm sure I would like to dive into this tradition. I would like to live two hundred years and really enter the English literary tradition. I'm fascinated, for instance, by English Romanticism, and I know that if I had time I would be totally captured by it. But, well, it's too late now.

Northrop Frye

2
Northrop Frye

"I think that criticism is still bound up to ideology, and consequently much more concerned to develop the language of argument and thesis than really to embark on the empirical study of literature."

Northrop Frye was born in Sherbrooke, Quebec, in Canada, in 1912, and grew up in Moncton, New Brunswick. In the late 1920s, he left the Canadian Maritimes for Toronto, to compete in a national typewriting contest. While there, he enrolled at Victoria College, in the University of Toronto, where he graduated in Philosophy and English in 1933. In 1936, Frye was ordained in the United Church of Canada, but soon thereafter won a scholarship to Oxford. He returned to Toronto in 1940, after taking a First in English at Merton College, Oxford, where he was tutored by Edmund Blunden. Since then, Frye has taught at the University of Toronto – where he is now University Professor – and served a long term as Principal of Victoria College. The recipient of numerous awards and honorary degrees, he has resisted offers to leave Canada permanently, but has taught terms at many American universities, and at Oxford.

Frye's first book, *Fearful Symmetry: A Study of William Blake*, was published in 1947. This was a time when, due to the influence of T. S. Eliot and the old New Critics, Romantic studies (as well as the reputations of the Romantic poets) were in decline. Against this trend, *Fearful Symmetry* – which remains the most influential book ever written on Blake – argued for Blake's centrality in the English poetic canon, and for the centrality of the Prophecies in Blake's canon. From Blake, and primarily from the Prophecies, Frye extracts a whole neo-Romantic "argument" about the poetic imagination:

> Nearly all of us have felt, at least in childhood, that if we imagine
> that a thing is so, it therefore either is so or can be made to become
> so. All of us have to learn that this almost never happens, or
> happens only in very limited ways; but the visionary, like the
> child, continues to believe that it always ought to happen. We are
> so possessed with the idea of the duty of acceptance that we are
> inclined to forget our mental birthright, and prudent and sensible
> people encourage us in this. That is why Blake is so full of
> aphorisms like "if the fool would persist in his folly he would
> become wise." Such wisdom is based on the fact that imagination
> creates reality, and as desire is a part of imagination, the world we
> desire is more real than the world we passively accept.
>
> (p. 27)

Against the claims of T. S. Eliot and others who found Blake's
vision too "chaotic," *Fearful Symmetry* attempts to establish the almost
obsessive orderliness and structure of Blake's symbology. In its closing pages, the book even claims Blake's work as providing a gateway
to the structure of literature as a whole, and as comprising an
"iconography of the imagination" (p. 420):

> Blake's doctrine of a single original language and religion implies
> that the similarities in ritual, myth and doctrine among all
> religions are more significant than their differences. It implies that
> a study of comparative religion, a morphology of myths, rituals
> and theologies, will lead us to a single visionary conception which
> the mind of man is trying to express, a vision of a created and
> fallen world which has been redeemed by a divine sacrifice and is
> proceeding to regeneration.

Frye continues: "It is conceivable that such a study – the study of
anagogy, if a name is wanted – would supply us with the missing
piece in contemporary thought which, when supplied, will unite its
whole pattern" (pp. 424–5).

These sentences, near the end of *Fearful Symmetry*, lead directly into
Frye's next and greatest book, *Anatomy of Criticism* (1957), which is
precisely a study of myth, ritual and anagogy (or absolute vision) in
literature. With magisterial confidence, in a series of brilliantly witty
arguments supported by copious examples, the *Anatomy* slaughters a
veritable herd of New-Critical sacred cows, including the following:
that each poem is the realization of some sort of *pre-poetic* mood or
emotion or experience; that the proper perspective for criticism is
microscopic linguistic analysis; that each poem is a self-contained
unity; and that criticism and value-judgment are inseparable.

Against these beliefs, Frye argues: that criticism should "stand back" far enough from the poem to be able to perceive its archetypal or mythic connections with other poems; that these patterns serve to unify literature *as a whole* and comprise a "literary universe" or "order of words" created by the poetic imagination; that the poet does not imitate nature, but rather draws on the reservoir of archetypes and conventions contained in the literary universe; and that the proper role of criticism is not to make pronouncements of value, but systematically to describe the literary universe and its internal configurations. The central, unifying concept of Frye's system – its "transcendental signified" – is the idea of myth. In a series of radio lectures in 1963, he said that his "general principle"

> is that in the history of civilization literature follows after a mythology. A myth is a simple and primitive effort of the imagination to identify the human with the non-human world, and its most typical result is a story about a god. Later on, mythology begins to merge into literature, and myth then becomes a structural principle of story-telling.
>
> (*Fables of Identity*, p. 45)

Frye's work since the *Anatomy* has moved in three principal directions. First, he has applied the techniques of myth-criticism which he discovered in Blake, and systematized in the *Anatomy*, to a wide variety of other poets, publishing detailed studies of Shakespeare, Milton, Yeats, T. S. Eliot, Wallace Stevens, and many others. Second, he has extended his ideas into a liberal-humanist social analysis, proposing the study of myth and literature as keys to understanding the whole shape of culture or civilization. Here, the argument has been that myths, unlike legends or folk-tales, tend to cohere into a *mythology* – something deeper than any ideology – which comprises all of a society's deepest convictions about where it has come from and where it is going. Frye often talks about a social mythology of this kind as a "myth of concern," which he described in 1971 as a "fully developed or encyclopaedia myth" which "comprises everything that it most concerns its society to know" (*The Critical Path*, p. 36). Third, and most recently, Frye has been re-examining the Bible as the preeminent "encyclopaedia" or storehouse of Western imaginative myths. *The Great Code* (1982) is a study of biblical typology from a literary critic's perspective; a companion volume, currently in preparation, will explore the influence of the Bible on Western literature.

Frye's own influence has worked in two different ways. First – and only semi-intentionally – he had the effect of upsetting the whole basket of New-Critical, Eliotic, "neo-classical" literary values that

preceded him; and thus he inspired a new surge of Romantic studies
so powerful that we are only now beginning to see the counter-
movement (in, for example, the renewed interest in eighteenth-
century studies). Second, as the most systemic treatise on poetics
since Aristotle, the *Anatomy* was one of the great forces behind the
establishment of the field now called "critical theory" – a field which
has since grown so crowded that periodic crises can be announced in
it. The *Anatomy* demonstrated that, even if we cannot agree about
critical methodology, we can at least *dis*agree about critical
methodology, and the institutional effects of this demonstration can
now be seen in the English curriculum of every major university in
the world.

The following interview, which took place in Toronto in September,
1985, is the third that I have recorded with Professor Frye. To lift
a Fryean joke: it should therefore, on the model of folk-tale, be the
successful one. There can be little argument about the fact that Frye
has been the most influential critic since the Second World War, and
not *only* because he is the most urbane, widely read and imaginative.
There is another quality as well. Near the beginning of *Fearful
Symmetry*, addressing the common claim that Blake was mad, Frye
says: "What Blake demonstrates is the sanity of genius and the
madness of the commonplace mind, and it is here that he has
something very apposite to say to the twentieth century, with its
interest in the arts of neurosis and the politics of paranoia" (p. 13).
I remember coming across an old review of *Fearful Symmetry*,
published in a Toronto tabloid under the headline: "Toronto Don
Discovers Sanity of Genius in Blake." Those who read this interview
will surely discover something of the genial and unshakeable sanity
in Frye.

Imre Salusinszky: Well, I'm going around talking to a series of
people about the social and institutional contexts of contemporary
criticism. I'd like to talk to you first about the role of criticism in
society, and I've been thinking of what you've written about
"concern" – the things that a society thinks it needs to know about
where it's coming from or where it's headed – and the relation of
criticism to concern. I want to talk about three of the concepts with
which your names always has been, and most likely always will be,
associated within criticism. First, the notion of myth or archetype.
I know that this a very general question, but I want to ask you to
summarize briefly the main steps or landmarks or intellectual
moments which brought you to your view of myth or archetype.
Northrop Frye: I suppose that, autobiographically, it was largely a

matter of what I happened to be most interested in studying and teaching. When I began here, I was trying to write a book on Blake and trying to teach Milton, and both of them being very intensely biblical poets led me to see something of the infiltration of the Bible into English literature. I think that what gradually dawned on me over the years was that most people start out with a social context as an ideology, and feel that literature fits within the ideology and to some degree reflects it. Well, that is true, but I think that an ideology is always a secondary and derivative thing, and that the primary thing is a mythology. That is, people don't think up a set of assumptions or beliefs; they think up a set of stories, and derive the assumptions and beliefs from the stories. Things like demo-cratic, progressive, revolutionary, Marxist political philosophies: these are comic plots, superimposed on history.

IS: Does ideology differ from "concern"?

NF: Well only to the extent that I regard mythology as prior to ideology, and ideology as taking its shape from the mythology that it derives from. A Christian ideology comes from a Christian myth, a collection of interconnected stories that Christianity tells – and similarly with other religions.

IS: The second, very central concept that comes out of your work in the 1950s and 1960s is the "order of words," or the idea of an overall structure to all of literature. What brought you to that?

NF: I think it was somewhat the same principle. I soon realized the priority of mythology to ideology in a culture, and then I realized that a mythology is an interconnected series of myths, and that the distinguishing characteristic of the myth – as distinct, say, from the folk-tale or the legend – was that myths tended to link together and to form a mythology. I felt that there had never been a corres-ponding term for works of literature. Because, as literature grows out of a mythology, and is the most direct product of the mytho-logy, it also has a group of stories which are interconnected by convention and by these recurring units that I called archetypes.

IS: If mythology is prior to ideology, why do we find clashing ideologies within a given society, which has a shared mythological structure?

NF: Well, that's the point: you can't *stay* at the mythological level, because you can't argue about a story. You can merely say whether you think it's true or false. But as soon as the secondary ideological development takes place, then you're in the realm of proposition and thesis, where every statement implies its own counter-statement. The Bible begins with a story that God made the heaven and the earth. That leads to the ideological statement, "There is a God." And that in turn leads to the possibility of saying, "There is no God." Judaism and Christianity differ on the question of whether an incarnation of God is possible, but mythologically they're just about the same religion.

IS: The third and final theme in your work which I wanted to pick up in this way was the argument in the *Anatomy* about the need for criticism to be systematic and progressive – for criticism to become, I suppose, a social science. What was the development of that idea?

NF: It developed out of what I call the "stock market," the way in which criticism was being used tactically, by people like T. S. Eliot and Wyndham Lewis, to boost certain names and denigrate certain others, in connection with certain literary movements they were promoting. I noticed that, particularly in painting, for example, these "isms" and schools were a sign of immaturity and of not properly established authority. Consequently, it seemed to me that they were all really pseudo-structures, and that the real, genuine advance in criticism came when every work of literature, regardless of its merit, was seen to be a document of *potential* interest, or value, or insight into the culture of the age. It simply arose from my observation of normal scholarly practice, which is that if you're "in" the eighteenth century, you read everything in your field, regardless of its merits.

IS: How has the fact that the critical schools seem to be warring as fiercely these days as they were during the 1920s, 1930s and 1940s affected your view? In other words, is this something you still think can be broken?

NF: Well, your question assumes that I've got very much more cynical about the willingness of critics to tackle the essential jobs of criticism as I see them, and that is quite true. I think that criticism is still bound up to ideology, and consequently much more concerned to develop the language of argument and thesis than really to embark on the empirical study of literature.

IS: What would you say are the reasons for that?

NF: It may have different reasons in different communities. In Great Britain, when I started thinking about the things connected with the *Anatomy*, I thought it had a social reference, and that criticism was bound up with the conception of gentlemanliness. If you were a gentleman, you were a cultivated person, but you didn't actually work systematically at a job. Or, if you were a person of not quite that social class, but trying hard to be a gentleman, like F. R. Leavis, you were even more defensive. With France, I dare say it's different. The cultural traditions there are so Cartesian and anti-Cartesian, and the French critics tend to start out with a philosophical position and then rationalize.

IS: In the *Anatomy*, you say that "a public that tries to do without criticism . . . brutalizes the arts and loses its cultural memory" (p. 4). Is criticism, then, a *mediator* between society and the arts?

NF: Yes, criticism has to be a mediator between literature and society, because its essential job is to examine first the literary and then the social context of whatever it's studying. But, as I keep saying, the mediation has to take account of the difference between the ideological and the mythological. For one thing, that's the only way to account for the fact that so many great writers have been ideological fat-heads: Yeats, Pound, Lawrence – you name them.

IS: You've kept fairly distant from the specifics of critical struggles of recent times, but I wanted to get your reactions to two of the currently very influential critics. First, Harold Bloom and his poetics of influence. Bloom has very readily acknowledged, at least in his early work, your influence upon him. But clearly the current Bloom would not accept that the New Testament is the great code of art. The patterns he's finding now are much more Hebraic ones, both normative and gnostic. What do you think of them?

NF: My whole early training focused on the structure of the Christian Bible because, as I say, my original job was writing about Blake and teaching Milton. That, to me, holds together as a mythological pattern, but I'm not prepared to say that it's the right one or the true one or the most complete one. I'm merely saying that it's the one that seems to me to be central in the traditions of English literature that I'm most concerned with. I think there is some danger, perhaps, of painting yourself into a corner once you decide that a kabbalistic tradition, for example, is the more authentic, the more right, the more true one. I remember disagreeing with Bloom, very early on, over his conception of the "authentic Romantic," and feeling that it didn't matter a damn whether one was authentic or not.

IS: Can you understand Bloom, and other Jewish scholars, becoming uncomfortable with what has been, after all, a very Christianizing tradition of English literary criticism?

NF: Well, I think that Bloom was certainly uncomfortable with what he found at Yale at the beginning, the New Criticism there. But that, of course, was in a line of Christianity that I don't have a great deal of interest in myself. As I say, I'm interested in the mythological structure; I'm not interested in the ideological content.

IS: But when you talk about the "secular scripture" and so on, your "economy of concepts," as the popular saying goes, still has a Christian framework – that is, a displaced Christian framework, which a Jewish scholar might conceivably still feel was not a comfortable one.

NF: Yes, he might very well. I've just been compelled to write out
my undergraduate lectures on Shakespeare, for a publisher who
demanded them, and there I found myself unable to proceed without thinking of the kind of assumptions that Shakespeare's original
audience would have brought into the theatre with them. If I were
Jewish, I would be made exceedingly uncomfortable by a play like
The Merchant of Venice, but it *does* exist; it did represent something
which the audience of its time accepted. I think that there you can
point to Shylock and say: this is an utterly skewed and corrupt
notion of Judaism; but it was there, it's a historical fact.

IS: If Bloom has, to some extent, challenged the Christian direction
of English literary studies, it is Derrida who has challenged the
persistent Platonism that one can also see running through English
literary studies. Criticism has always tended to think of any great
literary work as possessing unity, with some sort of closure, and
as being in some sense seminal. Now Derrida seems to have
opened up a whole range of new possibilities, where instead of
closure and insemination he has his concepts of dissemination, of
trace, of displacement. Derrida, however, is a philosopher, and I
wonder if you regard his present influence as merely one of those
enclosure movements which you describe, in the *Anatomy* (p. 6), as
coming from outside criticism and wanting to take it over.

NF: It certainly seems to be the way his influence has operated, yes,
but I don't think that it's entirely fair to Derrida that it has
operated that way. I think he's genuinely interested in opening up,
as you've just said, new possibilities in criticism. The thing is that
I don't see why the sense of an ending and the sense of wholeness
and unity, and the kinds of things that he's talking about, should
be mutually exclusive. I don't see why you have to have an
either/or situation. It's like those optical puzzles you look at, which
change their relationship when you're looking at them.

IS: In the days of the *Anatomy*, you faced more than a few hysterical
reactions. Does the reaction of the "critical establishment" to
Derrida seem to you to have some traces of hysteria about it?

NF: Sometimes it almost does seem to. I thought there were some
very curious words being used – "parasitic" and so forth. I don't
understand what all the hoopley-do is about. I can understand that
certain disciples and followers of Derrida might get lost in a
morass, but then people said that my disciples got lost in a morass,
so what the hell?

IS: I think I mentioned to you that I was going to do a sort of I. A.
Richards exercise; instead of showing an unseen poem to first-year
English students at Cambridge, I was going to travel the world and
show an unseen poem to the most famous literary critics. This is

an exercise which, if it works, I hope will give those outside criticism a sense of the alternatives within the field, and the way they affect practical interpretation. When you face up to a poem like "Not Ideas about the Thing but the Thing Itself," by one of the poets who has been closest to you right through your career, how do you begin to work with the poem, what processes do you take it through, what are we looking for?

NF: What are we looking for? I suppose I'm really looking for, in this case, a poem which illustrates the title: the fact that, when you're dealing with ideas about a thing, you're dealing with statements which have a tendency to become self-enclosed. And that when you are using the metaphor of the "thing itself," the metaphor of vision, the metaphor of eyesight, you are speaking of something which keeps shifting from the inside, where your eyes are, to the outside, where the thing is. So my eye would be caught first of all, I think, by the dots after "snow" and "papier-mâché;" and by the musing "It would have been outside," and then again "The sun was coming from outside;" and yet realizing that that statement can't possibly be as simple as it looks, and that what he's after is a "new knowledge of reality," where you get past the whole inside/outside tail-chasing.

IS: I see it as a somewhat personal poem. I suppose it's hard to avoid that, because it comes at the very end of the *Collected Poems*, and we're tremendously moved by the very old Stevens writing this. How much of the personal element in the poem can criticism retain – or does it have to wash it entirely clean of the personal element?

NF: No, it doesn't: that's an either/or situation again. Stevens had a personality, and there is an aspect of that personality which is his business and peculiar to him. There's another aspect of it which gets into the poem, and is transmissible: that's the personality which I am capable of absorbing.

IS: You know, it struck me when I was conceiving the present project that almost all of the critics I wanted to interview for the series have been very heavily influenced by Stevens. What do you think the great attraction of Stevens is for the more theoretical and more romantically oriented critics like you, Hartman, Bloom, Hillis Miller?

NF: Well I think, again, there is no point of closure in his mind. He's always, even in his very last poem, looking for a new knowledge of reality. I didn't realize how often I'd quoted Stevens in *The Great Code* until I got an interview from Sydney, Australia, where they asked me this over the telephone, why the hell I referred to Stevens so often – I hadn't realized I did. He seems to me to have the kind of representative culture for a person of my generation. He's just, exactly, what speaks to me with the voice of contemporary poetry. Of course, that comes from back in the *Harmonium* days, a generation behind people of your generation.

IS: Regarding what you say about Stevens as, even in his very last poem, looking for a new knowledge of reality: this seems to me to be one of the many respects in which you resemble him. Stevens spent his later years trying to write out a version of the "supreme fiction," and you are presently working on your own equivalent, the "great code." You've mentioned being affected by *Harmonium*, but Stevens's long meditations on the supreme fiction are the product of his sixties and seventies: have these late, long poems acquired any additional resonance for you as you have entered the same period of your own life?

NF: Yes, the conception of the "supreme fiction" in Stevens has acquired a good deal of resonance for me, though I get this resonance less from the long meditative poems than from shorter ones: "Prologues to What Is Possible," "Forms of the Rock in a Night Hymn," the paramour soliloquy, the last poem, "Of Mere Being."

IS: There's one thing I've never understood fully about Stevens: his relentless unpopularity; his not being, at all, a "popular" poet. This struck me when I was passing through Hartford recently, and thought to drive past the house on Westerley Terrace where he lived. I was surprised that, while America is happy to erect plaques and memorials to every old thing, Stevens's house just sits there without any public memorial or plaque or plate on it. (Actually, in what I suppose is an irony, it's now the Deanery of the Hartford Episcopalian Church.) Why do you think Stevens never caught on with the public?

NF: I suppose because he's so studiously oblique. His work is *all* "asides on the oboe."[1] You're never quite sure just what you are hearing. You said a moment ago that Derrida is perhaps the first non-Platonic critic; well, when you read a poem of Stevens saying "beauty is momentary in the mind . . . but in the flesh it is immortal," people just blink.[2] That's not what he's supposed to say. He's supposed to say it's momentary in the flesh, but it's immortal in the mind.

IS: I think he was worrying at that Platonic dialectic right through his life. I think the influence of contemporary philosophy on Stevens has been overrated, at the expense of his obsession with the Platonic contrast. I mean, obviously his imagination/reality

---

1 See Wallace Stevens, "Asides on the Oboe," in *Collected Poems* (New York: Alfred A. Knopf, 1954), p. 250.
2 Wallace Stevens, "Peter Quince at the Clavier," op. cit., p. 91.

dialectic is in some way derived from it.

NF: I think that's very close to the truth about him. The point is that he was aware of it as a problem. It wasn't just an unconscious assumption.

IS: I would like to move on and talk about criticism in its institutional context, the university. You are in some ways in a unique position, because you have been in a position of leadership in the university through a very difficult period. And you've seen the changes which have come over the university through a very long period, because you've been involved in the university since the 1930s. When one reads over your early professional history, it can function, these days, almost like a lost pastoral vision. You went to Oxford, and then you returned to the college where you had been an undergraduate. You were welcomed back there. You were given all the time you needed to publish your first book, which became the major study of Blake. As we know, this sort of leisure, and this sort of pattern, is not typical of what's faced younger scholars in the last ten years. How has the tightening, the shrinkage in the university, the competition for jobs, the competition through publication, affected the universities and the sort of work done in the humanities?

NF: It has, really . . . "destroyed" is a strong word . . . it has *transformed* them into places of labyrinthine arguments. I read so many articles which *are* arguments, which don't seem to get anywhere in particular, but which are sufficiently coordinated to be publishable as arguments. One feels that the reason for their existence is simply to get them on a dean's list, and that the notion of the pursuit of a structure, or of knowledge, so that it gets clearer in the mind, is just something you haven't the time for.

IS: There's a very unhappy irony in what you've said. Society cuts back funding to the universities, because it wants them to be more socially relevant, more socially responsible. Instead, that simply produces more highly specialized, irrelevant work.

NF: That's exactly right. And I think you're quite right in what you implied: that is, that a great deal of what I've written about education has been an attempt to recapture my own pastoral myth. Because I know that there was something genuine about the college that took me in when I was nobody, took a chance on me simply because they knew me, then sat back and waited for me to get that infernal Blake book off my hands. I know that that position wouldn't have been possible in very many universities even then, and wouldn't be possible anywhere now.

IS: I was always particularly influenced and moved by what you've written about the university, but when I left graduate school and

actually entered the university, and the job market, I found it hard
to square with reality. Is an idealistic story about the university
becoming a harder line to push?

NF: In a sense it is. It must have been very difficult to believe in
Christianity during the Thirty Years War, but perhaps the original
dream was still there, in some form or other.

IS: The Thirty Years War ended: will this work itself through?

NF: I profoundly hope so. I think, in the natural course of events,
it will. The only thing that keeps me reconciled to life in my seventies is my realization that everything does go in cycles.

IS: Is academic freedom severely compromised by the tightening of
the budgets?

NF: Oh yes. The question, for example, in Canada, is whether
Canada should get into Reagan's Star Wars schemes or not, and
whether this would be accompanied by contracts let out to universities. Well, hell, there was a time when no university that valued
its reputation would even think of such a thing. It would mean
classified information, and the universities are not supposed to
deal with classified information. If you want to work on that stuff,
you get the hell out of the university.

IS: Talking of that, when you were the managing editor of the
Canadian Forum, you were very involved at the centre-left of
Canadian politics. Was there a period in your development when
you were attracted to Marxism?

NF: I suppose everybody's attracted to Marxism in the sense that it
gives you a kind of outsider's viewpoint on bourgeois society. That
part of it is something totally inescapable. The difficulty, of course,
is the difference between Marxism as a critique of bourgeois
society and Marxism as the instrument of a Marxist government.
As I never felt the Soviet Union was making very much of a bid
for human freedom or independence of thought, I was never
attracted to political Marxism of that particular kind. Following a
party line: I never wanted to buy that at all. I think that Marxism
has been, or certainly should be, incorporated into the Western
imagination as an essential part of its thinking – just as Darwin,
or Nietzsche, or anybody else should be.

IS: During the ''McCarthyist'' days in America, there was a similar
tendency for witch-hunts going on in Canada. I know that the
Canadian Forum was very outspoken, and I know that the universities were very much under investigation and attack then. Those
must have been strange and difficult times. What are your
memories of them?

NF: I wasn't as involved in them, because I was never marked out
as a Marxist. Earle Birney, a Canadian poet, has written a book

called *Down the Long Table,* which evokes the time when he was here during the 1930s and the early 1940s. He was a Trotskyite, and he summons up those days very well, I think. I was never in that aspect of the movement, but it was certainly going on all around me. I think that Canadians have a lot to be grateful for in their own cold-bloodedness. The country is so big, and so sparsely populated, that it just can't work up the kind of hysteria that America can.

IS: You've said that academic freedom "is the only form of freedom, in the long run, of which humanity is capable," and that it cannot be obtained unless the university itself is free ("Definition of a University," p. 59). How can the university be free when, after all, the state and, increasingly, various corporations hold the purse strings?

NF: Freedom is a relative term, and the degrees of freedom are of immense importance, simply because complete or absolute freedom is out of the question. The university will always, to some extent, be controlled both by government and business influences; but there's an immense difference between a professor's being able to speak his mind and get away with it and hold his job, and his finding himself in a concentration camp.

IS: In the same essay, you write that it's the university's task to define the vision of society (p. 57), and in your 1976 Presidential Address to the MLA you say that the university works to dissolve all élites into the classless society that is the final embodiment of culture (p. 386). Increasingly, Marxists within the university are telling us that the university is one state institution among others and that, far from working for a classless society, it simply passes on a sophisticated version of the very ideology which the bourgeoisie needs in order to preserve its own privileged class position. How do you react to that?

NF: Well, again, I think it's a half-truth. It implies that those who are trying to speak their own minds and tell the truth as they see it are still incapable of realizing the extent to which they may be speaking for a bourgeois hierarchy. I think that rather underestimates the intelligence of many people.

IS: What does society want, or think it wants, from the university? And what do we, within the university, think that we want to give society?

NF: I think that there is a great deal of respect for the university in society, in so far as it can become a community, where truth and learning are pursued as such, though not necessarily for their own sakes. I think there is such a thing as a moral majority, even if the people who call themselves that aren't it. I sense this kind of respect for the university, and I see the loyalty of the alumni, which I've had some experience of as an administrator and which I've always been very touched by. I think that what the university wants to give society is not really very different from that. They realize that what they are doing will perhaps be oblique in its social impact, but that that doesn't necessarily undermine its genuineness.

IS: I'm thinking about what you've spoken of as "phoney mythology": propaganda and advertising, things that society is trying constantly to force down our throats. I suppose that, in that sense, the university always has to be at odds with the society within which it exists, because it's working to . . .

NF: Oh yes, always, always . . .

IS: Why is it tolerated, then?

NF: It seems to be part of the democratic process. Democracies seem to depend on advertising, and dictatorships on propaganda. The difference is not so much in the rhetoric, as in the fact that advertising is more open to the spirit of criticism.

IS: There is a lot of feeling now that the specialization within the humanities is counter-productive, in that it cuts the humanist off from the social context. I know you've always been an opponent of specialization in criticism.

NF: I'm not really opposed to specialization in itself. I'm opposed to the cutting-out of the perspective. A person can be specialized, and still be a very broad and humane scholar. I have a former student who sends me offprints on analytical bibliography, which is about as specialized a discipline as you could ask for, but I know that he's a genuine scholar, in the sense that the perspective on knowledge has not vanished for him. He's working within that. It's the absence of the perspective that I'm opposed to.

IS: And what are the causes of that, when it occurs?

NF: I suppose the causes are, again, the competitive spirit of the graduate schools, the fact that so many articles exist for the sake of existing – that kind of thing. Practicing that is bound to corrupt one's vision, and to instill in its place a kind of cynicism.

IS: In closing, a couple of biographical questions. I asked Derrida whether his great fame had affected his work. In this respect, among the group I'm talking to, only you really compare to Derrida. It's a very unusual position for a humanist to be in; it's almost unique. How has it affected your own work?

NF: It's bound to have affected it. I think it affects it mainly in the fact that the question which had always been latent very deep in my mind when I'm writing – what kind of audience am I addressing? – comes much closer to the surface. You are continually thinking in terms of somebody who hates your guts; or, more rarely, of somebody who'll take this as gospel, and therefore you ought to make sure it isn't fatuous.

IS: I also asked Derrida what he saw as the main events in his life, and rather to my surprise he came out with a reading list. I know your work somewhat better than I know Derrida's, so I'd be less surprised if your answer was along those lines. Would it be?

NF: I daresay it would be, fundamentally, yes.

IS: And what are the landmarks?

NF: The discovery of Blake, which happened in my adolescence. And there would be a variety of things. The art show at the Chicago Art Center in 1933, during the World Fair, when I was 21 and seeing all those glorious pictures for the first time in my life. A great deal of it has to do with the novelty of impact. The time when I first read Spengler, for example, knowing with every page I turned what a stupid, thick-skulled Teutonic ass he was, and yet nevertheless fascinated by that kind of perspective. Samuel Johnson said that all wonder was the effect of novelty upon ignorance, and I think that whenever novelty has hit my ignorance, that's been the turning-point.

IS: How did the Second World War affect the composition of *Fearful Symmetry*?

NF: Well, I think if you look carefully at the book, and even more at the footnotes, you'll see it's a very anxious, troubled book. It's written with the horror of Nazism just directly in front of it all the time. When I first read Rosenberg's *Myth of the Twentieth Century* – the big Nazi bible, about the Atlantis myths and the Nordic heroes and so forth – it just sent the shudders up my spine. If this kind of thing had prevailed in the world, everybody would not only be reading him, but thinking that Blake thought that way too.

IS: Did the Cold War have anything like a comparable effect on the *Anatomy*?

NF: Not so much on the *Anatomy*, which grew directly out of my work on Blake. The most fruitful part of that I was doing at a period before the Cold War really set in, still in that period of hope between 1945 and 1950. I think that that came out more in my articles on education and the universities.

IS: I remember hearing you give a talk in Chicago once where you said that, whenever you were asked to commit yourself to a talk sometime in the future, you gave it a title that reflected where you hoped to be, intellectually, when the time came around to give the talk. Where do you hope to be, in the next few years?

NF: The rest of my life will be what Jerome Bruner calls a "spiral curriculum," revolving around this successor to *The Great Code*, which has gone up in metamorphic flames several times (so did the other one). So, I imagine it will be just a series of revolutions, bringing me back to somewhat the same point, but nevertheless tracing out a circumference in the meantime. The only thing is that one does get very much aware of the passing of time when one gets into the seventies. Besides, there must have been times when even the noble and pure-hearted Sir Galahad said, ''Bugger the grail.''

IS: You haven't looked beyond the second volume of *The Great Code?*

NF: That's about it, that's the main thing. The first book was of two kinds. Half of it had been on my mind so long that it was obsessive; just really to be excreted, to be dumped. The other half were things that were really coming in, and were new in my mind. This one I'm not going to let go of until I'm ready to let go of it. I don't know where I'll be after that.

Harold Bloom

3
Harold Bloom

"'There are no texts. There are only ourselves."

Harold Bloom was born in New York in 1930. He studied at Cornell University and earned his Ph.D. at Yale in 1955. He has been on the Yale faculty since then, and is now Sterling Professor of the Humanities. He is the editor of more than thirty anthologies, and the author of sixteen books, including *Shelley's Mythmaking* (1959), *The Visionary Company* (1961), *Blake's Apocalypse* (1963), *Yeats* (1970), *Agon* (1982), and an important "tetralogy" of books on poetic influence: *The Anxiety of Influence* (1973), *A Map of Misreading* (1975), *Kabbalah and Criticism* (1975) and *Poetry and Repression* (1976). Bloom is now preparing more than two hundred introductions for the Chelsea House Modern Critical Views series, of which he is General Editor, and is also working on a full-scale study of all of Freud's major writings, under the title *Freud: Transference and Authority*.

In *Shelley's Mythmaking* and *The Visionary Company*, the young Bloom joined and extended the campaign against the poetics of Eliot and the New Critics which had been started by Frye in the late 1940s. For Bloom, this particularly involved challenging the New-Critical reduction of all poetic rhetoric to irony, the distrust of the long poem (especially in such poets as Milton, Shelley and Blake), the disparagement of discursive or unambiguous thought in poetry (particularly, again, in such poets as Milton, Shelley and Blake), and the denigration of all of the Romantic poets in favour of a "neoclassical" line.

This was the line which, it was said, ran through Jonson and Donne to Pope – skipping Milton – and then conveniently jumped more than a century to comprehend Eliot and Pound themselves. In response, the recanonization of the Romantics was itself brought forward into the twentieth century: just as Frye did a great deal in the 1940s and 1950s to establish the reputation of Wallace Stevens against the claims of the anti-Romantics, so Bloom was later to play the crucial role in establishing the reputations of such followers of Stevens as John Ashbery and A. R. Ammons. However, while Frye's intention – whatever his effect – had never been to institute a Romantic literary hierarchy (the Fryean sense of tradition is apparently all-inclusive), Bloom was, from the beginning, a fierce *proponent* of romanticism – agreeing with Eliot, at least on this score, that there are "definite positions to be taken."

In place of irony, there now began to be a renewed interest in romance. Against the New-Critical fixation with lyric, there was now a special investment in such poems as *The Faerie Queene* and *Paradise Lost*, in Blake's prophecies, Shelley's dramatic poems and Stevens's late meditations. And there was to be no more sneering at the theoretical or discursive poem: in fact, romanticism itself came to be thought of as a kind of argument. Above all, the neo-Romantic campaign involved the reinvigoration of what Bloom, in *The Visionary Company*, called the "apocalyptic ambition" of romanticism: "to humanize nature, and to naturalize the imagination" (p. 8).

However, with *Yeats*, and even more with *The Anxiety of Influence*, Bloom quickly began to individuate and distance himself from Frye, becoming increasingly skeptical of such key Fryean/Romantic notions as the autonomy of the poetic imagination from the poet's ego, and of Frye's view of romanticism as a "displaced" or secularized Protestantism. Instead, Bloom now came to see a "gnostic" element in all "strong" poets, by whom he means those who have managed to assert themselves against an over-burdened English literary tradition. Such an assertion will always involve a canny "misreading," by the would-be strong poet, of the strong precursor poet whose influence is most troublesome to him. In these terms, a poem like, say, *The Prelude* comes to be seen as a "strong misreading" or "misprision" of *Paradise Lost*, and its success can only be judged by the extent to which it has managed to elbow that earlier text away from itself.

So, in *The Anxiety of Influence*, Bloom proposes a "wholly different practical criticism" (p. 43), an "antithetical" methodology relying on six "revisionary ratios" – or tactically defensive tropes – which trace the "anxiety of influence" within any poem towards its precursor. Later, in *Kabbalah and Criticism*, he discovers analogues to these ratios in the six "behinot," or interpretive stances, of Jewish gnosticism. (With this move, Bloom becomes the first critic in the

English tradition willfully to assert his Judaism, instead of
sublimating it.) Still later, in *Poetry and Repression*, as Freud assumes
an increasing importance in his thoughts, Bloom shifts the emphasis
away from the six ratios and on to a revisionary triad of limitation,
substitution and representation.

The quest of the ephebe, or potential poet, is always designed to
evade the power of the precursor and discover self-identity – which
for the poet must necessarily take the form of a representation. When
we look at this quest from a slightly different angle, as a desire for
individuation or self-reliance, we realize why Nietzsche and Emerson
have also been so important to Bloom's vision. And just as Frye, in
the 1960s, built an entire social philosophy around his particular
brand of Romantic-Christian-Platonism, so Bloom since the late
1970s has been extending his vision from poetry out into all areas of
social life, religion, politics and philosophy: in all of these arenas he
discerns the *agonistic* struggle for individual assertion.

Among the American general public, Bloom is the best known of
literary critics – a result of his engaging and polemical style, as well
as of the fact that he publishes regularly in such journals as the *New
York Review*. Of course, Bloom styles himself as the pariah of
American academic literary criticism, but if this is true at all, it is
true only of the critical generation that precedes his own: among
younger American critics, no one is more admired, or more influential, than Harold Bloom. What is the source of this influence? I
would say that it has little to do with the technologies of an "anxiety
of influence," perhaps even less with any "Romantic revivalism."
Instead, I would trace its source to a stance and a style. If Wallace
Stevens showed, *contra* Pound and Williams, that a poem is not a
"machine made out of words," then it has been Bloom's achievement to remind everyone – by the example of his writing *and* teaching
– that the critic is not a thinking-machine. Like the poet, the critic
knows what it is to think *and* feel; what it is to fall in and out of love
with poems; and, above all, what it is to struggle towards voice.

The following interview was recorded in the middle of November,
1985, at Harold Bloom's home in New Haven. In much of it, we can
see Bloom vigorously distancing himself from the entire "critical
profession." This is a move which describes a gathering tendency in
his recent work (and which includes the "pariah" motif). Bloom is
better suited to the posture of "Romantic visionary" than to that of
"convention delegate." To subsume our troubled dialogue with
tradition under professional rubrics, including critical "schools," is
to execute a fall and a reduction, and to sacrifice the burden of
prophecy for weak role-playing. Here we may recall that Sartre's

most memorable example of "bad faith" is a professional example:

> Let us consider this waiter in the café. His movement is quick and forward, a little too precise, a little too rapid. He comes toward the patrons with a step a little too quick. He bends forward a little too eagerly; his voice, his eyes express an interest a little too solicitous for the order of the customer. Finally there he returns, trying to imitate in his walk the inflexible stiffness of some kind of automaton while carrying his tray with the recklessness of a tightrope-walker by putting it in a perpetually unstable, perpetually broken equilibrium which he perpetually reestablishes by a light movement of the arm and hand. All his behaviour seems to us a game . . . But what is he playing? We need not watch long before we can explain it: he is playing *at being* a waiter in a café. There is nothing there to surprise us.[1]

Or, as Stevens says in a late poem: "X is an obstruction, a man/Too exactly himself."[2] Re-reading those lines from *Being and Nothingness*, and then the closing pages of the following interview, we realize that the central subject of this interview is never directly mentioned in it: it is a hymn to good faith.

Imre Salusinszky: Two nights ago, I dreamed that we were doing this interview. Instead of living in a relatively normal house like this one, you lived in a vast palace, full of reception rooms and ballrooms. Every time I got ten minutes into the interview, you would have to rush to some antechamber to take a telephone call, and I would straggle after you with my notes and my tape recorder . . .

Harold Bloom: I hope that there will be no phone calls, my dear.

IS: At all events, in the dream interview I asked you many incisive questions, a lot of which I probably wouldn't dare to ask when we were both awake . . .

HB: I will answer any question within reason, Imre. It is not for nothing that I am known as the truly outrageous contemporary critic.

IS: A question that I remember clearly from the dream is one that, I'm sure, would interest a lot of your readers. I asked you: "How is it possible for someone to be as prolific as you've been, to produce as much text as you have produced?"

HB: Sleeplessness.

IS: Sleeplessness?

---

1 *Being and Nothingness*, translated by Hazel E. Barnes (New York: Philosophical Library, 1956), p. 59.
2 "The Creations of Sound," in *Collected Poems* (New York: Alfred A. Knopf, 1954), p. 310.

HB: Insomnia.

IS: Good . . .

HB: And many, many enemies. If someone is as consistently, abominably, weakly misread, as viciously reviewed and written about as I am, and believes as I do – and I've maintained this throughout my whole life – that one should never reply to anybody, then the only effect of this chorus of catcalls upon one might be to stimulate a little productivity.

   You know, this goes way back. I started publishing things back in 1958, with a little essay on Blake's *Marriage of Heaven and Hell*, my first and only publication in *PMLA*. It was greeted by a storm of angry letters, some of which were printed in the next issue of *PMLA*. They asked me if I wanted to reply, and I said "Certainly not." I have maintained that for these nearly thirty years now, and will go on maintaining it. I realized early on that the academy and the literary world alike   and I don't think there really is a distinction between the two – are always dominated by fools, knaves, charlatans and bureaucrats. And that being the case, any human being, male or female, of whatever status, who has a voice of her or his own, is not going to be liked. Only if your voice blends into everybody else's voice, and only if you make the proper gestures of self-negation, are you not going to run into these barbarians.

   I'm very used to this. In my early years, I didn't like the sort of reviews and reactions I got. Then I went through a very long period, really from the publication of the Yeats book onwards – it must have lasted about ten years, from 1970 to 1980 – when I positively welcomed it; when I felt that, after all, these mental defectives were doing my work for me. But I find that, in the last five years, I don't give a damn one way or the other. Since I am convinced that literary criticism is a purely personal activity, that it has exactly the same status as lyric poetry or narrative writing, why should I care about the response to it, one way or the other? Praise or blame, alike, is beside the point.

IS: I want to come to that, but from another direction. The first thing I want to ask you about – and I'm sorry to ask as disarmingly general a question as this one – is the concept with which your name is still most strongly associated: the activity of poetic influence, the anxiety involved in it, and the revisionary . . .

HS: Although I can write, and probably will write, my dear – if I live – another thirty-five books, I am reconciled to the fact that to my dying day and beyond I will be regarded as the author of one book: *The Anxiety of Influence*.

IS: At all events, even right back in your very earliest work, one can detect some hints of this idea. For example, in *Shelley's Mythmaking* there's a phrase about Shelley being in "corrective competition" with Milton (p. 53). How did you come to this idea?

HB: I think the notion was in my head from the time I was a kid, when I was 12 years old and reading Hart Crane, with his palpable assertions of Whitmanian influence, but with the poetry's enormous and not-so-covert struggle against the abominable Eliot. I think I was aware of it even then, and that is back in 1942.

The relation to Whitman is ideological on Crane's part and, to a certain degree, a screen. Anxious or not, the relation to Eliot is palpable. Although I myself believe – and I must be the only person alive who believes this – that Hart Crane is a much more powerful and enduring poet than Eliot, even at Eliot's rare best, there's no question that in Crane's case *the* precursor poet is Eliot. For Crane, the crucial poem is "The Waste Land." But then, I don't think you could *be* a real poet of Hart Crane's generation and not have, as the fundamental archetype of the poem, "The Waste Land." As, I suppose, the fundamental archetype of the poem for William Butler Yeats was the "Ode to the West Wind" and the "Ode to a Nightingale," and as the fundamental paradigm of the poem for Shelley and Keats themselves was undoubtedly "Tintern Abbey" and the "Intimations Ode." "The Waste Land" simply occupied that place.

IS: Was there a reading of something else that brought the notion of an influence-anxiety forward? Of the Kabbalah, or Freud?

HB: No, it was personal. It is true that I had a mid-life crisis when I was 35, in 1965. Never mind what, but it was a severe emotional crisis, and I entered analysis, which lasted intermittently for some five years. But it had, I believe, nothing to do with that. When I was 35, I did begin, for reasons that I still can't understand, to read for hours daily in two authors above all: Emerson and Freud.

But as to the genesis of the book *The Anxiety of Influence*, it was published in January, 1973, but most of it was written in the summer of 1967, and indeed the original draft, "The Covering Cherub, or Poetic Influence," I lost, and then recovered, because my friend Joe Trapp who is the head of the Warburg Institute discovered it there. I'm now going to republish it in a selected volume of my work. I lost the earlier version – I have some notebooks which have much of it in them – but there was an even crazier version of that crazy piece.

I had a ghastly nightmare, about the time of my birthday: July 11, 1967. A simply ghastly nightmare, in which I had this sensation that I was being suffocated by some great winged creature which was pressing down on me. I woke up the next day and, after I had cleared my head, I started writing a long dithyramb called

"The Covering Cherub, or Poetic Influence." And then, throughout the summer of 1968 a year later, I elaborated on the first
notion of "clinamen," and the other five tropes or ratios came into
play. I didn't publish the book for four or five years more, partly
because everyone to whom I showed it – including that great man
the Ayatollah Hartmeini – shook their heads and assured me that,
whatever this was, it was neither literary theory nor literary
criticism. Hartman, in particular, told me to just junk it. I never
believed I ought to junk it, and it made its way into the final
version of the Yeats book, and into the book of essays I published
a year later in 1971, *The Ringers in the Tower*. Throughout 1972, I
kept tinkering with it, trying to see if I could not so much tone it
down as rationalize it and historicize it a bit. I think, now, that that
was a mistake, and if I could I would recover the whole of the
earlier version. But I would have to work endlessly with notebooks,
and so on, and I'm not going to do that. I like it as a book. I
haven't read it in years, but I like the fact that even I, the last time
I tried to read it, could not quite figure out what was going on in
it. I repeat: I like that very much.

IS: When people outside the academy, including the poets you talk
to, ask you, "What is the anxiety of influence?" what explanation
do you give them?

HB: They don't ask me that: they simply tell me they don't have it,
whatever it is. And if I'm close enough to them, particularly if they
are ladies, I hug them and say, "Forget about it." Even if I'm not
close to them, I simply shrug and say, "Don't give it another
thought." It's not their business, as it were; it's your business and
it's my business, but it's not their business. Why diagnose their
disease for them when, in fact, it's better for them not only to have
the disease, but to have it in a pure form?

IS: You have deprivileged direct allusion in poetry: what is gained
by privileging indirect, or revisionary, allusion in its place?

HB: I think I've learned not to bring this too directly even into the
graduate classroom. I have talked about this, in particular, in that
essay called "The Breaking of Form" in the *Deconstruction and
Criticism* volume that I shared with my remote cousins, intellectually speaking. What *we* call a poem is mostly what is not there
on the page. The strength of any poem is the poems that it has
managed to exclude. No poem, not even by Shakespeare or Milton
or Chaucer, is ever strong enough to totally exclude every crucial
precursor text or poem. If that way of talking about poetry has any
force – and I'm probably still unique in the world in believing it
has more force than any other way – then clearly what you have
called "indirect" or "revisionary" allusion would be considerably

more relevant than overt or calculated allusion.

IS: Soon after you'd come upon this new terrain . . .

HB: Is it a new terrain? You know, there's an irony in this. I well
remember the reviews that *The Anxiety of Influence* got throughout
the first half of 1973. With a handful of honorable exceptions, the
air was full of cries of charlatanry and willfulness and obscurantism
and nonsense. I find that the characteristic attack upon the book
now, twelve years later, is to say: "Boring, inconsequential, we
knew it all along."

IS: That's a revisionary ratio in itself. But, for you, when you
entered this terrain, there soon began to be a feed-in from your
reading of Jewish gnosticism.

HB: No, I think that went along with it. When I was a child, I was
raised high Orthodox, and indeed trained to be a Talmudist. It is
impossible to be in that tradition and not encounter all kinds of
strands which lead you into speculations that, very gradually, you
come to understand are gnostic. I think I first was aware of
kabbalistic texts and traditions at about the time when I first
became passionately involved in reading Hart Crane and Blake,
when I was about 10 or 11. In an attempt to make some sense out
of it, from a perspective that would help me, I started reading
Scholem when I was about 13 or 14. These interests have been
with me for a very long time. By the time I was a Cornell
undergraduate, at the age of 17, if anyone had asked me what my
own religious stance was, I would have said "Jewish gnosticism."
I cannot, of course, read Coptic, but from the time I was very
small I could read Hebrew and even Aramaic.

IS: Scholem says that the Kabbalah was the first thing that the European Jews let go of, in the process of assimilation. In that case,
isn't your use of gnosticism a "return of the repressed," to use the
most overworked of phrases? Instead of just injecting a Hebrew
sensibility into literary criticism, you have injected the part of it
that a Christian community can least easily swallow.

HB: But who's repressed it? It was never repressed in me, and I
believe that the equivalent of it has never been repressed in the
poets. I'm puzzled as to whether or not it is a Jewish element.
Scholem spent his entire life passionately insisting that the
Kabbalah was nothing if not Jewish, and indeed he pressed
towards the notion that Jewish gnosticism was indeed the essence
of Judaism: a sublime and outrageous position. But Kabbalah,
whatever its historical origins, is essentially a blend of two traditions, neo-Platonism and gnosticism, both of which are fundamentally Alexandrian. There was certainly a vast and flourishing
Jewish community and culture in Alexandria when these doctrines

arose, so there may have been a Jewish input. Nevertheless, it seems to me that all that neo-Platonism and gnosticism – which are, of course, fundamentally in opposition, as Plotinus's denunciation of the gnostics demonstrates so eloquently – all that they have in common is that they are both strong misreadings or misprisions of Plato.

But, of course, to say what is Jewish or what is not Jewish is finally like saying what is Christian or what is not Christian. Every tradition is so powerfully syncretic that once you start to trace out its origins you run into all kinds of antithetical bewilderments. I remember once trying to discuss this with Northrop Frye, and making very little headway indeed. Certainly, back in the days a few years ago when I ventured to give a few lectures on matters like this to Jewish groups, I met such outrageously hostile receptions that I discontinued lecturing before such groups.

What I said that always gave most offense, and yet what has been demonstrated overwhelmingly by normative Jewish scholarship of the twentieth century, is that what is supposed to be the very essence of normative Judaism – which is the notion that it is by study that you make yourself a holy people – is nowhere present in Hebrew tradition before the end of the first or the beginning of the second century of the Common Era. It is perfectly clear that the notion reached the rabbis directly or indirectly from the writings of Plato, because it is a thoroughly Platonic notion. And yet it has become more characteristic of normative Jewish tradition than of any other Western tradition still available to us. I take that to be an instance of why one should distrust any statements about the ontological or historical purity or priority of any spiritual tradition whatsoever.

IS: However, I know one surely kabbalistic fact, which I only discovered yesterday. On the same day that you were born in the Bronx, fifty-five years ago, in far-away Algiers another . . .

HB: Of course: Jacques Derrida. Four days after me, actually. I was born on the 11th of July, 1930, and Jacques was born on the 15th of July, 1930.

IS: Is there anything of the kabbalist about Derrida?

HB: Well, I remember remarking in *Kabbalah and Criticism* (p. 52) that Jacques was to some extent a kind of kabbalist-after-the-fact, because what he asserted was original in him – which was a question never raised before, he said, in Western metaphysics – is in fact the fundamental postulate of Kabbalah: Jacques' notion of the "trace" is a purely kabbalistic notion. There are obviously strong elements, in the *Grammatology* and *Speech and Phenomena* and the other early writings of Jacques, which are wholly contrary to the neo-Platonic element in Kabbalah, absolutely contrary to it. But what could be called the gnostic side of Kabbalah finds many parallels in what Jacques does. But Jacques, of course, does not have, in any special sense, a religious sensibility, whether normative or esoteric. Jacques is a professional philosopher of the Parisian variety, or of *a* Parisian variety: indeed, in his case a variety that he has largely managed to create for himself.

IS: Can we imagine such a thing as a gnostic university? Can we imagine gnosticism *without* the university?

HB: Gnosticism is an Alexandrian phenomenon. Therefore, since the university is an Alexandrian phenomenon, I don't see how we can keep the two aside from one another. There is, I think, something fundamentally gnostic about the very idea of the post-Platonic academy, and we all of us live and teach in post-Platonic academies. A great deal of what now passes itself off for normative Western religion is frequently closer to second-century gnosticism than it is to second-century orthodoxy.

IS: I suppose that what I meant was: can gnosticism survive without a normative opposition to itself?

HB: You know what that is, ultimately? That is like my dear old teacher and old friend M. H. Abrams's denunciation of Derrida, and even as my own sad poor self, not to mention the Fishy-foo, in a piece that he did strangely linking the three of us as so-called "new readers." And also in his endless and, to me, misleading debates with my other good friend, Hillis Miller. It's like Mike's perpetual notion that without the traditional accounts of reading, and the traditional humanism of the West, none of these departures have any coherence and make any sense. Of course, I would not counter this the way Hillis does, since it strikes me that Mike and Hillis are merely disputing degrees of irony. I've said many times – and I feel it more strongly than ever today – that all formalisms are one. So that, finally, New Criticism, Mike Abrams's kind of refined historical criticism, deconstructive criticism as practiced by the late Paul de Man and Hillis and all of their disciples, are very hard to distinguish from one another.

As for Mike's argument, what is fundamentally wrong with it is that it is based upon the notion – which he shares, I believe, with the academy in general – that what we call "humanism" and so-called "secular" imaginative Western literature are displacements from what were originally religious categories. To this I can only say two things, but I believe that they are quite definitive. One is that no displacement has ever taken place, or could take place. There is no distinction between a sacred text and a secular text; I regard that as a purely political distinction, and I am not interested in political distinctions when applied to imaginative literature. You can either say that all literature is sacred, or you can say that all literature is secular, but you do not gain anything by trying to distinguish between the two.

The other notion, having to do with Mike's notion of historical priority, is this: what mattered in the first place, surely, in any theology, Western or Eastern, is merely William Blake's point in *The Marriage of Heaven and Hell*, when he says that all forms of worship are derived from, or codified from, poetic tales. What comes first is what you might call the "psycho-poetry," which is then rigidly codified into a theology The only vital force, all that allows that theology to be memorable, is the poetry. Mike is finally making the ghastly Arnoldian point that we should have been done with a long time ago. But all these people, you know, remain the heirs of Arnold. I do not credit this notion that there is anything revolutionary about Jacques or Paul or any of the Continental modes. All I see are Arnoldian formalisms, and they do not interest me.

IS: I want to ask you about the other big feed-in into the influence tetralogy, which is your reading of Freud. I suppose that when one hears that a literary critic is heavily influenced by Freud, one expects to find notions to do with the symbolism of the unconscious, the Oedipal complex and so on. But your interest in Freud seems to be so centered on the theory of transference.

HB: I am not a Freudian literary critic. I think there is no such thing as a Freudian literary critic. Of all the many jokes I have put into my books, the one I like the best, so that I've repeated it frequently, is that Freudian literary criticism is like the Holy Roman Empire: not holy, not Roman, not an empire; not Freudian, not literary, not criticism. My interest in Freud comes from the increasing realization that Freud is a kind of codifier or abstractor of William Shakespeare.

In fact, it is Shakespeare who gives us the map of the mind. It is Shakespeare who invents Freudian psychology. Freud finds ways of translating it into a supposedly analytical vocabulary. I have, during the last several years, been intensively reading and teaching – and am now beginning to write – about Shakespeare. It is something I had always intended to do, but knew I had to put off doing, for many reasons. A growing conviction that I've had since I started to read Freud intensively, more than twenty years ago, now seems to me wholly confirmed. I understand, better and better, why Freud, in his final phase, became so passionate an advocate of the theory of the gentleman so marvelously named Looney: which is, of course, that the Earl of Oxford had written Shakespeare.

IS: Why is the theory of transference of such interest?

HB: Well, what is transference? Transference is the carrying-over from earlier figures to later figures. And what is that but a way of talking about the history of imaginative literature?

IS: I'd like to quote something to you from the piece on Wallace Stevens in *Figures of Capable Imagination*:

> Poets influence us because we fall in love with their poems. All love unfortunately changes . . . we also get hurt when we abandon, or are abandoned by, poems. Criticism is as much a series of metaphors for the acts of loving what we have read as for the acts of reading themselves.
>
> (p. 103)

Is there a transference as between the reader and the poet, as well as between the poets themselves?

HB: Oh yes, and there are also, of course, negative transferences moving in every direction. You know, what I have favored increasingly – in reading Freud, teaching Freud, writing about Freud – is the ancient Roman stage trope, "contamination." I think Freud is *about* contamination, but I think he learnt *that* from Shakespeare, because Shakespeare is about nothing but contamination, you might say.

The Roman stage trope of contamination has to do with taking characters, with the names that they have had in other plays and in history, and giving them the same names but making them wholly different characters. It is the way we live, it is the way we write, it is the way we read. It is, alas, the way we love: we are always taking the names of dead or past characters and applying them to others.

IS: Are the transferences between the strong poets different in nature from the transferences between those poets and their readers?

HB: I think they differ only in degree, not in kind. They are yet more obsessive, they are yet more ambivalent, they are yet more zealous, more impassioned, more intense – and finally they are, I believe, both more destructive and more creative. They are, indeed, catastrophe-creations, because more power, more pathos, more sublimity goes into them.

IS: This raises the question of the relation of poetry to criticism. Within your work, there's a definite movement on this. You say of critics, in *The Anxiety of Influence*: "In relation to the poets we are not ephebes wrestling with the dead, but more nearly necromancers, straining to hear the dead sing" (p. 65). By the time of

Agon, however, we've got "poetry is verse criticism" (p. 45): obviously a strong trope, designed to provoke.

HB: What is memorable about criticism? Surely what is memorable about other genres – greater genres, if you would have it so. What is memorable, I think, is what gives sufficient pain, in terms of the pleasure-pain principle, so that you cannot let go of it. As Nietzsche would say: if you've suffered it enough, then it will be memorable. I have preternatural powers of verbal recall. If I ask myself what it is that I remember in criticism, it does not differ from what I remember in poetry. The critics who in the end matter most in the English language, I'm convinced, and the three greatest critics in the English language beyond any doubt, are Dr Johnson, William Hazlitt, and John Ruskin. That is because they do precisely what the poets do: they are idiosyncratic, and they are on one level or another engaged in a tremendous *agon* with every text that they read – as well as, finally, with their own tradition, which is that of commentary or exegesis.

I guess I've slightly evaded answering your question, because it really interests me less and less. I don't know what people are talking about when they think that an imaginative fiction – a poem or a novel or a story or a drama – is one thing, and a critical essay is something startlingly different. It comes, of course, from an ideology on their part, or a defense – what is an ideology, except a defense? – and it just does not interest me. I don't even care to give offense on this matter any more; I regard it as a dead issue: someone who cannot see it cannot be taught anything, and that is not my concern.

I take it for granted that, increasingly, the academic study of literature – and indeed what most literary persons think is or ought to be the proper study of literature – and what I do, cannot be brought together. I know that frequently when I say that, I am called a hypocrite or a charlatan. They say, "Well, then, why does he earn his living as Sterling Professor of the Humanities at Yale University?" My reply would be: "Well, what are all these other persons doing here?" From my point of view, *they* are not legitimate, because I am doing what I believe a teacher should do, and I do not know what it is that these other people are doing, whoever they are. I don't think I am at all bitter, but I am deeply weary of these debates. I am not concerned to be polemical any more. I have learned that all that the competing critical schools have in common is their secret agreement with one another, and that is why I am anathema to all of them, and they are of no interest to me – even if a lot of them happen to be very nice guys and girls, and therefore good friends. I don't think that I am

paranoid – I think I've gotten past that stage also. I suppose this
is the really pragmatic difference between me and a figure whom
I greatly honor, the foremost living student of Western literature,
Professor Northrop Frye. The most fundamental difference
between us is that he sees criticism, and literature, as a cooperative
venture: *I do not*. I think that idealizes.

IS: You mentioned your memory: it seems to function like some
kind of absolute concordance to all of literature. Here you do
resemble Frye, though his prodigious memory functions more like
a "Key to All Mythologies." These hidden linkages that you have
managed to find between poems: aren't they things which only
Bloom, with his vast accumulation, could ever hope to see? Does
your experience of literature relate at all to the common
reader's?

HB: Memory is not only a mode of cognition, it is *the* mode of cognition in literature and literary study alike – and I don't think there
is a distinction between literature and literary study. Memory is
an active process. Perhaps it cannot be distinguished from cognition, in the area of literature or literary study. Let me point out
that the critics I have learnt most to revere – Johnson, Hazlitt, and
Ruskin, as well as other figures who mean a great deal to me, like
Pater – do not verify their quotations: they quote from memory.
Mr Christopher Ricks has published at length denouncing both
Pater and myself for inaccuracy, because we insist upon quoting
from memory. It was Hazlitt who remarked that if a critic cannot
quote something from memory, then he has no right to quote it at
all, and ought not to do so. I firmly believe that.

As to what this has to do with the common reader, you know
the paradox as well as I do. The strength of Johnson – who after
all invented the phrase – and of Hazlitt is that they show us that
there is no distinction between the uncommon and the common
reader: to be a reader is to be uncommon. Reading is a frightfully
élitist activity. It always has been, and it always will be. Mr Frye
has, thank heavens, nothing in common with the Marxists,
pseudo-Marxists, neo-Marxists, *und so weiter*, but like them he has
idealized the whole question of what might be called – to use his
own trope for it – the extension of the franchise in the realm of
literature and literary study. Idealization is very moving: it is also
very false. It allows profound self-deceptions, at both the
individual and the societal level. Literature does not make us
better, it does not make us worse; the study of it does not make
us better, it does not make us worse. It only confirms what we are
already, and it cannot authentically touch us at all unless we begin
by being very greatly gifted.

IS: On this subject of memory, Angus Fletcher said to me years ago:
"Ask Bloom what it's like to have all that stuff perpetually battling
away there in his head." Does your own total recall – the fact that
the poets are always battling for preeminence in your memory –
have anything to do with the combative nature of the poetics you
have developed?

HB: I don't think so. Are we to forget the pseudo-Longinus: are we
to forget the true beginnings of Western literary criticism, and the
true origin of the dubious Bloom, which is the treatise "On the
Sublime," which I would translate simply as "On Strong Poetry"
or "On Literary Strength," and which talks about nothing *but* the
agon, including the *agon* between Plato and Homer? I don't think
it has anything to do with recall, total or otherwise. Are we to
forget Burckhardt and Nietzsche, on the *agonistic* spirit among the
Greeks? I haven't invented what you might call "literary agon-
istics." Think of Hesiod. Think of Homer himself. Think of the
relationship between Euripides and Aeschylus. Think of Aristo-
phanes, on Euripides and Aeschylus. The ancient understanding
of literature is that it is as profoundly *agonistic* as athletics or
warfare or politics or class-struggle. There's nothing new in this.
It is sentimentalism, it is social-dialectics of various sorts, which
attempt to eliminate this palpable struggle for priority and for
power from our minds. But literature is nothing else.

IS: Since we've now run over the terrain of influence and anxiety,
I want to take this moment to discuss very briefly this Stevens
poem, "Not Ideas about the Thing but the Thing Itself," with
you. Is this a crisis-lyric?

HB: It follows the great Western Romantic paradigm of the Word-
sworthian poem, beyond a doubt. It is a wholly typical Stevensian
modification of the Wordsworthian-Whitmanian crisis-poem, yes.
What else could it be? It is handled in a completely different mood
or mode – it is actually an extremely genial and self-celebratory
poem. Indeed it is the characteristic trope of very late Stevens. It
is the trope that is repeated with even more power in the very great
lyric, "The Course of a Particular": the cry of the leaves there is
the scrawny cry from outside here. By the way, I've always come
to understand, and may even have said so in print – at least I can
show the modesty of saying that my memory of my own vast six-
or seven-thousand page output by no means features total recall –
that the lines "It was part of the colossal sun,/Surrounded by its
choral rings" are an allusion to Blake:

"What," it will be questioned, "When the sun rises, do you not
see a round disk of fire somewhat like a guinea?" Oh no, no,

> I see an innumerable company of the heavenly host crying "Holy, holy, holy is the Lord God Almighty."[3]

IS: I'm trying to point up to readers who are, perhaps, not terribly schooled in literary criticism, what critics of different persuasions look for when they are confronted with a poem. How do you work with an object, or a process, like this?

HB: "Process," of course, is better than "object." Better even than "process," I would say "series of relationships" or a "happening" in which one is very much involved oneself – not "happening," of course, in that recent faddish sense, but something ongoing. "Process" always sounds so natural.

IS: To ask one of your own favorite questions: "What is this poet trying to do for himself, as a poet, by writing this poem?" Obviously, it's so late that he's done most of what he's ever going to do for himself, by this time. What's left?

HB: What's left is to make the next poem possible, which is what is always left; to rally what remains, in the grand Miltonic-Satanic tradition; to rouse up one's fallen forces. What he's doing here is fundamentally what he does, say, in the very great piece, "An Ordinary Evening in New Haven": it is to vary again his characteristic themes, it is to practice, it is to rehearse again an overcoming of the perpetual crisis which always will come again. "Crisis," as I use the term, particularly in "crisis-poem," is indeed what I mean by the trope or term "crossing." It does not mean, "Shall I run away with another man's wife?" or "Shall I hang myself at four p.m.?" or "Do I have cancer?" or "Where is God?"

IS: Or "Where can I find a plumber on a Sunday?"

HB: Yes, it doesn't mean that at all. This poem is a "crisis-poem" because, to use the Emersonian term for it, power resides in the shooting of a gap, in the crossing to an aim; power exists in the moment of transition: it, too, records the power which is gain and loss, loss and gain, in a moment of transition. It too is a fiction of duration, or trope of temporality.

IS: Is the image of the sun, here, what you would call a "trope of discontinuity?"

HB: Yes, it is that attempt of trying to make a natural trope, or trope of natural repetition, into an emblem or metalepsis of discontinuity. Indeed it is trying to make the sun of Blake into the sun of Nietzsche's Zarathustra. It's a rather Nietzschean poem, for surely that is the way that Nietzsche most affected Stevens: by

---

3 "A Vision of the Last Judgement," in *Complete Writings*, edited by Geoffrey Keynes (Oxford: Oxford University Press, [1969] 1976), p. 617.

giving him an emblem of the overman's thrust towards the discontinuity of freedom, or the freedom of discontinuity, in the metalepsis of the solar trajectory. Of course, in teaching it, one would emphasize the revisionary element in regard to Stevens himself. It is most palpably, from its very look on the page, an authentic and heartening revision of "The Snow Man." He tells us that quite overtly in the eighth line: "No longer a battered panache above snow." It is a poem of superb self-recovery, and to that extent it's a poem of having healed one's own reductiveness, of having dispelled the "Mrs Alfred Uruguay" in onself. Most Stevens critics don't wish to see that: they wish to see him as a powerful reductionist, because they are impotent reductionists. But never mind.

If I had to give the poem an epigraph, and speak of its truest precursor – again the repressed precursor, the precursor not quite evaded – then the true anterior text which I would urge my student to regard is neither Nietzsche nor Blake nor Wordsworth: it is that marvelous moment of moments in "Song of Myself" where our father Walt Whitman cries out: "Dazzling and tremendous how quick the sun-rise would kill me,/If I could not now and always send sun-rise out of me."[4] If I were not as great a sunrise, in myself, now and always, then, dazzling and tremendous, how quick this would kill me! Though Stevens would have bitterly protested the notion that that was the text upon which he was writing a variation, it is what I would say is being excluded here – not quite successfully.

IS: I want to go over some of the ground we have already covered, from a different perspective. In the 1950s and early 1960s, you were obviously very uncomfortable with the New-Critical orthodoxies. What was the atmosphere at Yale in the late 1950s?

HB: An Anglo-Catholic nightmare. Everyone was on their knees to Mr T. S. Eliot and, no matter what you read or how you taught it or how you wrote, you were always supposed to gravely incline the head and genuflect to the spirit of Mr Thomas Stearns Eliot, God's vicar upon earth, the true custodian of Western tradition.

IS: Frye believes that your discomfort with the New Critics at Yale explains the strong effect of his early work on you. In your first couple of books, Fryean phrases – romanticism as a "displaced Protestantism," the "autonomous imagination" and so on – are everywhere.

HB: Certainly: all Frye, all Frye. But in fact he's wrong: the effect

4 "Song of Myself," in *Complete Poetry and Selected Prose*, edited by James E. Miller (Boston: Houghton Mifflin, 1959), p. 43.

goes back much earlier. *Fearful Symmetry* came out in 1947. I, who
had always been fascinated by Blake, was then a freshman at
Cornell University, and had not encountered the Yale scene. My
teachers were romanticists, and Cornell was not a hotbed of the
New Criticism.

Frye's effect was much more personal, I must admit. In terms
of my own theorizations, one would have to say that one's attempt
to find precursors here and there merely evades the truth, which
is that the precursor proper has to be Northrop Frye. I purchased
and read *Fearful Symmetry* a week or two after it had come out and
reached the bookstore in Ithaca, New York. It ravished my heart
away. I thought it was the best book I'd ever read about anything.
I must have read it a hundred times between 1947 and 1950,
probably intuitively memorized it, and will never escape the effect
of it. I wouldn't want to go and read it now, because I'm sure I
would disagree with all of it – but it doesn't matter, agreeing or
disagreeing. To compare lesser things with greater, my relation to
Frye's criticism is Pater's relation to Ruskin's criticism, or
Shelley's relation to Wordsworth's poetry: the authentic precursor, no matter how one tries to veil it or conceal it both from
oneself and from others.

Frye is surely the major literary critic in the English language.
Now that I am mature, and willing to face my indebtedness,
Northrop Frye does seem to me – for all of my complaints about
his idealization and his authentic Platonism and his authentic
Christianity – a kind of Miltonic figure. He is certainly the largest
and most crucial literary critic in the English language since the
divine Walter and the divine Oscar: he really is that good. I have
tried to find an alternative father in Mr Burke, who is a charming
fellow and a very powerful critic, but I don't come from Burke: I
come out of Frye.

IS: What interests me is that, even right at the beginning – in your
review of the *Anatomy*, for example – there are the seeds of your
later departure from Frye. In the review, you say that he's too
much of a reconciler, and not enough of a quarreler, where the
New Critics are concerned (p. 133). You are clearly a quarreler,
rather than a reconciler.

HB: Oh yes. In 1959, Frye and his wife kindly came to have dinner
or tea with us in London. I see now, retrospectively, that it was
a little hilarious, because I was trying to push him into my own
open war against Eliot and the New Criticism. He wouldn't have
it. He obviously had, then as now, mixed feelings about Eliot as
a cultural prophet. I remember remarking, rather too nastily, in
A Map of Misreading, that Frye's "myth of concern" is a sort of Low

Church version of Eliot's High Church myth of "tradition and the individual talent" (p. 30). I would phrase it a little more genteelly now, out of respect and affection for Mr Frye, but it is true: one of them is the Low Church version of the other. The fundamental difference, in terms of literary theory and practice, between Eliot and Frye, is the difference between an Anglo-Catholic and a United Church of Canada, "Inner Light" version of your seventeenth-century Protestant. I'm not saying that one sees Mr Frye riding to Armageddon on a white horse behind Major-General Thomas Harrison of the Fifth Monarchy men, but it *is* the "Inner Light." Surely the Emersonian single candle of the imagination must be, on some level, what most deeply moved Frye towards Stevens.

IS: Whereas your quarrel with Frye is that he is a reconciler, his quarrel with you is that you are a quarreler. You know: he said when I interviewed him that he didn't like your idea of an "authentic Romantic" – which, interestingly enough, I traced to a remark you made about Stevens in *The Visionary Company* (p. xxv).

HB: I find that very curious. What can he mean? Obviously there are *inauthentic* Romantics. Matthew Arnold is an inauthentic Romantic, surely. I wonder what it is about the word "authentic."

IS: It is the emphasis on value. Frye's mission was to banish value-judgment from criticism. Here, you parted ways with him very severely. It's the Dr Johnson element in Bloom – the separation of the genuine from the inauthentic – that Frye cannot . . .

HB: Well, we were born different people. Johnson and Hazlitt were very pugnacious fellows. Frye may be the first great critic in English literature whose pugnacity is diverted to other purposes. He may not want to face it any more, but one of the things that first attracted me to him was the real pugnacity that was there. In a review of Allen Tate which I still treasure, Frye, unable to stand this Anglo-Catholic, Eliotic bit a moment longer, cries out that this is nothing but the myth of the "Great Western Butterslide."[5] It's a marvelous moment. The chapter called "Antique Drum" in his little book on Eliot is marvelous. Those ironies! Mr Frye is, in his own charming way, a very vicious ironist indeed.

You cannot banish value-judgment. How can you get it out? To have written as he did on Blake is an enormous act of value-judgment. To exalt romance above the other modes, while denying

5 "Ministry of Angels," in *Northrop Frye on Culture and Literature*, edited by Robert D. Denham (Chicago: University of Chicago Press, 1978), p. 132.

64   Criticism in Society

that you are doing so, is an act of value-judgment, and Frye is a
romance critic above all else. The cruelest thing I've ever said
about him, I'll stick to: he is the great homogenizer of literature.
I really don't like that. I dislike that book *The Secular Scripture*, and
of course the single book by him I dislike the most is *The Great Code*.
The man's powers are undiminished in *The Secular Scripture*, and
even more in *The Great Code*; but I deplore, at this time in
particular, a reading of the Bible in which the Hebrew Bible
vanishes, and there is only the Christian Bible.

IS: I put this question to Frye, and said that Bloom was bound to
be uncomfortable with this Christianizing, New-Testamentary,
"Great Code of Art" view of literature. He gave the example of
Shylock to imply that the poets *have* worked with a Christian
framework, not with a gnostic or Jewish or Hebrew one.

HB: Yes and no. The answer to Shylock is Barabbas, is it not?
Marlowe does not work with a Christian framework, in spite of the
absurdity of Marlovian scholarship. Marlowe is a mad hermeticist
who hates Christianity, obviously, as he hates heterosexuality – he
even links the two.

I do not read Shakespeare as a Christian poet. His is the most
comprehensive of Western consciousnesses. Is Hamlet a Christian? Shakespeare is so much larger than any other poet, any other
writer. Larger than Plato, infinitely larger than Freud. You'd have
to take the whole of the Bible together to get any representation of
consciousness as wide as Shakespeare's. I think that, in Shakespeare too, there is, as it were, a naturally gnostic element which
comes from the poet-hood. He puts it in scattered places. The one
place where he lets it take over completely is *Macbeth*, which to me
makes sense only as a kind of gnostic universe. It cannot be an
accident that Shakespeare goes out of his way in that play to make
everyone, with the possible partial exception of Lady Macbeth, so
uninteresting compared to Macbeth. I take it that the play is an
implicit critique of why we find Macbeth so interesting. It's a critique of imaginative solipsism, of the near-alliance between the
imagination and solipsism, of why we are always more interesting
to ourselves than anybody else can be interesting to us. That
terrible inwardness of Macbeth, we go into; and he is very
interesting indeed, as we are interesting to ourselves.

IS: In *A Map of Misreading*, you call Frye's "myth of concern" a "lie
against time" (p. 30). Geoffrey Hartman has said that, in order
to overturn Frye, you had to reintroduce the "sour-myth of Time"
back into literary criticism (*Fate of Reading*, p. 46). It's certainly an
unusual view of time, though, isn't it? Because it doesn't include
social history.

HB: Oh no. I think that – especially these days, with the neo-Marxist revival in American academic literary criticism – I get more battered on that score than on any other. It just makes me more pugnacious and more combative. There is no social dimension to what we do. I insist upon that more and more strongly.

Reading, writing, teaching, being taught: the experience of literature is the experience of an isolate and solipsizing glory. We're just fooling ourselves and trying to assuage our bad consciences. It is the greatest and most superb of narcissistic self-indulgences: *and why should it not be?* What is wrong with that? It restitutes our wounded narcissism. That is a phrase I've used before, and everyone has pounced on it, saying: "Aha! A 1970s narcissist!" Bugger them: because they don't know how to read, because they've never had the joy of reading. It is a solitary and inward joy. It is an overwhelming joy. It is indeed a gnosticizing joy. It surely is our most authentic experience of poetry. It is down to the person alone. That is what Dickinson's poetry is all about, which is why it is so superb and honest. It's a solitary transport, which in the end we desperately try to communicate to others. But we can no more communicate it to others than we can communicate our love for others to them.

IS: If I could try to articulate my problem with all that: Platonizing critics, like Frye, believe in a realm of the imagination; poetry, and the dialogue between poets, takes place, for them, in some completely idealized world of forms. You have de-idealized that vision, and . . .

HB: I know what's coming: I insist upon throwing that into the social sphere and, if that is the case, can you then try to push the social sphere out of the act of apprehension, in which criticism begins?

I don't think I socialize, in any way, the *agon*. I think that societal *agon* is a parody of the inward *agon* that reading and writing constitutes. I don't believe that I am a mystic. I do believe that I am, in my gnostic Jewish way, religious. I've been haunted my whole life long by a great sentence from Meister Eckhart, which goes, "We are all asleep in the outward life."[6] I take it that the only pragmatic way of not being asleep in the outward life is to read poetry, to teach poetry, to talk to one another about poetry – in the broad sense of what poetry is. I do not believe that there is any social utility to that. I do think that there is no cooperation, even in that sphere. I believe that there is *agon*, even in that sphere.

6 I have been unable to trace this quotation.

I think that when we first fall in love with poets – as I first fell in love with Hart Crane and with Blake – it is like first love between men and women.

IS: But first love between men and women is a heavily socialized activity.

HB: I don't think so. Think of those glorious first loves which are rather like Dante's love for Beatrice. They are not even idealizations: they are purely inward matters. Some little girl whom you and I saw on a street somewhere in a city when we were 8 or 9: we carried the image in us for years after, but perhaps exchanged only one glance. That's not social, is it?

IS: Any love, to get past square one, has to assume social forms – courtships, rituals – which change with history.

HB: Well, if you're going to make a living out of the reading and discussion of poetry, then you go into those rituals. But I don't know that that is not equivalent to being asleep in the outward life. I'll tell you, dear Imre: what I understand least about the current academy, and the current literary scene of criticism, is this lust for social enlightenment; this extraordinary and, I believe, mindless movement towards proclaiming our way out of all introspections, our way out of guilt and sorrow, by proclaiming that the poet is a slum-lord – whether he wants to be or not – and that there is no distinction between Yale University – or the University of Melbourne – and the New York Stock Exchange.

This is clap-trap. The poet is not a slum-lord; the critic is not a hireling of the stock exchange. I am weary of this nonsense, and will not put up with it. It has nothing to do with *my* experience of reading poetry, of writing criticism and of teaching other people how to read poetry and write criticism. If they wish to alleviate the sufferings of the exploited classes, let them live up to their pretensions, let them abandon the academy and go out there and work politically and economically and in a humanitarian spirit. They are the hypocrites: the so-called Marxist critics, and all of this rabblement that follows them now in the academies. They are the charlatans, they are the self-deceivers and the deceivers of others. If that is bitter, it understates my contempt for them.

IS: What's the source of that contempt?

HB: I am a proletarian; they are not. I'm almost the only person I know at Yale University who was born and raised in a working-class family. I'm the son of a New York garment worker, who was an unwilling member of the International Ladies Garment Workers' Union, which he always despised.

These critics are American versions of that Parisian intellectual and social disease I can least abide – it is responsible for almost all

French literary and critical attitudes, including deconstruction, from the middle nineteenth century to the present day – which is the high bourgeoisie being unable to stand its status as the high bourgeoisie, while continuing to enjoy it in every possible respect. I am more than weary of this, and I'm especially weary of the self-righteousness that goes with their hypocrisy. How is it that they don't bore themselves to death? I can walk into the Yale Library periodical room any afternoon I want to, and I swear that I can read fifteen to twenty fresh attacks upon me for forgetting that the social world exists. They thus proclaim their critical originality and genius, by simply discovering what I say all the time anyway. Which is: forget it; it is not your function; you deal with a solitary pleasure which it is immensely difficult to impart usefully to others.

The only critical wisdom I know is that there is no method except yourself. Everything else is an imposture. There is only oneself. Denying it, or trying to claim that the self is a trope, talking about social processes, waving *The Eighteenth Brumaire* at me: it just doesn't make any difference, whether it be Fred Jameson or Jacques Derrida. The best critic and best human being I've known in my life was my dear friend Paul de Man. "The trouble with you, Harold," he would say with a smile, cupping my head in his hands, and looking at me with an affection that always made me want to weep, "is that you are crazy: you do not believe in the 'troot.' " I would look at him, shake my head sadly and say:

"No, I do not believe in the 'troot' because there is no 'troot,' dear Paul.

"There is no method: there is yourself, and you are highly idiosyncratic.

"And you clone, my dear: I dislike what you do as a teacher, because your students are as alike as two peas in a pod."

I've never had two students who really studied with me who resembled either me or one another in the slightest. All that a teacher can do is to help someone discover what his or her own personality is. If that is sentimental humanism, let it be sentimental humanism. If that is selfishness, if that is high capitalism, if that is mercantilism: I don't care. Pragmatically, it is where and as we live. If that is a palpable ideology, why not? If that is mere selfishness, narcissism, call it what you will. I would call it something else: I would call it telling the only truth that one can tell, which is a subjective, narrow, limited, personal truth.

IS: You've mentioned de Man, and I wanted to ask you about your relation to deconstruction, which has always been a major source of confusion.

HB: There is no relation whatsoever.

IS: You got into the volume.

HB: I devised the volume, I created the volume, I thought it up, got the publisher, brought everybody together and gave the book its title, *Deconstruction and Criticism*. I am a comic critic, and all I get are serious reviews. The title was my personal joke, which no one can ever understand: I meant that those four were deconstruction, and I was criticism.

I have no relation to deconstruction. I never did have, I don't have now, and I never will have. Nothing is more alien to me than deconstruction.

IS: But you were close to Hartman.

HB: Hartman and I began as close personal friends, from about 1955 on. We were, both of us, Romantic revivalists; but I think he was always more of a European formalist than I was; he believed in comp. lit. and *wissenschaftlich* and all that stuff; he was always more of a historicizer than I was; let's face it, he was always more respectable than I care to be.

IS: Can you read his work now?

HB: Hartman's work through and including the essays brought together as *Beyond Formalism* is the work of one of the four or five best critics in my own generation. From *The Fate of Reading* on, my friend Geoffrey Hartman is, in my view, the largest single American casualty of the influence of Jacques and Paul.

IS: Turning, finally, to some questions on teaching and the university, I want to ask you a question which you ask yourself in *A Map of Misreading*: "What is the larger subject of which the study of poetic influence is only a part?" (p . 63).

HB: Western revisionism. Or that large subject we haven't got a name for, that has to do with both the glory and the horror, not only of Western literature, but of Western culture: which is the deep split between the fact that its religion and its morality are Hebraic-Christian, and its cognition and aesthetics – and therefore its dominant imaginative forms – are Greek.

IS: It's presumably in the direction of this larger subject that you are gesturing in *Figures of Capable Imagination*, when you write: "To say that a poem is about itself is killing" – a reference to the New Critics – "but to say it is about another poem is to go out into the world where we live" (p. 140). Is that because the competitive revisionary ratios which apply to poetry are of the same kind as the competitiveness which applies to all areas of social life?

HB: It's a question of memorability. I think this is what I find most contemptible, intellectually as well as humanly, about the derivative forms of Marxism. What I find most trivial about them is their not seeing that competition is not merely an engine for exploitation; that, particularly in the realm of the spirit, it is the inevitable answer to the question of life being limited and time being limited. What are we to do? Why, after all, do we have one friend rather than another? You must choose. It isn't chosen for you. Why do we read one book rather than another? Why, for that matter, do we read one critic rather than another? Time is very limited. You can read all your life, for twenty-four hours a day, and you can read only a portion of what is worth reading. You can know only so many people. You can look at only so many sunsets. A fresh poem written now, a fresh critical essay written now, a fresh story or novel, competes against a vast overpopulation. That, I think, is what criticism must address itself to. But that is not the class-struggle: it is the question of how we individuate.

IS: What almost surprises me is that, when you had this original vision of the poetic landscape as being a battle to individuate, a battle to assert, a battle to become self-reliant, you didn't recoil in horror from the vision. We have been accustomed to think of the poets as the final repositories of a benign, liberal humanism. This is a much darker picture. It's almost a poetic analogue to fascism.

HB: I reject that completely. It has nothing to do with fascism.

IS: Strength, the battles of strength . . .

HB: That's Nietzsche.

IS: Well?

HB: It's like those people who thought that Nietzsche was a forerunner of Hitler. He certainly was not: he was not an anti-Semite, he was not a totalitarian. He was an individualist, trying to teach individualism. But he knew what élitism was. Elitism is not protofascism. Elitism is the condition of the spirit, as it is the condition of literature.

IS: What about Reagan?

HB: Reagan is mindless.

IS: Yes, but he's one result of Emersonian individualism.

HB: Henry Ford is one result of Emerson, and Walt Whitman is another.

IS: But Reagan is Emerson's ideal of the politician: instinctual, self-reliant . . .

HB: I don't believe so. Emerson is not inhumane. Emerson, you must remember, fought long and bitterly and memorably against his own state's accepting the fugitive Slave Law, and broke with his hero Daniel Webster on exactly that basis. I think you are confusing two very different matters. The social quarrel between gnosticism and the early church was the quarrel between élitist intellectuals – who thought that you could be saved never by faith,

but only by a complex, inward and very cognitive knowing – and
those who felt that you could be saved, however dumb or insen-
sitive you were, by mouthing some formulae. The quarrel
continues.

     People cannot stand the saddest truth I know about the very
nature of reading and writing imaginative literature, which is that
poetry does not teach us how to talk to other people: it teaches us
how to talk to ourselves. What I'm desperately trying to do is to
get students to talk to themselves as though they are indeed
themselves, and not someone else.

IS: All I was gesturing at before was: can you exalt individualism
    and Emersonian self-reliance, and then disavow Reagan?

HB: Yes, of course. Waldo does not tell us that the poor ought to
    be starved. He only tells us that you are not to spend your life and
    all your energies, if you have other things to do, fighting for the
    poor.

     By the way: you who have so keen an ear must be aware that
    part of the cosmological, psychological and rhetorical joke of the
    tetralogy was my own shock, my own dislike, at and of what I was
    saying; my own feeling that these are intolerable truths.

IS: Yes, there is a slight recoil. It is the difference between the Chris-
    tian motif of having a vision and then marrying it, and having a
    vision and then trying to divorce it.

HB: There was a considerable recoil in me, from about 1965 to
    about 1975.

IS: You've now learnt to marry what you've made?

HB: During this last decade? I wouldn't say that, but I've taken to
    heart Kierkegaard's great statement: "Only the truth which
    edifies is truth for you."[7]

IS: You were talking before about the saddest truth being that
    poetry can only teach us how to talk to ourselves. Wouldn't the
    saddest, gloomiest, most demystifying truth that we could possibly
    teach be the Marxist truth: that history really does determine art?
    That would undo not only the formalists, but almost the whole
    academy.

HB: Why is it a Marxist truth? Since that is itself a moderately
    strong misreading of a Hegelian truth, and that Hegelian truth is
    itself a moderately strong misreading of a Heraklitean truth, why
    not go back to the Heraklitean truth itself: *ethos* is the *daimon*.
    That's the real overdetermination: there are no accidents. Marx is
    a shadow on the face of Hegel, and Hegel is an enormous shadow

7 *Either/Or*, translated by Walter Lowrie (Princeton: Princeton University Press, [1959] 1974), II,
p. 356.

on the larger face of Heraklitus. And who knows what Heraklitus
is?

IS: You're clearly troubled by what your own wisdom constitutes as
a teacherly thing. In the essay in the *Deconstruction* book, you say
that poets make others free by teaching them the stances or positions of freedom (p. 3). In that "Covering Cherub" lecture, you
say that "discontinuity is freedom." Aren't our universities more
dedicated to teaching the triad of continuity, repetition and
homogeneity? Can a lesson about discontinuity be taught within
the university?

HB: I teach at Yale University, and that's what I teach.

IS: But is there a good fit between you and Yale University?

HB: No. I've been a maverick since I arrived there. I'm now a
maverick who's been here since 1951, and been on the faculty
continuously since 1955. I don't think there's a "good fit." Why
did I leave the English Department? I couldn't bear it, and they
couldn't bear me. No department could accommodate me, and I
couldn't accommodate any department. But the university has
learnt to accommodate me, and I've learnt to accommodate the
university. What else, but a university, could have accommodated
me? Had I become a rabbi, even of a reconstructionist or Reform
kind, they would long since have thrown me out – or I would have
thrown myself out.

Mr Frye never did defrock himself, as I understand it. Once I
asked him: "Are you still a minister of the United Church of
Canada?" "Sure," he said. I said, "What do you do with it?" He
said, "I marry and bury my students."

IS: Is the freedom of discontinuity a freedom from society and social
ideology? In that case, the freedom that revisionary criticism
teaches would be the opposite to Frye's view of criticism: he sees
criticism as the mediator between society and the arts.

HB: Absolutely not. That is my split from him: I do not believe in
his "myth of concern." Criticism is as solitary as lyric poetry.
Hazlitt is no more or less social than Keats, and no more or less
a mediator. Is Ashbery someone who mediates between society
and the individual? I suppose a thoroughgoing Marxist would say,
"Sure, otherwise he would have no coherence." I would say,
"Absolutely not, otherwise I would not love his poetry as I do."
I do not think there is the slightest difference between Ashbery and
myself, in that respect.

IS: Scholem points out that, although gnostic knowledge may be
more conservative than normative knowledge, there is always a
troubled relationship between the gnostic and institutionalized
religion. This brings us back to the discomfort which you clearly

feel within this institution. I believe you've described yourself as the "Yiddish Dr Johnson." One can, in fact, see you as more comfortable within an Augustan, pre-institutional context – jockeying for a word in the coffee-house, writing for *The Rambler*.

HB: We do change. If someone had said to me in, say, 1955: "Which is a more vital and great poem, 'The Dunciad' or Blake's 'Jerusalem'?" my mouth would have slung open and I would unhesitatingly have said, "Blake's 'Jerusalem', of course." Now my mouth would sling open and I would unhesitatingly say, " 'The Dunciad'." Pope seems to me a more powerful poet even than Blake. I would never have dreamed, thirty years ago, that I would say that.

IS: The eighteenth-century scholars in Oxford will be running for cover when they hear that Bloom's now going to take over Pope.

HB: I've written a glowing introduction to Pope's poetry for a Modern Critical Views volume that is not yet out.

IS: Aren't you going to leave anything for the "Moldy Figs?" Leave them Dryden.

HB: No, no: not a poet of Pope's stature, but I will take their Dryden (when I have time). Dryden is a great poet. Shenstone: they can have Shenstone. Matthew Arnold! For God's sake, let them have Matthew Arnold! They *are* Matthew Arnold! Let them go poke around tombstones in the Swiss cemeteries looking for who Marguerite was or was not.

IS: You'd let them have Pound, wouldn't you? They're having a good time with Pound right now, with their appalling "Centenary Observance."[8]

HB: I mean what I've said, that Eliot and Pound are the Cowley and Cleveland of the age. Eliot is a better poet than Cowley or Cleveland, but Pound is not. Pound is as good a poet as Edmund Waller. They have much in common, as Pound I think recognized. My favorite prose sentence by Mr Ezra Pound is in one of his published letters: "All the Jew part of the Bible is black evil."[9] And they ask me to take that seriously as a Western mind? "All the Jew part of the Bible is black evil." The prophet Isaiah? The tales of Jacob? The Book of Psalms? The Book of Job? The "J-writer?"

IS: One last question about teaching. There is a phrase at the beginning of *Agon* saying that you neither want nor urge others to apply, or even to accept, your own critical terminology (p. 38). Of course,

8 A reference to a series of festivities, in honor of the great man, held at Yale during November, 1985.
9 "To Henry Swabey," May 9, 1940, *Letters of Ezra Pound*, edited by D. D. Paige (New York: Harcourt, Brace, 1950), p. 345.

Frye's main justification for the *Anatomy* was always that it could be taught. Your point is the opposite. So what – if not a structure or a methodology – *are* you concerned to teach your students?

HB: What Emerson is always telling us: which is that every received text – even Shakespeare, even the Bible – is secondary. *They* are primary. *They* are the text. The Bible or Shakespeare is a commentary upon them. There are no texts. There are only ourselves.

Geoffrey Hartman

4

Geoffrey Hartman

"I think the intellectual effort is always against enchantment, but that doesn't mean that every enchantment must be rigidly resisted, as a matter of Superman-like honor. Then the cure is worse than the disease."

Geoffrey H. Hartman, who was born in Germany in 1929, is the Karl Young Professor of English and Comparative Literature at Yale. Further biographical details are provided in the interview itself. It was recorded early in December, 1985, in Hartman's office (which is as crammed with books and manuscripts as his texts are with puns and allusions). Like Frye and Bloom, Hartman was an important part of the "Romantic revival" movement of the 1950s and 1960s. But, unlike them, his early (and abiding) attachment was not to Blake and Shelley, but to the milder version of romanticism found in Wordsworth. And two decades later, again unlike Frye or Bloom, Hartman would come to play a leading role in a completely different movement: American deconstruction.

The reasons for Hartman's interest in Wordsworth, as for much else in his career, are doubtless tied up with the impact of European fascism and anti-Semitism on his own life. By the time he arrived in the United States in 1946, Hartman had probably seen too much of apocalyptic yearnings and unconstrained idealisms to be initially much attracted by Blake. Instead, he turned to a poet in whom an apocalyptic idealism is being continually qualified by a recognition of those things – nature, other people, experience – which are always outside the imagination, and will not be controlled by it. In Hartman's first book, *The Unmediated Vision* (1954), there is already an implicit awareness of the way in which an *unqualified* romanticism, where the imagination has become a total circumference and a vehicle for final truths, can drift towards the intellectual habits of fascism:

> Art . . . has this advantage over the other modes of knowledge: it, alone, is in the service of no one, not even of truth. For truth, even when sought for its own sake, will surely destroy in the searcher his consciousness of human responsibilities. Abstraction is never less than total. Great poetry, however, is written by men who have chosen to stay bound by experience, who would not – or could not – free themselves by an act of knowledge from the immediacy of good and evil.   (p. xi)

Wordsworth's sense of an unending dialectic between nature and imagination, irresolvable by any act of abstraction, is the central subject of *Wordsworth's Poetry*, published in 1964. Early on in the book (p. 33), Hartman points out that critics of Wordsworth have generally had him choosing one or the other side of this dialectic, and so have portrayed him either as worshipping nature (as in Blake's derogatory view), or as utterly opposed to nature (Bloom's argument in the contemporary *Visionary Company*). Hartman's own picture of Wordsworth is of a poet who, having sensed the human cost of any such choice, has *learned to live with* the dialectic itself:

> One part of him said, leave nature and cleave to imagination. The other part, fearing that imagination could not be cleaved to, indeed that it would take him beyond human-heartedness even out of this world, answered, cleave to nature and leave vision and romance, those errors of the childhood of poetry.   (p. xiv)

Since *Wordsworth's Poetry*, in his most influential phase, Hartman has turned increasingly to the essay, rather than the "unified" book, and has concentrated his efforts on practical criticism and critical history. He has resisted "critical theory" proper, being suspicious of the totalizing, reductive impulse in any theory that would claim to have mastery over literature. In *Criticism in the Wilderness*, published in 1980, he admits to remaining skeptical about "the possibility of a truly comprehensive literary theory or literary history," and says that the style of contemporary reading to which he adheres

> aims at a hermeneutics of indeterminacy. It proposes a type of analysis that has renounced the ambition to master or de-mystify its subject (text, psyche) by technocratic, predictive, or authoritarian formulas.   (pp. 299, 41)

Hartman's eventual move towards Derrida and *différance* is simply an extension of his longstanding distrust of totalization and transcendence, and of his sense that a text will always surprise those who think that they have pinned down its meaning or restricted its valency. Through Derrida, he has been able to inscribe *différance* – permanent delay and deferral – on to the more traditional "delay" of the reader-response chain. Delay does not lead to eventual determination; meaning does not cease its wanderings, nor criticism its wonderings:

> indeterminacy does not merely *delay* the determination of meaning, that is, suspend premature judgements and allow greater thoughtfulness. The delay is not heuristic alone, a device to slow the act of reading till we appreciate . . . its complexity. The delay is intrinsic: from a certain point of view, it is thoughtfulness itself, Keats's "negative capability," a labor that aims not to overcome the negative or indeterminate but to stay within it as long as is necessary.
>
> (*Criticism in the Wilderness*, p. 270)

Hartman's interest in *différance* has also, at the level of practical criticism, worked to liberate another trait that was already present: a fascination with wandering puns, etymologies, double-entendres and euphemisms. In a recent essay, Hartman considers one of Wordsworth's most mystifying "Lucy" poems, "A Slumber did my Spirit Seal," and discovers a series of funereal motifs hovering beneath the surface of the poem. Lucy, says Wordsworth, "neither hears nor sees" but is "Rolled round in earth's diurnal course,/With rocks, and stones, and trees." "Diurnal," suggests Hartman, divides into "die" and "urn," while "course" suggests "corpse." The whole image of "gravitation," meanwhile, whispers the word "grave." In addition, Hartman discerns a "subvocal word" that is "uttered without being written out." It rhymes with three of the words actually in the poem – "fears," "years," and "hears" – and is an auditory anagram of the final word, "trees": "tears" (*Easy Pieces*, pp. 145, 149–50).

But Hartman's most important theoretical application of *différance* has been to the traditional opposition between literary criticism and the art it deals with. Here, the influence of Derrida has merged comfortably with Hartman's sense of the inseparability of commentary and text in Hebraic biblical exegesis, as well as with his sense of Wordsworth's continuing alternation of reality and imagination. All of these strands now come together into a new view of the relation between poetry and criticism, which is a challenge to the "objective" style that has dominated from Arnold to Frye:

The situation of the discourse we name *criticism* is . . . no different from that of any other. If this recognition implies a reversal, then it is the master–servant relation between criticism and creation that is being overturned in favor of what Wordsworth, describing the interaction of nature and mind, called "mutual domination" or "interchangeable supremacy."

Hartman views criticism now as being "within literature, not outside of it looking in," and projects a vision of the critical essay as an "intellectual poem" (*Criticism in the Wilderness*, pp. 259, 1, 196).

He has been as good as his word, here, by investing his own style with puns, neologisms, ambiguities and other devices normally reserved for poetic discourse. This has placed Hartman at the most "ludic" end of deconstruction; so that, in substance and in style, he is the American critic who has most freely exploited the possibilities for dialectical liberation opened up by Derrida. And in his latest book of essays, in a gesture that is properly a *nostos*, Hartman has not hesitated to extend the complicity of poetry and criticism to a point where the latter may now share something of the anti-totalizing, anti-authoritarian power so long ago attributed to the former:

> Our experience of modern propaganda methods, their ability to program or brainwash entire nations, is as frightening, in its way, as the modern superweapons. . . . The dictatorship of the propagandists, their manipulation not only of the mass media but also of scholarship, became a reality in Nazi Germany and Stalinist Russia, and is the one historical fact that must not be forgotten in any general consideration of the emergence of literary theory as increasingly anti-ideological.
>
> (*Easy Pieces*, p. 214)

Imre Salusinszky: Your writing career encompasses much of what's happened in American criticism since the early 1950s, and I hope that in the time available today many of the issues that have led to this book might be clarified. In this case, however, I want to lead off with a biographical question. To be frank, I've never been completely clear on where you were born, where you were educated, and what course of events brought you to the United States.

Geoffrey Hartman: I was born in Germany, in Frankfurt-am-Main. I had to leave at the age of 9, about six months before the war, because of the persecution of the Jews. I was lucky enough to find a refuge in England, where I received my education. All my secondary school education took place in Aylesbury, where I went to an English grammar school.

In a sense, I was stranded in England during the war. Just before sitting for the competition for Oxford and Cambridge, I decided to join my mother who, in the meantime, had gone to the United States. I came to New York in 1946. I received advanced standing and completed my BA at Queens College in 1949. This was after half a year at Hunter College evening classes: I came to America at the moment of demobilization, and it was very hard to find a place, even in the City University. When I graduated, I was not quite 20. I then went to Yale from 1949 and – with a Fulbright year in France – received my Ph.D. in Comparative Literature in 1953. After that I spent two years as a draftee in the United States Army, where they called me "Doctor Private." I was asked to return to Yale in 1955 and started teaching.

IS: So *The Unmediated Vision* is a version of your Ph.D.?

GH: *The Unmediated Vision* was my Ph.D. plus two months of summer revision before I had to go into the army. I remember reading proofs in boot camp.

IS: Were your parents intellectuals? Professional people? Working people?

GH: A mixture. My grandfather had his doctorate, and taught Religious Studies at the Philantropicn, which was a famous Jewish school in Frankfurt. My father was a businessman. I wouldn't say that either my father or my mother were intellectuals in the sense that my grandfather was.

IS: I want to discuss a few important moments in your writing and then, towards the end of the discussion, come back to some of these big questions about the social function of criticism which are the focus of this book.

During your early years as a writer, Frye was becoming the major figure on the scene of American literary criticism. You haven't had anything like the struggle with Frye that Bloom has had, but with both you and Bloom one can find the seeds of some of your later positions in some of your earlier responses to Northrop Frye. We have seen how this works in Bloom. What I'm referring to, in your case, is the essay on Frye in *Beyond Formalism*, where your critique of Frye is that there is no "pure myth," there are only displacements (p. 37). Does that seem to you, now, a "proto-deconstructive" critique of Frye?

GH: Now that you mention it. But I was never a person conscious of movements, until around 1970. I'm sure I responded instinctively to the intellectual atmosphere around me. I must have, because the preface to *The Unmediated Vision* is very direct about institutional factors. I became a polemicist rather late. Polemics, for me, was engaging with the texts of critics as intensely as one would with the texts of literature – I've maintained that position – rather than forming a group, or trying to refine and extend the work of a group. But, now that you mention it: yes, there was life before deconstruction. What happened with Derrida – it didn't happen to me only – was that the consciousness of American criticism was raised by several notches. I've complained about that: not that it shouldn't be raised, but that there should be such a strong divide of before and after. I consider myself an engaged historian of criticism, rather than a theorist, and I probably did not engage with Derrida fully until *Glas* came out. I don't think I read Derrida before 1969 or 1970. It was only around 1973 or 1974 that he meant something significant to me, in terms of the history of criticism.

IS: You said that your reactions, early on, were instinctual. So there wasn't the feeling of oppression by the New-Critical school, here at Yale, that Bloom had?

GH: No. First of all, I didn't go through the English Department; Bloom did. I had two courses. One was in Anglo-Saxon, which didn't leave much room for Christian humanism. The other did: I had a course from Louis Martz which, however, I appreciated for the way it marched me through the poetry of the Renaissance. I was, I think, living sufficiently in my own textual world not to be particularly upset by what was around me. Moreover, because I had had a connection with Auerbach, and knew something about European stylistics, the New Criticism had always appeared to me as something small within a much larger pedagogical and cultural enterprise. It didn't single itself out for me, as having to be combatted.

IS: Regarding what you said about movements and schools: there is, of course, a thing now referred to as the "Yale School." Does it exist? If so, what are the advantages and disadvantages of being associated with it?

GH: It's still a mystery to me, why something was denominated or targeted as the Yale School. It was the middle of the 1970s when we found ourselves identified as such. There was a review, by Poirier, of *The Fate of Reading*, which was one of the first signs of this. Up to that point, Bloom, Hillis Miller and I simply enjoyed each other's work, and perhaps committed the sin of reading each other's work, and not being afraid to refer to it. So I had no problem in reviewing Bloom, or de Man for that matter. I thought that was part of the intellectual enterprise. It may have

contributed, though, to a feeling on the part of other people, that
there was something going on at Yale. The focus had been on Yale
anyway, because of the New Criticism.

What happened then was that we contributed to the identification, by publishing *Deconstruction and Criticism*. We did this, partly,
to "show them that we're very different from each other." Of
course, that was silly. I remember arguing with the publisher that
there should not be a blurb saying that this is a manifesto. I said,
"Call it an anti-manifesto, and you'll get the same publicity effect,
and it will be closer to the truth." But you can't fight the advertising industry. (By the way, the original conception of the book was
that we would all write on Shelley. Derrida, although increasingly
intrigued by English romanticism, felt uncomfortable, so he did his
thing. I found myself lacking time, so I did another essay on
Wordsworth. Only Paul de Man ended up writing on Shelley.)

So I think that we contributed, by allowing ourselves to be put
under one cover, to the perception that there was a Yale School.
What difficulties has this brought? I think about what psychological or sociological need this sort of identification points to. To
me, it really doesn't make a difference. I would have read the way
I did, and the authors I did, anyway. It doesn't embarrass me; nor
does it particularly inspire me. I don't get the same kind of love–
hate reviews as Bloom, so I think that each of us would probably
reply in a different way. I would understand if Harold Bloom were
more upset by it than I, because generally people who talk of a
Yale School decide that this or that one is going to be the target,
the *chef d'école*. I am enough of a mediating sort of a personality –
or slippery – that they have difficulty with me. They try to give
me a kick here and there, but I am not targeted as much as some
of the others.

IS: Talking of being a mediator, one consistent strain in all your
work is the mediation between Continental, or more theoretical,
modes of criticism, and the Anglo-American or practical modes.
This is also reflected internally, at every stage, in the reverberation
between close textual analysis and theory. The earliest major
Continental influence on your work was phenomenology. Who
was the main influence, in the first couple of books?

GH: I took phenomenology to mean describing one's responses and
feelings as directly as possible. It wasn't reader-reception, though
I can see that reader-reception has a modified phenomenological
element in it. Phenomenology meant being aware of the poet's
world, trying to enter that world, and respecting the verbal and
other difficulties. In a sense that meant, not leaving one's
sensibility at the door, but becoming aware of one's own presup-

positions by trying to enter the world of others. I read Hegel and
Husserl, but I don't know how much of that rubbed off, because
I don't think I'm very cultured in philosophy. I have the same
direct, instinctive relation to philosophy as I have to literature. I
enjoyed reading Hegel's *Phenomenology* immensely; I was very
moved by it; I saw it as a curious form of poetry. I found much
more difficulty with Husserl, but I liked his toughness of mind,
and Husserl sent me back to Descartes.

I don't know whether that is felt in *The Unmediated Vision*. The
non-literary intellectual sources were Continental: in a minor way
Husserl; in a more significant way Hegel; and then, to some
extent, Buber. Buber, not so much because he was Jewish, but
because I read him as coming out of the Romantic movement with
which I was already connected, in terms of affinity. It surprised me
later, when I met Harold Bloom, that he too had been nourished
by Buber. The difference is that I had a more easy relation to
Continental philosophy.

IS: Just having an interest in Hegel, in the early 1950s, would have
put you outside the Anglo-American "lit. crit." habits of that
time.

GH: I had the advantage of studying with René Wellek, who was so
vastly erudite a person that, when I gave him a paper on *Hamlet*,
I found mysterious scribbles in the margin: "Hegel, Hegel,
Hegel." I said: "Could it be?" I remember my astonishment
when Wellek told me, "I can see you're making progress; how
your reading is coming into your criticism." I wasn't aware of it.
Wellek understood that these realms were adjacent, although he
tried to keep criticism apart, for the purpose of his *History of
Criticism*. I had no such methodological hygiene.

I also had no one here at Yale. I knew Bloom, but Bloom really
wasn't interested in philosophy. So my companions were books.
Sartre, for instance. The excitement of discovering Sartre's *Situations*, especially the first volume, and the way that he managed to
bring philosophy together with literary perception, was very
significant to me. It made a very strong impact: that it could be
done so well, with due respect to both sides of the equation. But
I don't remember a colleague, at that time, who had similar
interests.

IS: In your early work, there is a strong interest in voice. In *The
Unmediated Vision*, you say of poetry: "Instead of giving conventional names to things, it would, like the painter, take them away
and render instead the immediate 'figure' of the senses, which in
this case especially is that of speech as pure voice" (p. 163). About
a decade later, in the essay on Frye in *Beyond Formalism*, you say

that the great work of fiction "recalls the origins of civilization in dialogic acts of naming, cursing, blessing, consoling, laughing, lamenting, and beseeching" (p. 39). Those acts have remained very important to your work.

As every schoolboy knows, however, voice as the "immediate figure of the senses" has been shown, by Derrida, to be caught up in the displacements, mediations and *différance* which are the features of "writing-in-general." Could you describe the history of voice in your work, and its accommodation of Derrida?

GH: That's a very good question and, you know, almost impossible to answer. When I tackled Derrida, that aspect bothered me least, because I felt from the beginning that it was a reaction to what I was talking about; just as, when I called my book *The Unmediated Vision*, I was perfectly aware that I was haunted by the opposite. I felt that these two things went together, and that they would never be resolved. In Derrida, I just didn't respond to what most people have taken up. I responded to the style, and to the quality of the commentary. Then, when the essays on *Glas* became *Saving the Text*, in the "Words and Wounds" section, I took on Derrida directly and said, "He *is* interested in voice; it's the energy of the *phoné* that keeps haunting him." I still think so. About the same time as I was writing that, he was giving lectures in France on "otobiography": the life of the ear. That you critique something doesn't make it go away: it makes you aware of it. This is already obvious, say, in André Malraux's *La Condition Humaine*, when one of the revolutionaries discovers "otherness" by hearing himself recorded. He doesn't recognize his voice, and he realizes the narcissistic intimacy of voice and self. And my attitude is: you can critique it, you can perhaps avoid certain errors, but that's not going to change our thinking constitutionally.

IS: And that is why you've always been haunted by "the energy of the *phoné*?"

GH: Yes, always. But I don't feel threatened by it. It is one of the elements in the human situation, just as one has a body and one has senses. In *The Unmediated Vision*, I don't even emphasize the centrality of voice, although Rilke has a finely imagined piece in which, instead of the sun, you have sound in the center. In that book I'm mainly concerned with the centrality of visual representation, and with how one can think of symbolic process as going against the tyranny or dominance of the eye. But I didn't say the dominance or tyranny of the voice. Voice was the second important factor. At that point, it seemed to me that visuality defined us more than voice in terms of a preponderance that had to be balanced.

IS: In *Easy Pieces*, you say that Derrida shows that there is no
"unmediated vision," and no "transparence of thing to thought"
(p. 194). Is that a reference to your own early endeavors?

GH: Yes. I don't want to diminish the contribution of the
individual, but the real excitement in criticism is to find a certain
wave, and wavelets within the wave, and how things move and
move back – the entire weather-map of intellectual affairs. I've
been forced to think about myself much more than I did in the
1950s or early 1960s when, as I said, I was an instinctual kind of
person when it came to literary criticism. But since I was forced
back on myself – and with age that would probably happen
anyway – I began to see that at the time of *The Unmediated Vision*
I must have been in a similar situation to de Man and Derrida.
Even though none of us three were in contact. De Man, when I
met him in 1959 or 1960, said that *The Unmediated Vision* had meant
something to him, not because it was right, but because it had been
written. It covered an area that he was deeply interested in.

IS: And this area which the book covered, and which Derrida and
de Man were also thinking about at that time, was the general
question of mediation.

GH: Yes: the mediatedness of whatever, especially the self, which
Derrida to some extent translates in the mediatedness of the voice
(though not as Harold Bloom understands it): how it is already
pre-mediated by writing.

IS: Some of the voices which your ear has picked up have been
pretty spooky, to do with hidden words, euphemisms, seances:
generally, the terrain of the magical. This applies to your recent
as well as to your early work: there is the hidden theme of mourning, for example, which you discover in Wordsworth's "A
Slumber did my Spirit Seal," in *Easy Pieces* (pp. 145–50). In *The
Fate of Reading*, we are told that "nothing is so disturbing as the
idea that all, not just figurative, language is magical" (p. 262):
again, very much a proto-deconstructive, "white mythology" kind
of statement. This interest in magic has made you vulnerable to
charges of obscurantism. So I'd ask you to clarify this magical
element in language and literature.

GH: I wonder whether you would call Cervantes an obscurantist,
because he is interested in enchantment and disenchantment.
That's what I'm interested in, too. Obviously literature has an
enchanting effect; obviously there are many things in life that are
enchanters, and life may be a process of disenchantments. What
I've found is that there's no progress in that; that one falls from
one enchantment into another through a method which one thinks
is going to disenchant one. Poetry is more courageous, in this.

Here I can quote de Man, and say that literature is not afraid of the fallacy of unmediated expression – it doesn't pretend that it can get beyond that – and in that sense it may be less naive than philosophy. So I would answer it that way: how can you read great poetry, how can you read Shelley and Blake, without giving yourself, to some extent, to that strange fire which you called "magic?"

The question then is, how romance fights against itself. That is the enlightenment theme. Very early on, I thought that those who misunderstood Romantic poetry took it too literally. They took it literally because they wanted to take it literally and so condemn it; they weren't willing to give it up. If you privilege the eighteenth century – it's silly to play these periodizing games – or Donne, you find yourself having to put childish things that you want to leave behind, but haven't, somewhere else: and they dumped them into the Romantic movement. Whereas I see the Romantic movement as being post-Enlightenment: very clearly post-, but also counter-Enlightenment, and working this out. The Romantics put themselves back into romance, but from an Enlightenment perspective; they tried to bring it forward. This is a purification pattern, but very much against absolute purification. One of my themes is that there is no absolute purification. Those who want purification too much fall into a certain kind of political fundamentalism. Much of politics is fundamentalist.

IS: This movement of falling continually into new enchantments: this is where you part ways, isn't it, with a figure who's been very influential to you, Freud? He would reduce enchantment entirely, if he could.

GH: If he could. But in *Civilization and its Discontents*, he makes peace with the fact that *eros* is what *eros* is, and that if there is an alignment of love and death, that's how it is: he has to be realistic. I think the intellectual effort is always against enchantment, but that doesn't mean that every enchantment must be rigidly resisted, as a matter of Superman-like honor. Then the cure is worse than the disease. It's a very human matter to assign something to the realm of enchantment, and not to assign it in such a way that you say: "Enchantment is over there; I've overcome it; it's wrong." Think of Wittgenstein, and his language bewitchment, and the way he always put himself back into language.

IS: From magic to religion. I realized, as I was formulating my questions, that all the people I've interviewed so far in this series – Derrida, Frye, Bloom and yourself – could be said to have theological affinities. (So, with the New Year, when I interview Edward Said, I'll move into the Enlightenment, since he's a proponent of "secular criticism.") Derrida does not attach himself to any theology, but in *Saving the Text* you connect him with Hebraism through his choice of the notion of writing as his "polemical instrument" (p. 17). Bloom was very straightforward about this when he said that his own religious stance, in his work as in his life, was Jewish gnosticism (if you can call that straightforward). Your answer?

GH: Except for being born into a religion, my religious background is minimal, yet reinforced by the fact that persecution did not allow me to assimilate, and that gradually I became more and more interested in my heritage. I did not start with a strong Talmudic or normative religious background, and I have no phrase to describe my position. It is certainly not what someone like Jonathan Culler thinks it is. If I am interested in Judaism, it is both because it is part of myself, as I have realized, and because I felt that the academy had excluded it to a surprising degree. And because *what* was excluded, in terms of major texts, seemed to me so marvelous. Finally, because of a certain type of reading and commentary which is one of the glories of the Jewish tradition. That tradition is really, basically, commentary. In almost nothing else is it so strong, after the Bible – whatever the relation of the strength of the Bible to permitting almost nothing but commentary until the contemporary period. So I've been meditating this. When someone comes along and says that dealing with the Bible makes you religious, it hardly needs refuting. Of course, you allow yourself to enter into the orbit of that commentary tradition.

For me, the Hebrew Bible has become more and more important, not in contrast to the New Testament – although I understand my colleague Bloom's polemic there, his attempt to challenge the privileging of New over Old – but in terms of the modern trend that asks, "Have we not left out too much, is there a way of expanding the canon?" My answer is that the most obvious thing that has been left out of the canon is where the idea of the canon comes from, that is the Bible. The Bible itself has been left out of the canon, in secular universities. So let's put it back in, not because it is canonical, but because in fact it's been left out. That is my point in studying the Hebrew Bible: not because it will give us religious enlightenment, but so that people are exposed to it. Even though the New Testament too isn't studied all that much, it filters in through Spenser and through the Christian tradition.

IS: Related to that, and also to your words a few moments ago about enchantment, you say in *Criticism in the Wilderness* that "the sacred has so inscribed itself in language that while it must be interpreted, it cannot be removed" (p. 248). This is where Culler comes in, saying that the role of criticism *is* this kind of removal, or

Geoffrey Hartman 87

demystification, and holding up Empson as a kind of model.[1]
Bloom, on the other hand, says that you can't secularize literature.

GH: You can't totally secularize it. Secularism turns back on itself
and becomes a religion, in the very intensity of the quest to do this.
The first thing the historical scholar realizes is that certain things
have happened, and that those things have ramifications. One
might not like one's father and one's mother, but one comes after
them. That's a family fact and a historical fact, although each
person may interpret it differently. All that "canon" here means,
and all that "sacred" here means, is that certain things have come
before, and unless you violently forget them, or revise history, or
liquidate them, you have to live with them. I prefer the Jewish way
of dealing with it by commentary: revision, rather than more
violent ways of denial, or trying to start *de novo* – or falsifying
history as has been done in totalitarian regimes.

IS: Is there any demystifying element in criticism, then?

GH: Yes, it is inbuilt. But often demystification goes through a
highly effective fictional stage, which is like a soft landing, and
which is one of the marvelous things about the human mind: the
inventiveness with which it demystifies itself. If we could demystify
ourselves totally, would any "self" be left to appreciate the fact?
But it leads to a great deal of invention, this activity of demystification. As I point out to students, if you met Blake's phrase – "The
dark religions are departed and sweet science reigns"[2] – by itself,
in an exam, and had to locate and date it, you would say the
English Enlightenment, or the eighteenth century. Now, in a sense
it *is* eighteenth-century, and Blake in that sense is a poet of the
Enlightenment, even though what he means by "dark religions"
may be different from the seventeenth-century reformer's
meaning.

IS: Related to this necessary recognition of the sacred element in
literature and language, could you briefly set out this current
interest you have in the relation of poetry to prophecy? It's a very
Fryean interest: he says that poetry is "man's revelation to man,"
and that criticism is the awareness of that revelation (*Educated
Imagination*, p. 105). How do you fit in with that?

GH: Frye is someone who is really witty, seriously so. His very late
works are maybe too schematic. One should posit old age in terms

1 See, for example, Jonathan Culler, "A Critic Against the Christians," *Times Literary Supplement*,
23 November 1984, p. 1328.
2 "The Four Zoas," in *Complete Writings*, edited by Geoffrey Keynes (Oxford: Oxford University
Press, [1969] 1976), p. 379.

of a genuine stage, and old age sometimes becomes schematic and skeletal. It's like those who have become thin. One can recognize, in late Frye, the more skeletal intentions. They satisfy me less than the Frye who has an anatomy I don't see quite so clearly, because of the marvelous verbal wit, the aphorisms, the play. This is a roundabout way of saying that I enjoy the quotation you've just given me, and I say "yes" to it as something enjoyably aphoristic. I might not put it quite that way, because I don't have that sort of connection with the word "revelation." For me, the word "revelation" sounds too much like the Book of Revelation. It has a Christian tonality, though that's really not fair, since it's a general word.

IS: It has an apocalyptic tone.

GH: Perhaps too much of an apocalyptic tone. Frye, like Blake, is always using it in a secular or demystifying way, but the word continues. I can say the following about poetry and prophecy. Prophecy expresses a disturbance of voice, and of the sense of time, and maybe of space: when one says, "Where *am* I; *where* am I; where am *I*; and what does '*am*' mean in this?" you're then in an area which is potentially religious or prophetic. It becomes prophetic only if you then become very inventive and anticipate. I don't make too much of a distinction between "prophetic" and "visionary" and "futuristic." My interest in poetry and prophecy centers on this disturbance of the voice, the disturbance of the sense of time, the disturbance of identity, and a pressure to do something about it.

IS: Is your interest in this centered, as so much of your work has been, in the Romantics – as it is with Frye and prophecy, and as it is with Bloom and prophecy?

GH: It seems to me that romanticism is where the issue becomes inescapable, because the institutional religious frame has loosened. So what is within the frame, what the frame tried to limit, over- flows. I don't think it becomes, therefore, "spilt religion," in fact to some extent you have more frames by virtue of the fact that the frame starts breaking up. The contained manifests itself, but part of the contained is the container. There is a reversal in which you become more aware of factors of repression, the previous framing devices, and so on. This is not a disadvantage merely, as Eliot thought in comparing Blake and Dante, but also an advantage. I couldn't sit here and judge between Blake and Dante. I have difficulty, like Frye, with evaluation. I oscillate. It's not that there isn't an evaluating or discriminating activity going on, but I can put myself behind someone like Blake absolutely, and then I can put myself behind Wordsworth, and then I can put Blake against

Wordsworth. I just don't have a standpoint where I can say – because it's intellectually important to say it, not because I say it – that we must choose between Blake and Dante. I don't dismiss Eliot's distinction, because it is done for the sake of the intellect as much as for the sake of what he could call belief, but for me it is only important for the sake of the intellect.

IS: To be able to make firm adjudications would imply that the interpreter is in a fixed or stable position, and that's denied throughout your work.

GH: That's right. That's my problem. It may be other people's problem too, like the reviewer who said "Hartman doesn't stay still long enough on the page for me to catch his meaning." That is how I am. I have enough trust in the conservatism of any mind, no matter how radical it is, that it will stabilize itself whether it wants to or not. Going into the classroom, I'm not afraid that students will subjectivate wildly, because I've found just the opposite: that they are out for a consensus, or something tangible. So that you open up things; you don't try to close up things. Similarly, when I write, I am not worried about where it will come out, because the necessity to have something stable will manifest itself.

IS: At several points you talk of deconstruction as a response to the failure of the Enlightenment, a response to the failure of humanism. And yet, in *Easy Pieces*, there is a fascinating hook left dangling: that deconstruction might be a rearguard humanism. This is suggested in phrases of this type: "Imagine a world in which you cannot think except by reading and writing. That is our world" (p. 187). Such phrases confirm a long-held suspicion of mine about Derrida: that, although his work has rendered the term "humanism" obsolete, he is our most humane, most liberating philosopher.

GH: "Humanism" is a word, like many others, which some people have wanted to demystify, or even suspend, because it has served deleterious purposes. For me it's still a vital word that should not be proscribed. After humanism pointed to an ethnocentric, central European tradition of high culture, which did not think beyond itself in any way, a movement came which said, "If that's humanist, we are not." Basically, I do feel, with you, that Derrida is saving texts, that he is renewing our ability to read. Of course, this may lead some astray: what movement, what strong intellect has not led people astray? It may result in mechanical operations and applications, but again: is not Bloom often applied mechanically? That seems to be a constant. What is interesting is that Derrida reads as closely as anyone I know. Sometimes he goes right through the text, as Blake says we see through the eye and not with it. I think strong interpreters have always done that. But interestingly enough, like the rabbinical tradition, he insists on the text. I guess I shouldn't define humanism as an insistence on the text, but that does distinguish humanism as against anti-humanistic movements which give the impression of wanting to leave literature behind. Literature and mystification are so identified by those movements that they would like to leave both behind. They all want to create their own, new mode of total, prosaic, sober, socially oriented, realistic literature.

IS: My next question was to do with this element in your work, this consistent opposition to totalizing ideologies and systems. This draws together many strains in your work, including the one in which you are skeptical about an ultimate truth which, you say in *The Unmediated Vision*, would destroy the seeker's sense of human responsibilities (p. xi). Another thing drawn in here is your own tentative style, which certainly executes high jinks at the rhetorical level, but in terms of the finality of its conclusions is tentative in almost an English way. But when we oppose ideology and totalization, don't we make the mistake of assuming that all ideologies were created equal? Can we totalize ideology, and reject it all?

GH: There is a way that ideology enters all our thinking. The question is whether one can have ideology and irony together. Those who are ideologues, in the modern sense, tend to forget everything else. I know that sounds sweeping, but I didn't like your saying that my tentativeness was English, so I'm immediately very apodeictic and sweeping. Think of the essay in which I tried to work with the ideology of Keats's "To Autumn" (*Fate of Reading*, pp. 124–46). There's only heterogeneity in this area, as when you talk about English ideology or German ideology. So my tentativeness is in the nature of the situation, not simply in the nature of my temperament. I would make it clear in each case what the ideological component is, but I would never go from there to talking about a political unconscious, or to a utopian premise, however much I may have certain wishes in that direction. It's a very simple matter. If you can have both ideology and irony, fine. Neither, by itself, will do. Irony by itself will simply strike most people as sterile, and therefore will be forgotten. Ideology by itself will exhaust itself in an action that probably won't succeed, or succeed for only a short time, or will seem so inflated that, however secular it is, future generations will say, "That's really a disguised religion."

IS: We've discussed your reception of and struggles with Derrida. The name "Bloom" will already be sprinkled across the text we have created to this moment, but can I ask you to summarize your struggles with Bloom?

GH: Harold and I have had a lasting intellectual relationship. It started in 1955, when I met him in the basement offices of the old campus to which we were both assigned as very junior members. I had never met him in graduate school, because I was not in English but in Comparative Literature. There was an immediate sympathy. I had published *The Unmediated Vision* and was struck by his ease and precision and warmth of response to it. This intellectual relationship has had stronger and weaker moments. One of its strongest moments was when I was working on Wordsworth, and I think he engaged with that work. I enabled him to overcome certain reservations, because he was totally Blakean and Shelleyan. And he in turn helped me to understand Blake. I had real difficulty with Blake; he had difficulty with Wordsworth. There was an interesting exchange from around 1959 to the time when I left Yale in 1962.

The second high point was when I came back, 1968 to about 1973. It was the period in which he was writing on Yeats. He had begun to shift on Blake. There was a kind of "revolution" in his mind, even a revulsion against Blake, but not yet against Yeats. He was intrigued with Yeats, and I thought the chapters on "A Vision" in *Yeats* were the strongest part of that book. They still strike me as superb. During that time he began to gestate the anxiety of influence thesis. Our intellectual correspondence, day by day, was extremely intense. I don't know how, retrospectively, he looks at this. I know how it looks to me. I remember that he gave me, quite early on, two pages which seemed to be a most remarkable, marvelous lump of mythological reflection – something out of which a novel or novella would come. When he later did write a novel, *The Flight from Lucifer*, someone reviewed it under the title: "Bloom's Gnovel." Well, this was a gnovel in miniature. He asked me about it, because he had some self-doubt, and I said, "I find it fascinating, but as such it really can't be published – there's something stirring there." I didn't doubt its value; I doubted the possibility of presenting it in that form.

What happened gradually was creation by division, by disentanglement, by analysis – an incredible kind of creative act. During the actual composition of *The Anxiety of Influence*, we were in almost daily telephone contact. I felt I was in the presence of someone giving birth: out came the baby, called "clinamen," and suddenly something else stirred, called "tessera," and there were twins, then triplets, then quadruplets, then sextuplets. He played off ideas against me. I remember distinctly that at certain points he was struggling for terms. He had found "clinamen" and "tessera," but there was a further stage which he was discovering, and I suggested the term "kenosis," that "emptying-out" which comes from religious tradition, referring to Christology. Two terms – "kenosis" and the "counter-sublime" – I helped with. I don't say this to take credit, because all the credit is his: it's an extraordinarily brave and important book.

Bloom has the strength to follow his ideas and to go as far as they lead. But it doesn't mean that he is not occasionally riveted by self-doubt. My temperament, as you well know, is that I'm not someone who says "absolutely yes" and "absolutely no." Perhaps it would have helped; instead of being a critical, sympathetic, maieutic observer, I would have said "no" or "yes" all the time. I did neither. I allowed the process to take place, and enjoyed it fully. This is my recollection of the most intense period: after that, I'm not sure which way it went. I think we are still strong intellectual friends. But Harold has not liked my engaging with Derrida. He has a strong personal friendship with Derrida, but intellectually he has distanced himself.

I engage with Derrida partly because I see him as an important episode in the history of commentary, and partly because I have a natural European affinity with him. He read the same things as I did in the 1950s, clearly: there is a correspondence there, however different our path. I was interested to learn that he wished he could get in touch with the English Romantics. In terms of philosophy, we read the same texts, except that he read them professionally, and I instinctually. But the literature was a very different kind of literature. I knew something about French literature, though my great liking and engagement were for and with English romanticism; whereas that was the one thing left out for him. He had French romanticism, and then German romanticism. When I look at German philosophy, it is in the context of German romanticism. He probably didn't read it in that context, but as philosophy. For me, poetry came first, philosophy second. But still, many of the same texts absorbed us. I can't figure out why Harold tends to be dismissive of, and overestimates, that aspect of my engagement with Derrida.

IS: As you know, it's a gimmick of these interviews to use the same poem to highlight how different critics begin the process of criticism, how they begin to work with a poem, and what they look for in it. There are voices in this poem, all right – a cry from outside. Criticism begins in the act of reading, but every reading is selective. We've talked about trying to get into the poet's world, we've talked about the sacred and the magical: can we focus these things into an act of practical interpretation?

GH: Yes, although I always jump off from the poem, and then weave reflections which can be theoretically and rigorously developed. Part of my method is to be immethodical – that is, to ask those with whom I'm reading a poem: "Where would you start?" The beginning point is a question in itself.

As I look at it now, I notice that "carliest ending," that it is a near oxymoron. Then I see it as a threshold phrase, and think about the threshold feeling, and am reminded that it is an old-age poem. It recalls the poem on Santayana, "To an Old Philosopher in Rome," except again it's skeletalized. It has the same feeling of being at the threshold; no one is there to lead you over. You're beginning to wake into sleep. There is a curious exchange of the idea of waking and sleeping, of inside and outside. That's what I would be exploring here. I would also pick up what happens to the internal rhyme, by which I mean that repetition of "cry," being then reduced to a "c," which is the first letter of "cry," and ending with a simile phrase: "It was like . . ." I almost wish it would stop there. "A new knowledge of reality" is a throwaway line; it's a conclusion that says "Something has to be concluded"; one can redeem it, but it does strike one as prosaic and lame.

IS: When you reduce "cry" to "c," I'm not completely clear on your point. Are you referring to "The Comedian as the Letter C?"

GH: No, I meant that "c" is the first letter of "cry," the first letter of "choir," the first letter of "colossal," the first letter of "choral." It's already an ending, although it's a beginning. It's something that reduces itself. It's the "c" of "abc." In other words, it's a poem that tries to reduce itself to a minimal sensuous ascetic, which is the tendency of Wallace Stevens. Sensuous, but ascetic; the "scholar of one candle";[3] that is the feeling that comes from the poem.

IS: The cry from outside . . .

GII: Scrawny.

IS: But I wonder if it relates to what you were saying before about confusions of "Where am I, where do I stand, who am I?" The cry from outside: where is it coming from, and where am I situated in relation to it?

GH: That's correct. Moreover, it occurs at the end of winter and at the beginning of spring. Stevens's attitude towards winter is not always to say farewell to it: there's a reluctance to cross the threshold to spring. There may be a sense here of "Will I make

3 "The Auroras of Autumn," in *Collected Poems* (New York: Alfred A. Knopf, 1954), p. 417.

it?'' or "Can I even suffer it, let alone the fullness of the colossal sun.''

IS: There was always a snowman in Stevens.

GH: Exactly. It's also, in that sense, defensive. It is a poem of minimal, but great, satisfactions. As though it were enough to say: "abc.'' He has come to "c" and that's enough; and out of that everything else is built, all these choral rings. When you read "It was not" and the "it was, it was, it was," that is a simplicity that you also find in Wordsworth, not quite so sterilized – the use of the copula can be strong. And "part of the colossal sun,/Surrounded by its choral rings": the stylized force of that makes one think of something heavenly, cosmic and visionary. But here it's casual; it doesn't really pressure us. Some of his poems do, but his poems often evade their own pressure. I guess that the poem this reminds me of is "The Course of a Particular," where the leaves cry, and also of "The Motive for Metaphor.''

IS: Where there is also "The ABC of being.''[4]

GH: Something insists: the cry insists, the outside insists, and won't let you go to sleep. Whether it really has the power to wake you, and what that waking means, whether there is a waking into something really real, remains implicit.

IS: Bloom, in the interview, said that criticism was a purely solitary activity, without any social context whatsoever. I don't think you agree with that. What is the social function and social context of literary criticism?

GH: The simplest way to put it is that it provides us with shared texts. We can't live unmediated with each other and, for the sake of the intellect as well as the imagination, need passwords. Some are complicated exchanges. I myself – it may be my own defect – cannot conceive of this taking place without the sharing of texts. That's enough of a social context with me, because as soon as you sit around a table and share a text, you are within a social context. You may go beyond that and say "Is it the Yeshiva kind of sitting around?'' or is it some other kind, and then you do get to institutional analysis, but I think the "abc" of it is that you agree to study texts together, you discover that these texts are interrelated, that one text has been behind many things. Moreover, some facts exist: there was something called "the Renaissance," and the Renaissance is indelible in English literary history – and you go on from there. However, you must have one essential agreement, an unstated contract that you want to share the text. Bloom insists on the other side of that: even though you share a text, and make

4 "The Motive for Metaphor," op. cit., p. 288.

it common, and keep it alive, the reading is still an individual act. You have to pass through an intensely alone moment, solipsistic or not. And you have to find a way of separating yourself from prejudice and predetermination. Bloom insists on that moment against others who see it as less deliberate and less *agonistic*. So I would agree there is this moment – in which one might have to lose oneself – of reading for oneself, as if one were the last reader. But, still, one does bring it back, and share it: one listens and intervenes. I wish to leave it at that: it could be a question of politics, but I don't like to bring in the word "politics" too soon.

IS: But what you have said raises the institutional question. In *Criticism in the Wilderness*, you say there's a rift between the imagination and the natural or social sphere (p. 39). But the university is a social institution – or do we go along with Frye's idealized story, where society has somehow forgotten to enclose or ideologize the university, so that prophecy can still emerge from there?

GH: In America the private universities have enough inner pressure, pressing against political and utilitarian forces, to lend truth to what Frye says. However, I think one cannot generalize about universities on the basis of American universities, especially private ones. In that respect, the word "private" takes on a very important meaning: but they're the exception, rather than the rule. On the other hand, in America there are so many institutions of higher learning that their very multiplicity does have a de-ideologizing or pluralistic effect. That makes it hard for any one institution or group to take over the whole damn system.

IS: And that protects the system against attack from without, and presumably also against the internal critique of Marxists who would seek to ideologize all our work?

GH: Yes. There will always be that little voice coming from some corner of the university system, and suddenly you have to listen. This is not just a plea for naive pluralism, because that would weaken everything – although if I had to choose between pluralism and a "mono" form of system, I would choose pluralism. Certainly I am for an examination of structures of appropriation, which come as much from marxisant trends as from more subtle, free-market pressures. They are just different strategies. Perhaps Marxist or neo-Marxist secularism is more above board; one can grapple more with it intellectually. I don't find it interesting in the way that the Frankfurt School was interesting. One of the problems is that in the United States we haven't developed a good sociology of literature. America missed out somehow. It didn't go through the European phase, partly because of the European catastrophe. Except for the Depression, America didn't have that pressure period of the 1930s and 1940s. I'm not saying that nothing happened; Kenneth Burke and many other things happened. But the threat helped to produce, not just to depress, and somehow energized the intellect of those whom we now denominate as the Frankfurt School. And so we're back to Frankfurt.

Frank Kermode

5
Frank Kermode

"Criticism entails immediate encounter with particular texts, which is the sort of criticism I would like to do. I don't think that kind of criticism can possibly be called progressive. It may be an agent of change, but it can't be an agent of progress."

Frank Kermode spends half of each year teaching at Columbia University, in New York, and the other half in London. He was King Edward VII Professor of English at Cambridge University until 1982, when he resigned following a serious falling-out with the producers of the longest-running show in Cambridge, "No Speculation, Please, We're British!" The dispute centered, of course, on the tenure of a young don, Colin MacCabe, but in a broader sense was about the wisdom of allowing various theoretical modes, of Continental origin, a voice in the great and ancient British universities. Between 1980 and 1982 there was a general purging of such voices, fittingly leaving Cambridge to the towering and more objective geniuses of the "Peterhouse School."

   The irony in this situation is that Kermode's own attitude towards "theory" has always been skeptical, suspicious and pragmatic. Indeed, in the very *best* traditions of British empiricism, he has assimilated whatever has seemed useful to him in foreign modes, and rejected whatever has seemed reductive or purely abstract. In a "Prologue" to *The Art of Telling*, written in the immediate aftermath of the Cambridge fracas, Kermode proudly describes his own theoretical temperament as "recuperative" (the chief bogey-word among the dissident factions of certain poststructuralist splinter groups). Kermode has always been the most prominent mediator between British, Continental and American critical styles, as his further remarks on the Cambridge dispute indicate:

> Deconstructionism is, in part, a catastrophe theory, for behind it there is the assumption that the whole Western metaphysical tradition can be put into reverse. It is at this point that the orthodox, who dislike having to consider such unsettling propositions, man the walls with their dusty banners: principle, the imagination, the human world, though the most vocal of them are manifestly unacquainted with the first, lack the second and seem to know the third only by hearsay. . . . We lack a great man who might, like Eliot, hold together the new and the traditional, catastrophe and continuity; unfortunately we do not lack doctrinaire and unconsidering people on both sides of the argument. My own inadequacy as a mediator has already been adequately demonstrated. There is a war on, and he who ventures into no-man's-land brandishing cigarettes and singing carols must expect to be shot at.
>
> (p. 7)

As all of this would begin to suggest, Kermode is the most difficult of critics to "sum up," having neither formed his own school nor been incorporated into anyone else's. However, one thing that does connect him with Frye, Bloom, and Hartman is the determining effect upon his career of an early identification with a major poet: in this case, with Wallace Stevens.

Another thing that makes Kermode difficult to summarize is the extraordinary range of his interests, including Renaissance and seventeenth-century poetry, modern poetry, theories of narrative, and biblical poetics. Although trained as a literary historian and Renaissance scholar, Kermode wrote his first book, typically, on the continuity between Romantic and twentieth-century poetics. *Romantic Image* (1957) was enormously influential, because Kermode was among the first to identify the Romantic elements in the work of such strident anti-Romantics as Eliot and Hulme. This complicity is indicated in the terms of Kermode's definition of romanticism as "the literature of one epoch, beginning in the late years of the eighteenth century and not yet finished, and as referring to the high valuation placed during this period upon the image-making powers of the mind at the expense of its rational powers, and to the substitution of organicist for mechanistic modes of thinking about works of art" (p. 43).

The problem with the theory of the "Romantic image," according to Kermode, is its anxious exclusion of statement and idea from the realm of the properly poetic. This exclusion only serves to reserve poetry for an initiated élite, separating it off from wider human discourses and general human needs. It prevents the poet from performing the function allocated to him by Wallace Stevens: "to help people to live their lives."[1] Kermode announces that "the age of dissociation . . . must end," because art "was always made *for* men who habitually move in space and time, whose language is propelled onward by verbs, who cannot always be asked to respect the new enclosure laws of poetry, or such forbidding notices as 'No road through to action' " (p. 161). (These words surely place Kermode within the "Lucky Jim" generation, signaling as they do the typical frustration of lower-middle- and working-class academics with the "gentlemanly" protocols that still dominated the university study of English in post-war Britain.)

As in the case of Geoffrey Hartman's identification with Words-worth, Wallace Stevens – by showing ways in which mind and world could cooperate, instead of effacing each other – was to provide Kermode with a way out of Romantic entrapments, but a way which at the same time did not pretend to leave romanticism entirely behind. This is announced at the end of *Romantic Image*: "Recently Wallace Stevens has come to be more widely read in this country, and he is a poet who provides a unique, perhaps unrepeatable, solution to the image-and-discourse problem, by making the problem itself the subject of poems" (p. 152). Three years later, in his pathbreaking book on Stevens, Kermode defines reality as "that which the imagination, in different ways at different times and in different places, must contend with, compound with" (p. 38). We will realize, he says, how vast Stevens's claims really are if we think of "Mr Eliot,"

> who believes that art has frontiers, and that one goes on from it to other and possibly more important matters. Stevens' poet discovers an order which cannot be discovered by anybody else; religion, myth, were forms of poetic activity.
>
> (p. 84)

Although this had been precisely Northrop Frye's argument about the relation between Stevens and Eliot, Kermode, as the 1960s wore on, was to use Stevens *against* Frye, and against the idea of "myth." Kermode saw "myth criticism" as a denial of literary texture, and so of the reality of reading. To the Fryean idea of "myth," he would oppose Stevens's notion of "fiction." Like myths, fictions impose human meanings on the world, and human structures on the dizzy-ing openness of space and time. But unlike myth, fiction doesn't *deny* space and time, and is always willing to abandon its structures for new

1 "The Noble Rider and the Sound of Words," in *The Necessary Angel* (New York: Alfred A. Knopf, 1951), p. 29.

ones as life itself changes. Like Hartman, Kermode has problems with totalizing mythologies, which he sees as monolithic, unchanging, unaware of their own fictionality, reality-denying and ideological:

> We have to distinguish between myths and fictions. Fictions can degenerate into myths whenever they are not consciously held to be fictive. In this sense anti-Semitism is a degenerate fiction, a myth; and *Lear* is a fiction . . . Fictions are for finding things out, and they change as the needs of sense-making change. Myths are the agents of stability, fictions the agents of change. Myths call for absolute, fictions for conditional assent.
>
> (*Sense of an Ending*, p. 39)

The relation between fictions and reality is thus exactly the "mutual domination" or "interchangeable supremacy" that Hartman, following Wordsworth, ascribes to another interpretive relationship: the one between criticism and poetry.

Here, however, Kermode does not follow Hartman or Bloom. His own style is very much in the "objective" tradition, and to say that criticism is "inside" poetry – instead of being a rational discourse about it – would be to separate criticism off into its own mythy mystique, its own élitist and self-regarding "Romantic image." In a recent essay on "The Decline of the Man of Letters," Kermode has portrayed the contemporary university critic as "intent on establishing for himself a wholly novel position of dignity and authority, and a new sort of isolation from the larger literary public" (p. 206). Kermode himself has no interest in the isolated prophetic voice, nor any apparent anxiety about seeing criticism as a cooperative venture. In fact, criticism as a cooperative institution is what helps to keep literature alive, by discovering and validating those new "latent senses" and "secrets" which, in their very newness and adaptability, testify to literature's peculiar ability to *stay* alive.

Accordingly, of the critics interviewed here Kermode seems to be the one least interested in generating a "position" that will identify him as the author of his own books. He seems to enjoy dealing with the questions *as* questions, visibly wondering about them and working them through. This quality, together with his humor, lends a general atmosphere of surprise to his conversation. As I was leaving his temporary office at Columbia, following the interview, he presented me with a copy of a sonnet by John Peale Bishop, saying that I would discover a hidden personal significance in it:

Famously she descended, her red hair
Unbound and bronzed by sea-reflections, caught
Crinkled with sea-pearls. The fine slender taut
Knees that let down her feet upon the air,

Young breasts, slim flanks and golden quarries were
Odder than when the young distraught
Unknown Venetian, painting her portrait, thought
He'd not imagined what he painted there.

And I too commerced with that golden cloud:
Lipped her delicious hands and had my ease
Faring fantastically, perversely proud.

All loveliness demands our courtesies.
Since she was dead I praised her as I could
Silently, among the Barberini bees.[2]

Imre Salusinszky: Where were you born, and where have you spent
your life?

Frank Kermode: I was born in Douglas, in the Isle of Man, which
is some eighty miles from Liverpool. That's a very isolating factor.
I hardly ever set foot in England until I went to university; since
then, I've hardly ever set foot in the Isle of Man. That's the way
it goes. I was of a poor family, and went to Liverpool University,
which was the local university. I went straight from there into the
Navy, and emerged from the Navy in 1946, after five and a half
years of service. Then I became a graduate student, rather briefly
– I never finished my Ph.D. – and got a job at Newcastle, which
was then part of the University of Durham. I worked there with
John Butt, who was a hard but virtuous taskmaster, and then went
to Reading, because I wanted to work with Donald Gordon, the
Renaissance scholar, whom I greatly admired. From there I went
to Manchester, to a professorship, and then I wandered a bit; from
Manchester to Bristol, and from Bristol to University College
London – which is, I suppose, the foundation that I have most
respect for. Then I had some years at Cambridge – eight of them
in fact – all of which I somewhat regret, and left under a cloud in
1982. I'm still a Fellow of King's, but that's my only connection
with Cambridge. I have a loose connection with Columbia: since
1983, I've been here about half the time.

IS: You said that you were born on the Isle of Man: in what distant
epoch was that?

2 "A Recollection," in *Collected Poems*, edited by Allen Tate (New York: Charles Scribner's Sons,
1948), pp. 71–2.

FK: I was an armistice celebration, I suppose: I was born in
November, 1919. I was 66 the other day.

IS: Congratulations! If I can develop, for a moment, my own fiction
– which is that there is some sequence, or relation, or pattern among
the critics that I've chosen to interview – let me see if I can begin
to fold you into the mix. With Bloom and Hartman, I found that
we began by talking a great deal about Northrop Frye. That makes
a lot of sense because, in the first place, I completely agree with
what Bloom said: that Frye is the major figure in the literary criticism
of our century. In the second place, both Bloom and, to a lesser
extent, Hartman have had important intellectual struggles with Frye.
Frye was not even comparably as influential in England as here –
a fact worth discussing in itself. However, talking to you I am talking to the only significant British critic who did have anything like
a "struggle" with Frye. I'd even hazard to say that, back in the
1960s, your reading of Frye was quite an important moment in your
development. Could you summarize your reception of Frye?

FK: As far as I remember, when I read the Blake book I had pedan-
tic objections to it – it seemed hard to know where Blake stopped
and Frye started – but I felt the impact of Frye when the *Anatomy
of Criticism* came out. I was sent it to review by the *Review of English
Studies*, and was asked to review it in three hundred words. I read
it with amazement: I really thought it was an important work of
literature. So I told the editor that if he wanted it reviewed in three
hundred words he better get somebody else to do it, and he rather
surprisingly said, "Have as much space as you want." I did a review
that was more of a summary than anything else, with comment.
I think that Frye is certainly the finest prose writer among modern
critics. He has the expository force and some of the wit of Shaw.
Not much that he's done since *Anatomy of Criticism* has interested
me very much, because the great mass of it really was filling in the
detail, or developing the themes in different areas. I once said of
his book *Fools of Time* that, if necessary, he will depart from the major
systematic arrangements of the *Anatomy* and make up new ones. I
suggested that really they are a kind of memory theatre, just
mnemonic aids. He wrote me a rather snappy letter saying "Well
of course they are: what did you think?"

I don't like the recent books at all. You see, I disagree with Harold
Bloom and Geoffrey Hartman about the relative status of poetry
and criticism, but I do think that critics are like poets in this respect:
they will pick up anything that suits their plan. That's what I've
always done, and *Anatomy of Criticism* did suit me: the Polemical
Introduction made me think a good deal about how judgments are
arrived at, what their value is, what validates them, and so on –

and that left a mark. My own feeling is that Frye's apogee was in
the early 1960s. His influence and his interest have waned since that
time.

IS: Why was Frye, as well as all the subsequent theoretical modes
that have originated in America and France, rejected by British
critics? Why are they so resistant to theoretical criticism?

FK: I think they've probably been less resistant than that formulation suggests. There are people like Stephen Heath in Cambridge,
for example, who in his own individual way has followed the French
line. Culler is not British, but he's a product of the British academy.
At Cambridge, in my time, there was a great hunger among undergraduates for more of that kind of thing – that's why Heath's were
enormously popular courses. On the other hand, there was bitter
opposition to it. The animus against theory is very strong in the
English departments in England, especially among the older
teachers. Cambridge, of course, is exceptionally hostile to any kind
of thought at all, as far as the English Faculty is concerned. There's
always this feeling that you get among certain sorts of English critics
that all this French nonsense is something which you can blow over
with one good "huff." People like George Watson think that, just
as they can demolish Marxism in a twenty-page article, they can
demolish the entire French critical effort by the obvious exercise of
common sense.

IS: The career of French philosophy in Britain has been similar.

FK: It's not just French, either. For example, the neglect of Heidegger
in England has been very extraordinary. There is a certain insularity
there. Just as America is now the place where refugees go, it's also
the place where refugee European philosophers go. Derrida is in
that sense a sort of refugee. As he says in his own interview, he's
much more celebrated in the United States than he is in France.

IS: You're a critic who doesn't wear his influences on his sleeve.
Wallace Stevens has obviously been a major influence, but we'll
come to that. Another early and abiding influence seems to have
been Eliot.

FK: That's partly because the inoculation was so early. When I was
a student, Eliot was very much, not only the most authoritative
figure, but the latest thing.

IS: The Jacques Derrida of his time.

FK: I suppose so, though that's a rather odd way of putting it.

IS: In *Romantic Image*, you're working against the grain, though, by
trying to drag Eliot and his mates into the Romantic tradition.

FK: I suppose that's because I liked Milton, and of course Eliot didn't.
That book was peculiar, in that I never intended to write it. It just
happened one summer, and it's the only book I've written without

any kind of soul-searching, delays, multiple drafts or anything. It's an essay, not a piece of research. I wondered whether anybody would want to publish it. Indeed, I was advised not to publish it by Cecil Day Lewis, who didn't think it was deep enough. But then, it has been a rather successful book: a new edition is about to come out after twenty-nine years.

There was a feeling that one ought to get out a bit from under these Eliotic prescriptions, which had been imposed upon us so forcefully. It's rather hard to understand now, because everybody knows, or thinks they know, what's wrong with Eliot's criticism. But he did draw a new map. And then there was also Leavis: it's his early respect for Eliot which really informs a lot of Leavis's best criticism.

IS: One of the things that bothers me about bringing Eliot into the Romantic tradition is the nature of his social views. I wonder whether the critical establishment hasn't been a little too hasty to whitewash those, and to say that we can separate them from his poetics. After all, I don't see that sort of division of sensibility existing within ourselves.

FK: Take the more extreme case of Pound. The issue was localized in the question of the Bollingen Prize: should a man who holds such views – which were much more disgusting, at least in their expression, than any of Eliot's – be included in the pantheon? But wouldn't this be true, in a very minor way, of Stevens himself? There's no necessary correlation between romanticism and left-wing politics. Probably none of us share Stevens's politics, which were, as far as one can tell, rather narrow and very conservative.

IS: Yes, but I suppose it's harder to see those politics feeding through into Stevens's poetry than it is with Eliot. With Eliot's idea of tradition – which, he says in *After Strange Gods*, is "of the blood" rather than "of the brain" – it is easy to draw an analogy with some kind of racial myth or blood myth.[3]

FK: That's true, but it depends what you want to do to a poet. If you want to attack Eliot, that's the place where you'd probably get at him best. If I wanted to attack Stevens, I could say: "Here's a poet who's so indifferent to war and poverty that he can only treat them as metaphors for the world of poetry." Poverty is not a physical but a metaphysical notion, in Stevens, and so is war. So you can ask why we should pay any attention to this poet and think of him as so central – as many of us do – when he's so clearly deficient in this respect. There, you can say that the test case would be something like "Mr Burnshaw and the Statue," where he did actually try, for once, to come down to earthly politics: and it was a disaster.

3 T. S. Eliot, *After Strange Gods* (London: Faber & Faber, 1934), p. 30.

IS: There are many similarities between the tone and stance of your work and Geoffrey Hartman's. Both of you are concerned with re-creating the immediacy of the reading process, with close reading, and in both cases there is an extremely wide reference to all sorts of sources: Continental, British, American; philosophy and literature.

It is this question of the immediacy of the text which is behind your eventual rejection of Frye. When we take Frye's advice and "stand back," you say in your second essay on him, we lose "the breath of Hermione, the presence of Perdita" (*Continuities*, p. 121). What about Frye's argument that criticism simply can never recapture, in critical terminology, the immediacy of reading itself?

FK: It seems to me that that's subject to the empirical test of whether it ever does. To tell you the truth, I'm surprised by the parallel you draw between Geoffrey Hartman and myself, because I've never thought of it, and I don't suppose Geoffrey ever has either. It's something that you've come up with out of the blue.

Close reading, yes, from time to time: but what one really needs is a constantly varying depth of focus. There's nothing more tedious than endlessly close reading. I don't know whether one consciously aims at this, but habits form over the years, and I think that a vary-ing depth of focus is what one really does, whether one wants to do it or not.

IS: Let me develop the question of close reading, and the Hartman parallel. Lately, you've been talking a lot about "secrets" in a text, the "latent sense." Your recent reading of the secrets in *Under Western Eyes*, for example, is very much a close reading (*Art of Tell-ing*, pp. 133–5). These secrets seem to me to be very close to what Hartman talks about as "voices," or what we spoke of in the inter-view as "magic." Like Hartman's voices, these secrets of yours do create a disturbance of time: you say in *The Art of Telling* that secrets are "at odds with sequence" (p. 138). This interest in the secrets and latencies in a text seems to be a feature of your later work. One can't see it as a big factor in *Romantic Image*, or the book on Stevens. How did it develop?

FK: I don't know quite how it developed. I'd been thinking about *Under Western Eyes* for a long time. Conrad's novels, and perhaps Ford's, are peculiar in that they were trying to meet a popular or general requirement of fiction, which catered for the "under-reader." I don't think that Conrad really succeeded in that, even in things like *The Secret Agent* ("A Simple Tale"). They also wanted to please the wiser sort by concealing, and I think the whole process of deliberate concealment, which both Conrad and Ford did practice – various sorts of obfuscation, coming from temporal disjunctions and so on – actually does create a situation in which you get secrets. These are not, in the strict sense, planned (I don't want to get into the question of what's intended and what isn't) but are best thought of along Freudian lines, as involuntary condensations and displacements. So the work of reading them does rather become like the "third ear" work of the analyst.

I've been trying for a long time, also, to find some kind of common ground between the hearing of psycho-analytic discourse and the hearing of literature: that's where these things come together. I wouldn't like to say I've got very far with that. The next stage would be to talk about interpretive communities. They allow, just as a psycho-analytic community would allow, a good range of variety in the manner of interpreting within the community. The idea that there is a kind of stabilized, homogeneous form of interpretation seems to me wrong. There are forms of valuation which are institutional, and which are very hard to shake, and that's why I got interested in the canon question. One thing leads to another, in that way.

IS: If we talk about secrets, and the reading of secrets by a community of initiates, don't we open ourselves to claims of élitism and anti-democraticism? Frye's attempt, for example, has always been to make everything open, to democratize everything: isn't the idea of "secrets" going in the other direction?

FK: Yes, I think it is. You can only do the Frye kind of thing by abolishing valuation, which is what he does. At the other extreme, there is a form of élitism – I suppose you have to say that – or "election," to use a more neutral term. I think that must be so, and just is empirically so. We all know this. Why do we fool ourselves about such things? What we do, to satisfy our consciences, is to behave in our studies as if we were, in this very limited sense, members of an elect, and behave in the classroom as if we wanted other people to become members of that elect. Whether we achieve it or not is doubtful; and under modern conditions, even in important universities like this one, it becomes even more difficult to achieve than it used to be, simply because people are not prepared for it. There's no preparation, so your pastoral work consists far more of the sort of thing that used to be done in high school, than of really getting people on to the outer fringes of what you like to think of as your club.

IS: I remember once asking the students in a first-year class whether they knew the title of Homer's story about the Trojan war. There was a stunned silence, until one girl ventured the answer: *The Wooden Horse*. Being at the coal-face of teaching often makes one wonder about this stuff: literary theory, secrets, Bloom, Frye – whatever.

FK: I think that's a very important point. Fond as I was of Paul de Man, one thing that I differed from him very violently about was the notion that the study of literature should be confined to very small groups of people. Actually, the most important thing of all is what you call the work at the coal-face.

IS: Would you talk a little about your reading and reception of Derrida?

FK: I first read Derrida because I met Paul de Man in Paris in 1968, and he said that the most important French thinker since Sartre had appeared on the scene. Then I began to read *De la Grammatologie*. I was having a lot of trouble with it, so I asked Paul de Man how I could break into this book. He mentioned some page numbers. I said that I must have read those, and then I realized that I'd bought a defective copy of *De la Grammatologie* in which those pages were missing.

I didn't study the *Grammatologie* until the Spivak version appeared. I remember my wife and I reading *Glas* in a bookshop in Paris until they said, "Listen, either buy that book or leave." I've heard him lecture a good deal. He's someone whom I find very attractive in all sorts of ways. I find that the so-called "ludic" element is very baffling to me, particularly when it actually spoils something, as I think it spoils, for example, the brilliant essay on Heidegger and Meyer Schapiro. It seems to me to be one of the things he does almost as an obligation, and I don't understand that. I sharply differ, not by conscious decision but by temperament, from this type of criticism; not just Derrida, but all those like him – Hillis Miller will go on worrying at some pun – because I have a great prejudice in favor of lucidity. I think that people ought to be able to understand what you're saying without getting involved in some pseudo-poetry or pseudo-crossword-puzzle. This is a very simple complaint, but it seems to me a serious one, and I think that in the end it will be a destructive one.

IS: The ludic temper is certainly not the British temper . . . .

FK: We do have *Tristram Shandy* . . . .

IS: And *Private Eye*. But has anything in Derrida affected your own reading?

FK: Not directly, I don't think. That whole movement does affect the way one looks at a text. For example, the piece you mentioned about *Under Western Eyes* probably couldn't have been done the way it was done if there hadn't been deconstruction before it.

My acquaintance with all that really came up in London in the late 1960s and early 1970s. I had a very informal seminar there. We used to get novelists to come, and critics – we always had this contingent from Cambridge: Heath, Culler, Veronica Forrest-

Thompson. They were already committed to structuralist and post-structuralist thinking. A good deal of that kind of thinking was injected into the discussions; and then a good deal of rather more rigorous, Israeli kind of criticism: we got this surprising blend of two rivers which rarely flow into each other. The Israeli school of narratologists, with a few exceptions, keep apart from that other tradition. They are closer to Wayne Booth than they are to anything that's happened since *The Rhetoric of Fiction*.

IS: Your talk of secrets and latent meanings – as well as Empson's talk of ambiguity – seems to me to have more to do with deconstruction than with the common strain in normative British criticism.

FK: When *The Genesis of Secrecy* came out, Empson read it, and he liked it very much. He phoned me and said that he wanted to write a review of it. Then he re-read the book, loathed it the second time around, and wrote an extremely harsh review of it in the *London Review of Books*. I think that, obscurely, he was afraid of it, because he was afraid it was what he called ''neo-Christian.'' He thought it was drifting in that direction. Curiously enough, he also took me fiercely to task for, as he thought, misrepresenting the thought of C. H. Dodd, the theologian, whom I think he probably had some personal fondness for. A very complicated set-up. You never really knew where you were with William Empson, except that you always knew you were in the presence of someone very distinguished. I would say – I know that you agree with Harold Bloom's judgment on Frye – that in terms of pure intellectual capacity and force, Empson was the best critic of the twentieth century, in English. This is by no means to say that he didn't write an awful lot of nonsense in his time, because he did.

IS: From ''ambiguity'' to ''secrets'' is not an astonishing leap: has his work been very influential on you?

FK: I'm sure it was. Even the poems were. It goes back a very long way. I first met Empson when he came back from China, in 1953. I'd read *The Gathering Storm* as well as the two early critical books before the war. He and I never really got on. That has to be said, and that's quite important, in a curious sense. There was a kind of mutual suspicion. Mine was only a reflection of his. He had got me down as a neo-Christian long before, and he could never really quite forgive me for being that, as he thought. As so often, the judgment was a totally prejudiced one.

IS: What is your religious background?

FK: I was brought up as a low Anglican, as a choirboy. But I've had nothing to do with the church since I was about 14. Of course, that wouldn't answer Empson's point, because neo-Christians very often don't have anything to do with the church; they just think that it's nice to have a torturing God.

As for these admirations, the world is not that pure. You can see it in your interviews with Hartman and Bloom. We don't admire or dislike each other for the words on the page. There are feelings which people have about each other which affect their judgments.

IS: Lentricchia, in his preface to *Forms of Attention*, says that you're someone who waits for the fuss about a new fashion or mode to die down, and then picks up and employs whatever makes any sense (p. ix). I think there's some truth to that.

FK: Well, it's nice of him to put it that way, but it may be that it's far less creditable than he makes out. It may be that there's a kind of laziness, where you never identify yourself with anything that actually is going on. It's an informed laziness, I would like to think. The only school I've ever belonged to – and that was very briefly – was when I was an undergraduate and, under the influence of ferocious young teachers, became a Leavisite. I mimicked the jargon, and so on, but then saw that that's not a thing that you ought to do. You know, the blinkered Leavisites were all people who never developed themselves, no matter what their real gifts were.

IS: So a school, unlike an interpretive community, is not a good thing to belong to.

FK: Not really. The ones I'd have liked to belong to wouldn't have me – it's the Groucho thing. I would like to think of myself as having learnt most about the study of art, on a historical scale, from the Warburg Institute: but nobody at the Warburg Institute would ever dream of thinking of me as one of them.

IS: It occurred to me while you were speaking that Groucho's remark – "Any club that would have me, I wouldn't want to join" – would have to be the best and most concise summary I have ever heard of the theorizations of Harold Bloom.

FK: Except that Harold *has* formed a school. The world is full of Bloomians. There aren't any Kermodians in the world.

IS: I haven't met any. Another strain in your recent work, particularly in *The Sense of an Ending*, is the notion of the function of art as being the imposition of human forms and meanings on to the raw flux of reality. In this context, you say a lot of derogatory things about myth. Presumably, fiction is in some kind of commerce, or concord, with reality, and myth is not.

FK: That part of that book is often assailed. I still think it has some validity. I use the word "fiction" in a Nietzschean or Vaihingerian sense. Vaihinger was doing all this on his own, by the way, so it's clear that the notion of heuristic or protective fiction was in the air at the time. I got interested in that. It seemed to me that there is a very great difference between those benevolent or neutral fictions and the sort of fiction that is involved in anti-Semitism. And then I thought of myth as a useful fiction.

At that time, I wasn't actually thinking about Lévi-Strauss, but you would easily fit that in, because the whole diachronic exposition of mythical material, for him, really is a fictional version of some totally abstract, almost algebraic formula. The truth, in so far as he would allow the word, would be that formula. The fiction which enshrined the truth would be disposable. In that sense, what we *usually* think of as myths – the sorts of stories that he himself collects – really are heuristic fictions. Whereas a myth which actually solidifies social prejudice – whether for good or for ill – deserves a different sort of title from something as eminently disposable and malleable as a fiction.

I was reading a student's essay, only this morning, about mourning in *Hamlet*. About how the King and Queen want to impose upon Hamlet, and think that by imposing the ordinary forms of mourning on him they can get him out of his gloom. Well, that's a perfectly reasonable thing to do: that's what the ordinary forms of mourning are. They are ways of celebrating the acceptance of separation. It's not wrong to formalize, and in that sense to mythologize, death. In fact, it may be that modern society is wrong in having demythologized it. So although I use that example of anti-Semitism as myth, one could probably use benign examples also.

IS: Whereas myth is synchronic and unchanging, you would argue that it is the work of *fiction* to send out advance parties in the direction of whatever it is that *is* changing, and bring us back reports.

FK: Yes, and that's also the work of interpretation. That's why we all become obsolete. Stevens, to come back to him, was one of the few poets who had the nerve to go on saying that all poetry, including this poem, is going to be obsolete. He had an understanding of the temporal dimension in which these things operate.

IS: We could also describe ideologies as attempts to make some human sense out of the raw material of existence – which is how you describe fictions, in your recent work. How do ideologies differ from fictions?

FK: Well, for one thing fictions are provisional. They are probably conscious, in a somewhat Rortian way, of the fact that they are evanescent. I don't mean that they disappear: *The Odyssey* isn't going to vanish from the face of the earth. But it has to be kept in place by continuous efforts of interpretation. Ideologies have to be represented as permanent structures: they aren't, but they have to be represented as such. If they included a sort of self-destruct component, this would be too obvious for them to have their effect.

IS: In your description of fictions, the influence of Stevens is very apparent. In *Sense of an Ending*, you say that fictions allow us to impose "coherent patterns," but also have to take account of "things as they are" (p. 17). And you say that a critic's first qualification has to be "a scepticism, an interest in things as they are, in inhuman reality as well as in human justice" (p. 64). The influence of Stevens is clear in the phrase "things as they are,"[4] as well as at a deeper level. One of the many pleasures of your text, for me, is that you seem unable to write more than a couple of pages without quoting from Stevens.

FK: I think that *was* so. My old friend John Wain said of *Sense of an Ending* that it was a sort of love-letter to Stevens. In a way that was true: that was the time when I was most full of Stevens. I'd written that little book about him far too early, and have always rather regretted that. By the time of *Sense of an Ending* I knew a lot more about Stevens than I had then. I saw, in some later essays that I did on him, what was the fatal trap of Stevens, which is that everybody treats him as a kind of sack in which there's a philosophy hidden. Nobody examines the texture of the sack very much. So my whole feeling about Stevens changed. I'm still devoted to Stevens, and he's still the poet that I would read if I felt I had to read a poem right now.

IS: Talking of depictions of Stevens as philosopher, Hillis Miller does that in his book *Poets of Reality*, and comes to much the same conclusion about Stevens that you do: that Stevens is telling us how to live in a world where God is dead, but where the power that created Him has survived.

FK: That book, which I liked very much, belongs to Hillis's phenomenological stage, where he sort of pulls everything apart, as in that extraordinary essay on Conrad. I was rather opposed, actually, because I'm a great believer in time. I don't know what it is, but I believe in it, and this affects not only my whole view of the interpretive task, but also my view of plot. I've had a long-running, fruitless quarrel with Joe Frank about space and form, which cropped up again the other day on a panel I sat on with William Gass, who even said that logical classes are evidence of spatial form. This is nonsense. It may be true that when we visualize a logical class we think of some kind of figure, but it hasn't got any spatial dimension at all. It is very important not to fall into that, and not to lose the sense of temporal flow, both in the history of interpretation and in the history of individual texts. Also to understand that the intemporal isn't necessarily spatial.

IS: I've been interested by your continual questioning of spatial metaphors for literature. Although we are not suited to the long

4 See "The Man with the Blue Guitar," in *Collected Poems* (New York: Alfred A. Knopf, 1954), p. 165.

perspectives, time is our element, and this is presumably another
case where you feel that literature has to have something to do with
our element.

FK: I don't know that it has to: I think it just *has*. What foxes people
is that they like to think of a dimension of time in which a narrative
exists, and a dimension of myth in which time disappears. The best
treatment of this in modern criticism is in an essay by Yuri Lott-
man, where he talks about the plot of scandal as the temporal plot,
and distinguishes it from an intemporal plot. The best treatment
of it in *any* kind of interpretive literature is in the *Confessions* of
Augustine, where he has this notion of things passing through time
and then residing in some kind of – not space, he doesn't make that
mistake – repository, which resembles eternity in a way. I think
that about gets it.

Certainly, the interrelations of parts in the eternity bag are
different to those in the temporal bag: and the secrets are in the
eternity bag. In psycho-analytic discourse, there really is a plot of
scandal – it flows on and on – but the parapraxes indicate some
point where there is something at a different level; where the relationships between the constituents are not temporal relations.
They're not spatial relations, obviously. This was the great interpretive gain of *The Interpretation of Dreams*: that it actually started
making us think this way. What we've never been able to do is to
get that into poetics. We think of it as belonging to symptomatology,
but it really ought to belong to poetics, as Jakobson saw. We keep
on losing track of it, partly because of the seductions of the myth
of spatial form.

IS: You know, we may still end up with a ''Kermode School'' by the
end of this interview: the anti-Platonic ''School of Time.'' Stevens
had a tricky and troubled relation to Platonism, which came up in
the Frye interview. I'm surprised to hear you say that you regret
the Stevens book, because it was so pathbreaking in introducing
Stevens to a British audience. Why was Stevens, like critical theory,
so slow to take off in Britain?

FK: There were practical causes: the reluctance of anybody to publish
him. It used to be said, apparently wrongly, that the main obstacle
to the publication of Stevens in England was Eliot. That does not
seem to have been the case: he can't, on the other hand, have been
very keen, either. When the *Selected Poems* came out, they were
reviewed by Empson in *The Listener*, with great enthusiasm, but
mostly on the topic of Stevens as the exponent of the English blank-
verse tradition. Tennyson must be very formative for Stevens. We
do go on about Emerson – Harold is quite right to put Stevens in
a firmly American tradition – but he also belongs in that English

tradition: "Sunday Morning" is certainly a Keatsian/Tennysonian poem. The iamb is always around in Stevens.

I admire Stevens partly because of a general air of prescience that he has. Without actually ever going to much trouble about it, he always seems to know what's going on and what's going to go on in the general development of thinking. He's not a philosopher, and people who take him seriously as a philosopher obviously make a mistake, but he has a kind of peripheral awareness of the important issues in philosophy, which is more impressive in a poet than actually getting down and working them out. I suppose there's a kind of temperamental affinity that people have or haven't got; and it might have been harder in the 1950s, when people were just coming to terms with poets like Larkin, who is in many ways a far more exquisite poet than Stevens.

IS: But who is also a poet capable of the occasional Stevensian mood: "If I were called in/To construct a religion/I should make use of water. . . ./And I should raise in the east/A glass of water/Where any-angled light/Would congregate endlessly."[5] Mind you, this also works the other way. Larkin – who I would, until his death a fortnight ago, unquestionably have called the greatest living poet writing in English – is not widely read in the United States. It's strange the way that currency doesn't work.

FK: That's right. I was looking at a new journal called *Poetry New York* only this morning, and thinking that there wasn't anything in it that I would bother to read twice. This is because there's a whole lot going on in poetry in the United States that I don't really *want* to understand. I think the peculiar subtleties of Larkin are such that you wouldn't like them unless you liked people who were technically adept. And Americans don't like their own poets – like Wilbur, Hollander, Hecht – who are technically adept. Hollander and Hecht are not in Helen Vendler's new anthology.[6] That seems to me extraordinary, because if they were English poets they certainly would be in any comparable collection.

IS: Bloom dismisses Larkin, but at least Bloom has read him.

FK: Well, he may not have *read* him. It seems to me that anybody that knows about poetry cannot really read Larkin and dismiss him.

IS: He doesn't like that anti-Romantic, cautious . . . .

FK: No, I can see that he wouldn't; but that, I think, would stop him from reading it, even though his eyes had scanned the words. This is not a one-way process: there are lots of things that Harold Bloom

5 "Water," in *The Whitsun Weddings* (London: Faber & Faber, 1964), p. 20.
6 Helen Vendler, *The Harvard Book of Contemporary American Poetry* (Cambridge, Mass.: Harvard University Press, 1985).

gets a big charge out of that mean nothing whatever to me. Again, it's a temperamental question.

IS: Let's talk for a moment about the poem we don't have, because I forgot to bring it down from New Haven with me on the train.

FK: And I forgot to bring it from home.

IS: Maybe it will be an interesting exercise, considering that Bloom says we should never talk about a poem that we don't have by memory – which, in the classic formulation, is easy for *him* to say. If we *did* have "Not Ideas about the Thing but the Thing Itself" in front of us, where would you begin your critical work?

FK: It's a lovely little poem. John Wain once said, in conversation, that these little poems that come at the end were "fragments broken off the monolith of his dialect," which I think is a rather terrific expression. If you came across it in *Poetry New York*, and it was by Ann Jones or somebody, you wouldn't think anything of it. It has to have a corpus behind it before it really works. That little idiosyncratic playing with the letter "c," for example: that has a history. "It was like/A new knowledge of reality" is like Stevens coming home. I think Bloom said in his interview that it was a self-celebrating poem: that's right. There are other poems which end with some word about reality, like "An Ordinary Evening in New Haven," where reality is not something that is unequivocally good to arrive at: "It is not in the premise that reality/Is a solid. It may be a shade that traverses/A dust, a force that traverses a shade."[7] That poem ends with rather gloomy winds blowing through it: this one ends like waking up on a beautiful summer morning. In that sense it is a happy poem. If we all had the good luck to have a splendid final period, where we could just chip off poems every morning from the quarry-face, this is the kind of thing we should like them to be: not Sophoclean, but just having a sort of Santayanan contentment, which he's also looking for in the "Old Philosopher" poem. This poem really has that. "It was like": the use of "like" here is very Stevensian. He doesn't say it *was* a new knowledge of reality.

I particularly admire some of the last poems. "Of Mere Being," which seems to be the last poem, is absolutely extraordinary. I wish they would not change "distance" to "decor" in it, because distance is really important to it: he's very good on that, that sense of "The academies, like structures in a mist."[8] And the two Romes in the Santayana poem: that's what "Of Mere Being" is really about, except that instead of the rather conventional two-city pattern, you

7 "An Ordinary Evening in New Haven," op. cit., p. 489.
8 "Notes toward a Supreme Fiction," op. cit., p. 386.

have this extraordinary invention of the bird. Stevens never forgot that there is a very little difference between "as if" and "is," and that's why that "like" is so important in this poem.

IS: Let me finish with a few questions on the relation of criticism to society and the university. In *Forms of Attention*, you describe the work of criticism as follows:

> whatever preserves and restores some object of which the value may have been or may be in danger of getting lost is, however prone to error, good. . . . What is not good is anything whatever that might destroy the objects valued or their value, or divert from them the special forms of attention they have been accorded.
>
> (p. 92)

An essentially conservative task, then?

FK: Well, I suppose it has to be conservative in the sense that it says that things have to be conserved. I think that the book itself qualifies that in various ways. The idea is that there is a qualitative difference in the way that we attend to things which have been canonized, and things which haven't. This is best illustrated by the question asked by John Barton, the Old Testament scholar: try to imagine what would happen if the book of Ecclesiastes had been excluded from the Jewish Bible, and had turned up at Qumran. It would not be the same book, because it would not have had the same kind of attention, and it would not have the same context. That could never be restored.

The cost of this is that you are at the mercy of canonical decisions made by people long ago, for reasons that you don't understand and can't reconstruct. So there's a certain arbitrary quality. This means, for example, that there are books blessedly included, like the Song of Songs, which might not have been included, and which we can see good reasons for excluding for the sake of the canon. On the other hand, there are books of which it is hard to think of any reason for their being there: things like Jude. The important thing is the gain. The losses are harder to understand, simply because we've forgotten the reasons why they ever were there. The reason why the Apocalypse is in the New Testament is really pretty obscure, but there's no doubt that not only the history of literature, but the history of politics, would have been quite different if it hadn't been included. That's what I mean by saying that we have to make an act of acceptance in some cases.

IS: What are the forces working to destroy the valued objects that criticism is always working to preserve?

FK: There are very strong anti-canonical and rival-canonical arguments going on now. For example, the argument that was put

forward in the *Journal of Higher Education* here: that the most important influence on literary study in the United States over the next
years will be the work of Jacques Derrida, as it is relevant to Black
and Women's Studies. Now, that's not the first form of relevance
of Derrida that you would think of anyway. But still, letting that
pass, the man who writes the piece goes on to say that dismantling
the canon is the prime object of this enterprise. Well, of course,
deconstructors oddly don't deconstruct the canon: they have to have
something in its place. But he wants to remove works from the
canon, by which I think he really means the list of things studied
in English departments, names he doesn't specify that have been
foisted on to them, by white males, who tell half-truths about
everything. We've got to get rid of them, and replace them with
black women writers like Zora Neale Hurston and Toni Morrison.
Taking it to its extreme, this really means that he thinks that English
departments should stop teaching, say, Spenser – I don't know what
he had in mind: it might have been Wordsworth, it might have been
Dickens – and put in these other objects of attention instead. Then
he ends by saying that the purpose of this is, in the end, a political
purpose, a revolutionary purpose. I can't sufficiently express my
disagreement with such a view. I'm not expressing a disagreement
with the view that black women writers deserve critical attention.
It's a kind of upside-down Eliot notion: he thought that new books
joined some kind of timeless order of works; this view holds that
new books can drive old ones out, and that everyone ought to bend
his best efforts towards making sure that this happens. That seems
to me entirely wrong.

IS: That's an attack on the canon coming from within the academy. I thought you were going to talk – as Frye is always doing
– about the attack coming from such things as advertising and
television.

FK: You can't now turn the tide back in that respect, either: you can't
produce a generation of people who have not watched the television
when otherwise they might be reading. We have to face the fact
that, as you say, your students don't know the title of Homer's book
about the siege of Troy. You now take it for granted that, if you're
teaching Milton, the first thing that you have to talk about is the
first chapter of Genesis, because they don't know what's in it. All
the things that you could reasonably have expected people to have
at least heard of, or read, they've no longer heard of, or read.

IS: In *The Genesis of Secrecy*, you say that what must not be looked for,
in interpretation, is "some obvious public success" (p. 126). This
relates to the pervasive anti-apocalyptic tone in your work and, to
shore up my pathetic earlier point, connects you with Hartman.

There are at least two things involved in this rejection of the idea
that there will ever be a revelation in criticism to which everybody
will unanimously agree. First, it again splits you off from Frye, who
tried to give us a version of a critical revelation; second, from Marxist
criticism, where, again, there has been a revelation, so that all texts
can now be brought into coherence with it.

FK: I suppose that the flexibility of that situation is what people take
Marxism to be. That changes all the time. There is a wide difference between someone like Jameson and someone like Raymond
Williams. In so far as they take history into account, I'm all for
them, and always have been. This is why it's so preposterous for
people to call me a structuralist in the Cambridge row. But I don't
see, as they constantly adjust it, that their notions of the relationship between base and superstructure have any special validity.

IS: Like Marxist critics, though, you recognize the investment of all
criticism, via its institutionalization, in the social values that
surround it. In *The Art of Telling* you say that "such institutions as
ours do reflect the larger society which they somehow serve, and
it may be an unjust society. But how else shall we protect the latent
sense?" (p. 184). Does this leave criticism with any progressive, not
to say subversive, function?

FK: Criticism is a blanket expression that covers so many things.
Think of the sort of thing that was represented by Queenie Leavis's
book, *Fiction and the Reading Public*. I suppose you'd call that a work
of criticism; some might call it a work of sociology; I'd call it
something else. That was an attempt to do something about curing
a culture. But that's not really criticism. Criticism entails immediate
encounter with particular texts, which is the sort of criticism I would
like to do. I don't think that kind of criticism can possibly be called
progressive. It may be an agent of change, but it can't be an agent
of progress. I don't know how criticism could be subversive. I
suppose you could say that Empson on neo-Christianity or, more
recently, Culler echoing Empson on this point, are attempting to
subvert what they regard as evil social or intellectual tendencies.
But I couldn't understand what Culler was doing, really.

IS: You say in *The Genesis of Secrecy* that the discovery of latent senses
may appear to be a spontaneous individual achievement, but it is
"privileged and constrained by the community of the ear" (p. 5).
This is totally opposed to what Bloom is always saying: that it is
individual.

FK: It's a weak answer but, again: this is temperamental. I'm very
glad that Harold admires himself so much, and doesn't need support
from anyone else: that's what he's saying, really. Of course, he can
say that with comfort, because he has a large constituency, which

he chooses to discount when he's talking about himself. The solitary-madman figure doesn't seem to me to be very useful – and I'm sure that's a very bad description of Harold Bloom.

IS: You have continued to insist upon an interpretive community, as necessary to preserve valued objects and latent meaning, with an ever-increasing strength since the Cambridge fracas. This insistence strikes me, in the first place, as courageous, and in the second place as baffling. Didn't the Cambridge business show, if it showed anything, that there is no such thing, and never has been any such thing, as an interpretive community?

FK: I don't think the interpretive community would necessarily be a group of people all in one place at the same time. I always thought that a good deal of what was said during that scandalous episode was falsified by the fact that there *was* no community of the ear: nobody seemed to be able to listen to what the other person was saying. So the most absurd charges were made, publicly, which were flatly counter to the known and held positions of the persons to and of whom they were speaking.

The English newspapers are so disgraceful about this kind of thing. First of all, they make the false assumption that there's a strong intellectual content to a discussion like this. Second, they think that anything with a strong intellectual content is amusing in itself: "These peculiar dons, how they will fight for their absurd beliefs!" and so on. That was a double distortion, and no longer could you find out what people were saying. It became a matter of whether anybody was libeling anybody. There was even a suit, which I helped to get aborted.

It just shows you how much temperaments are involved in these things. There was a bitter opposition to MacCabe. People had undertaken as early as 1976 to get rid of him. It wouldn't have mattered if he'd written six wonderful books, instead of one indifferently decent first book. The only interest of this is that it puts a certain amount of human content in the idea of a College community: collegiality is not just being nice to one another, it's also being horrible to one another. But the importance of the Cambridge English Faculty, in the world of modern criticism, is close to absolute zero, so I don't know why so much attention has been paid to it.

IS: The public idea was that this was a big fight about something called "structuralism." Well, whatever it was about, it wasn't that. What was it all about?

FK: Well, I think you'd immediately move into all kinds of deep and difficult psychological relationships, as well as shallower problems like professional jealousy. Also, to some extent, they were right about there being a misguided but genuine political dimension to some of this. What I'm saying is that when you ask, "What was it about?" we immediately move away from anything you could recognize as an intellectual issue. If someone ever – God forfend – wanted to write a history of that episode, what they would have to do would be to treat it at that level of the personalities involved. My limited experience of being mixed up in controversies which have hit the newspapers confirms that the newspapers gratuitously get everything wrong. Immediately the newspapers come into it, you've got a different ball-game completely, because everybody begins to talk as if what the newspapers said was the case.

IS: Cambridge seems to have held these wars-in-heaven fairly regularly, perhaps on the model of the Olympic Games. One here again thinks of Leavis, so let's finish with him. This was someone also intent on preserving valued objects, against the Benthamite hordes. Did you ever meet him?

FK: Barely. He was not somebody who had any time for me. I was on his blacklist, I'm told. He had a hit list which, fortunately, he had no power to implement. He thought of me as part of that vague institution called the "London Literary Establishment."

IS: What attracted you to him?

FK: I had teachers strongly influenced by Leavis. Also, as Donald Davie remarks in his autobiography, there was a kind of convenience: it was very useful to be taught by Leavis because it meant there was so much stuff you could not only honorably ignore, but which it would be dishonorable actually to read. There really was some kind of weird notion that you could take over and run the society with people trained in this élite establishment. It's rather similar in structure to the old idea that solving diplomatic problems was a bit like writing Greek elegiacs – I know people who would strongly defend the position that experience gained in high-level problem-solving, like Greek verse, is transferable to diplomatic and political activities.

I think that the Cambridge problem is not so much a sort of Olympic Games cycle, but just Original Sin: the great rows in the Cambridge English Faculty have always been about something else; it's not as if the same subject keeps coming up; it's a different quarrel every time. There is no future for the serious study of literature at Cambridge as long as the bureaucratic forms remain as they are.

Edward Said

6

Edward Said

"The sense of being between cultures has been very, very strong for me. I would say that's the single strongest strand running through my life: the fact that I'm always in and out of things, and never really *of* anything for very long."

The work of Edward Said represents "practical criticism" in a new, powerful and, above all, oppositional mode. Said's has been the skeptical voice *inside* literary theory, constantly reminding it of how *im*practical its habitual strategies are, since they serve (like the older "practical criticism" associated with I. A. Richards) to split literature and criticism off from wider social practices. By conceiving of "literariness" or "the aesthetic" as isolatable affects open to formal theorizing, critics have marginalized both literature and themselves; and by failing to see the way in which literature – and criticism – are intercalated in a wider field of power and action, they have consciously or unconsciously served the interests of ruling-class power. Said writes against critical modes which, like deconstruction, have a tendency to substitute a pure theoretical consciousness for a critical or oppositional one.

Opposition, however, has been more than a matter of consciousness for Said. He is a Palestinian, born in Jerusalem in 1935, and is a member of the Palestine National Council (the Palestinian parliament-in-exile). As well as being a literary critic, he is well known in the United States as a writer, spokesperson and activist for the Palestinian cause, and has written several books on Palestine, Islam, and the treatment of these subjects in the Western media. Said came to the United States in the late 1950s, and was educated at Princeton and Harvard. He is now Parr Professor of English and Comparative Literature at Columbia University, where this interview was recorded at the end of January, 1986.

Said's first book, *Joseph Conrad and the Fiction of Autobiography* (1966), is based on his doctoral dissertation at Harvard. It does not offer many clues as to the course of his subsequent endeavors, except that, significantly, it broadens the discussion of Conrad from the realm of the strictly "literary" writings: it is a comparative (*not* a causal) study of the relation between the shorter fiction and the letters. Said's next book, *Beginnings*, did not appear until nine years later, but it immediately brought him to the fore among American interpreters of the new French thought. The beginning of *Beginnings* illustrates, I think, what is meant by calling Said a "practical" critic:

> The problem of beginnings is one of those problems that, if allowed to, will confront one with equal intensity on a practical and on a theoretical level. Every writer knows that the choice of a beginning for what he will write is crucial not only because it determines much of what follows but also because a work's beginning is, practically speaking, the main entrance to what it offers. Moreover, in retrospect we can regard a beginning as the point at which, in a given work, the writer departs from all other works; a beginning immediately establishes relationships with works already existing, relationships of either continuity or antagonism or some mixture of both. . . . Is a beginning the same as an origin? Is the beginning of a given work its real beginning, or is there some other, secret point that more authentically starts the work off?
>
> (p. 3)

The last of these questions suggests that it was Foucault, among the new French thinkers, who had come to exercise the greatest influence over Said. In *Beginnings*, Foucault is described as affirmative and progressive, in contrast to Derrida, who is "nihilistic" (pp. 342–3). At the other extreme, Foucault's "philosophy of decenterment" is proposed as a healthy antidote to Northrop Frye's centeristic Christian Platonism (pp. 376–8). Said was learning from Foucault that neither literature nor criticism is separable from history since history, like them, is discourse. It does not move in discontinuous periods separated by radical or heroic acts, but is constituted through large, anonymous, discursive movements whose function is essentially conservative. Such discursive formations can structure the thoughts and actions of any individual within a particular culture; more importantly, stronger cultures can appropriate weaker ones *in* discourse. This suggests that the demystification of cultural imperialism could take the form of a critical or counter-reading, and we begin to see how Foucault provides Said with an avenue for connecting his training as a literary critic with his specific historical situation.

A critical consciousness which *read* the cooperative hegemony between political, literary, scholarly, economic and other discourses, instead of merely reproducing it, would constitute a positive demystification, and a . . . beginning. The influence of Foucault – as well as of Deleuze, Vico, Chomsky, Fanon, and Lukács – is apparent in the terms in which Said sets up his continuing project, at the end of *Beginnings*. It will be an examination of

> the question of language as an object of speculation, as an object occupying for the writer a privileged first place; the formal and psychological questions of the interdependence of literary and sociological approaches in dealing with how English, for example, is at once a national and a world language . . . the question of the cultural domination of one intellectual or national domain over another (one culture is more "developed" than – having begun earlier and "arrived" before – another); and the questions of liberty, or freedom, or originality as they obtain in complex social and intellectual orders of repetition.
>
> (pp. 380–1)

Much of this project was to come to fruition in *Orientalism* (1978), Said's most scholarly, practical and well-known book. It describes the way in which European culture, since the eighteenth century, has increased its own strength by appropriating the idea of the Orient – and thus the Orient itself – as its mysterious, duplicitous, dark Other. Orientalism is the discursive imposition of a political doctrine over the Orient; it is the appropriation, transformation and, in short, occupation of a weaker culture by a stronger. The truly unsettling thing about Said's study, as far as its scholarly audience is concerned, is its demonstration of the way in which European Oriental scholarship, including that of our own century, has been a central part of this appropriation, rather than a descriptive account of it. This parallels many of Foucault's own findings – for example, that psycho-analysis was not the discovery and description of sexuality, but rather the production and transformation of it. So "scholarly" – or, supposedly, distanced – Orientalism turns out to be Orientalism proper:

> Taking the late eighteenth century as a very roughly defined starting point Orientalism can be discussed and analyzed as the corporate institution for dealing with the Orient – dealing with it by making statements about it, authorizing views of it, describing

it, by teaching it, settling it, ruling over it: in short, Orientalism as a Western style for dominating, restructuring, and having authority over the Orient.

(p. 3)

Orientalism implied that literary studies could apply its explicative techniques to uses of language that lie outside the literary canon, and could thus return to and immerse itself in the world by learning to read the relations between power and knowledge. In Said's latest book, *The World, the Text, and the Critic* (1983), this implication is explicitly theorized – to the chagrin of many of the book's reviewers. In *Orientalism*, Said had said that fields of learning, as well as works of literature, are constrained "by worldly circumstance" (p. 201), and the notion of "worldliness" has become increasingly important for him. It functions, within his work, like "fiction" in Kermode or "*différance*" in Derrida: it is that which criticism both deals with *and* is contained by. Criticism stands between culture and system, but outside neither. Literary texts, says Said in *The World, the Text, and the Critic*, "have ways of existing that even in their most rarefied form are always enmeshed in circumstance, time, place, and society – in short, they are in the world, and hence worldly" (p. 35). But critical texts are no less worldly:

> if we assume . . . that texts make up what Foucault calls archival facts, the archive being defined as the text's social discursive presence in the world, then criticism too is another aspect of that present. In other words, rather than being defined by the silent past, commanded by it to speak in the present, criticism, no less than any text, is the present in the course of its articulation, its struggles for definition.

(p. 51)

These insights have a potentially unsettling effect in store for both traditional *and* deconstructive approaches to criticism, since both tend to deal with texts in terms of varying accounts of textuality, rather than worldliness. In the poststructuralist concern with "intertextuality," says Said, one does not "encounter a serious study of what authority is, either with reference to the way authority is carried historically and circumstantially from the state down into a society saturated with authority or with reference to the actual workings of culture, the role of intellectuals, institutions, and establishments" (p. 172). More controversially, he holds that "it is no accident that the emergence of so narrowly defined a philosophy of pure textuality and critical non-interference has coincided with the ascendancy of Reaganism, or for that matter with a new cold war,

increased militarism and defense spending, and a massive turn to the
right on matters touching the economy, social services, and
organized labor'' (p. 4).

In Said's view, notions of pure textuality lead criticism back in the
direction of the mysterious, the transcendent and the religious. He
is an opponent of religiosity in intellectual, as well as in political life,
and proposes instead a ''secular criticism.'' Secular criticism aims to
arrive at ''some acute sense of what political, social and human
values are entailed in the reading, production, and transmission of
every text.'' It deals with ''local and worldly situations, and . . . is
constitutively opposed to the production of massive, hermetic
systems'' (p. 26). Secular criticism, in fact, constantly *undoes* theory;
it subverts the barriers which criticism erects between what is and is
not inside its own domain – barriers which simply displace religious
categories of profane and sacred, fallen and redeemed:

> The critical consciousness is awareness of the differences between
> situations, awareness too of the fact that no system or theory
> exhausts the situation out of which it emerges or to which it is
> transported. And, above all, critical consciousness is awareness of
> the resistance to theory, reactions to it elicited by those concrete
> experiences or interpretations with which it is in conflict. Indeed
> I would go so far as saying that it is the critic's job to provide
> resistances to theory, to open it up toward historical reality, toward
> society, toward human needs and interests, to point up those
> concrete instances drawn from everyday reality that lie outside or
> just beyond the interpretive area necessarily designated in advance
> and thereafter circumscribed by every theory.
>
> (p. 242)

Imre Salusinszky: The first time I met you, in a class at Yale, I
anticipated that you'd speak with a colorful accent, like mine . . .
Edward Said: I can do that too . . .
IS: But I was surprised at this New York persona: urbane and rather
assimilated. At all events, the story of your life must take the ear
strangely. I would like to hear how a Palestinian refugee becomes
an English Professor at Columbia: I think there must be more than
one step involved there.
ES: To describe me as a refugee is probably overstating it a bit. I
was born in Jerusalem, to a Jerusalem family. Because of my
family's business, we lived both in Jerusalem and in Cairo,
although after 1948 we were effectively settled in Egypt. I went to
a lot of schools because of these movements – we also spent time
in Lebanon, where my family had a summer house. So I went to

about nine schools by the time I left Egypt, in disgrace, in the early 1950s to come to America: I had been at a colonial English public school, and was effectively asked not to return because I was a troublemaker. Then, when I was 15, I came to America. I went to boarding-school here for a couple of years, and then I went to Princeton. My family remained in the Middle East, so I went back there in the summers; however, I'm the only member of my family who lives here.

Thus, my background is a very anomalous and peculiar one, and I've always been conscious of that. Although Palestinian, we were Anglicans: so we were a minority within the Christian minority in an Islamic majority setting. Then, because of my father's early years in this country (he had come to America in 1911 for a period of about nine years), we always had a kind of outlet to America, and for religious and cultural reasons to England. So England and America were my alternative places, and English was a language I spoke, along with Arabic, ever since I was a boy. There have always been the anomalies and strangenesses of being an outsider, but also of having, as years go on, no place to return to: I couldn't return to Palestine, for various obvious reasons, mostly political; I couldn't return to the Egypt I grew up in; and now I can't return to Lebanon, where my mother lives, and where my wife is from. My background is a series of displacements and expatriations which cannot ever be recuperated. The sense of being between cultures has been very, very strong for me. I would say that's the single strongest strand running through my life: the fact that I'm always in and out of things, and never really *of* anything for very long.

I studied literature because I've always been interested in it, and because it seemed to me that the things around literature, so to speak – philosophy, music, history, political science, and sociology – enabled one to be interested in a number of other human activities. It's been a very good life for me, and I haven't regretted it for a second. The alternative was always to go into business, which was my family background, but that was never a real alternative for me, because of the real social and political background of Middle Eastern business, which was always of a ruling-class type and which I more or less moved away from.

IS: What does your membership of the Palestine National Council involve?

ES: Actually, it involves practically nothing more than the symbolism. I was elected to it in 1977, by the council itself, as an independent member – I have no political affiliation with any official group. In 1977 I went to one meeting in Cairo, and was

there for approximately four days. I missed all the other ones until
Amman in November 1984 – the climactic meeting which sealed
the split within the Palestinian movement. I was there for two
days, essentially to make up a quorum. I'm a non-active member,
to all intents and purposes.

IS: Talking of displacements: if the Palestinian people were ever
successful in their national aspirations, for independence and for
a homeland, would you remain in the United States or return to
Palestine?

ES: I've thought about that a lot. I used to think that I would try
to return. Actually, the part of Palestine that I'm from is the
western part of Jerusalem: that's always been a part of post-1948
Israel, and it's not a section of the city I feel that I can return to
very easily. I really think, now, that the idea and the feeling of
exile is so strong in me that I doubt that I'd be able to appease it
by a return of that sort.

I'm not sure, in any event, that I believe in what would have
to be at the outset a partitioned Palestine. I've stopped thinking
that the solution to political problems is to divide up smaller and
smaller pieces of territory. I do not believe in partition, not only
at a political and demographic level, but on all sorts of other
intellectual levels, and spiritual ones. The whole idea of parceling
out pieces for communities is just totally wrong. Any notion of
purity – that such and such a territory is *essentially* the Palestinian
or Israeli homeland – is just an idea that is totally inauthentic, for
me. I certainly believe in self-determination, so if people want to
do that they should be able to do it: but I myself don't see any need
to participate in it.

IS: One of the things which comes across in reading *The Question of
Palestine* is, for me, a courageous position: you are one of the few
commentators within the whole debate who – while you are
uncompromising in your description of what Zionism has meant
for the Palestinians – continues to insist that the destinies of
Palestinians and Jews are interlinked, and cannot be separated
out. At the moment, though, what are the realistic outcomes?

ES: At the moment, there isn't really much to look forward to except
exacerbated conflict. I know a great deal about the Arab and
Palestinian situation, and there I think the sense of drifting and
hopelessness and uncertainty is very strong. I don't think that the
ordinary person has given up – there's a great deal of resilience in
the people – but what we're really going through is a crisis of
leadership, plus a singularly unfortunate and unfair conjunctural
crisis: all of the circumstances are against us. The role of the
United States, the role of the Soviet Union, the other Arabs, the

Israelis: all of these militate against any meaningful resolution in the near future.

But in the middle to far future, it's interesting that a number of Israelis and Palestinians are thinking along parallel lines, precisely in the way that I mentioned earlier: *against* the notion of partition and of trying instead to realize a democratic Jewish/Palestinian state. A lot of this, paradoxically, is due to people like Kahane, who has raised the problem and said that you can't have a democratic Jewish state: it's chilling, and people find it really hard to deal with. I was very interested in a recent piece by Meron Benvenisti, the former deputy mayor of Jerusalem, who has come to the same conclusion as me: we really can't talk about separate peoples, because our lives are interlinked in so many ways, at this moment principally by the dominance of one group over the other. But the whole idea of a separate, differential polity is a travesty of justice and of what was believed to be liberalism and a great social experiment.

That's where the future is: in the evolution, over time, of notions of community that are based on real interdependent experiences, and not on dreams that shut out the other person and half of reality. The principle of military thinking, which is so strong both in the revival of Jewish nationalism and in Arab nationalism, has to take its course over time and, if it doesn't destroy everything, be shown as completely washed up and ineffective. Until it's quite clear that military means are bankrupt – as one would have thought that the Lebanese experience revealed, for the Israelis and the Lebanese and the Palestinians – we're going to have these horrible dips in the lives of people. But I'm a great optimist, let's say for my son's generation.

IS: Your activism as a Palestinian must have in some ways made your work as a literary critic here in the United States more difficult to pursue. Two immediate reasons that come to mind are, first, that as a result, not of Zionist propaganda only, but of Zionist propaganda among other things, a synonymity between "Palestinian" and "terrorist" has been built up in the public mind here. Second, many of the people whom you deal with and are close to – including people like Geoffrey Hartman and Harold Bloom – are Zionists. And *any* feelings about this issue tend to escalate immediately to being violent and personal and passionate ones. So has it made your life as a literary critic more difficult?

ES: In perspective, one would have to say only slightly. If one sees it in the large perspective of a fairly bloody struggle between two peoples, then what I've had to go through is really quite mild in comparison. Obviously, one misses certain sides of a person if they're withheld because of hostility or fear. In the case of Harold, his ideas, as he told me many years ago, are those of a longtime Jabotinsky/Herut man. He's to the right of the right, but it hasn't inhibited us from talking about it. With Geoffrey, we've never discussed it. I remember being slightly pained during the summer of 1982, when I was with him at the School of Criticism. My entire family, and my wife's family, were in Beirut, being besieged. Not a word of compassion was said. I obviously couldn't say anything, and he didn't say anything. Those kinds of things are what trouble one, on a personal level. It was certainly the case with Trilling, who was a very close friend and a wonderfully generous colleague: a certain aspect of our lives was curtained off and not discussed. So you felt, always, that there was something missing.

On a more public level, the notion of being both a Palestinian and a literary critic is for some people an oxymoron: you can't be. To others, I gather that it's a thrilling and a rather peculiar pleasure to watch somebody who is supposedly a terrorist carrying on in a fairly civilized way. Here's a fairly impressive example. A Jewish psychiatrist, whom I'd met at some political meeting, had come to New York and was all the way down in the Village, but insisted on coming to visit me at my house. She came up – it was an hour by subway – and spent no more than about five minutes. Then she said, "I have to go back, I have another meeting." So I said, "Why did you come?" and she said, "I just wanted to see the way you lived." She wanted to see what it was like for a Palestinian to live in a city like New York, which was a strange proposition to her. She was interested in the fact that I played the piano and things of that sort.

The worst aspect of it is that you know perfectly well that people are attacking you for ideas that seem to abut on their notions of what Zionism is. The most horrendous and cruel irony is that I'm frequently seen as a kind of Nazi type, by people like Cynthia Ozick and the *New Republic* crowd. It is the most outrageous parody.

IS: What happened to Alex Odeh shows how dangerous it can be to speak to this cause here in the United States.[1]

ES: I've gotten death-threats, raids on my office, people trying to break into my house and so on. All of that is there, too. But even in the world we live in – non-political and literary – it's always creeping in. The American Jewish Committee did a review of my

1 Odeh was the director of the California office of the American Arab Anti-Discrimination Committee. He was killed by a booby-trapped bomb wired to his office door on October 11, 1985. The previous night, Odeh appeared on a local TV talk-show to deny the involvement of Yassir Arafat in the *Achille Lauro* affair.

book *The World, the Text, and the Critic*, in which the word "secular" was analyzed as really meaning the "secular democratic state" of Yassir Arafat, which really means (they went on to say) death for Jews, so Said is a terrorist, and so on.

IS: I remember that when I showed you the interviews with Frye and Derrida, last year, your response was: "If their problem is going about the world and always finding their own ideas already there to meet them, my problem is going about the world and always finding a distorted picture of my political position there to meet me." Discuss.

ES: It's very disturbing. Usually, when I go to give a lecture somewhere, a huge number of people show up, and there's always a question of security. Even though I'm going to speak on some literary or overtly non-political subject, there's always the danger of violence, of somebody rising in the audience and throwing something or firing a gun at me.

That's a problem. And you can't be private. I've been on the media often, and am fairly well known in that kind of world, so that one's privacy and one's ideas are totally out of one's control. In other words, it's not just finding them there; it's finding a whole institution which has already received and processed what it considers to be your views – whether from a sympathetic or an antipathetic point of view. It's a tremendous effort to control yourself, and not walk away in desperation, because it's very hard to break through into something resembling an exchange of views with people. That's true whether one addresses an Arab audience or an American audience. But, interestingly, if one talks with Israelis, as opposed to with American or even European Jews, then somehow there's a kind of liveliness there. With Israeli Jews, it's interesting, because there's a common experience, though of course it's an antagonistic experience. Still, it's something that you can actually talk about and deal with.

The most interesting thing, from a coldly political point of view – as well as from a philosophical and interpretive point of view – is to watch people talking about things that are not political and to see the question of Palestine interjecting itself. It's certainly the case in this country that, for a certain type of thinker, all questions of self-determination, human rights and so on are modified – sometimes implicitly – by the shifts in the fortunes of Israel. That's fascinating to watch, and one of the great challenges – not that I've succeeded in escaping from it – is to maintain a consistent position on such matters, on questions of principle, and not to twist them because the audience is friendly and expects you to do something else: nor to make exceptions. So that if you're opposed to religious madness of one sort or another, it would not only have to include Christian fundamentalism or Jewish fundamentalism, but also Islamic fundamentalism. In spite of my openly proclaimed views to the contrary, I'm considered a great defender of Islam, which is, of course, nonsense. I'm really quite atheistic.

IS: A question on your early work on Conrad: did your experience of colonialism have anything to do with bringing you to an author whose work and career are so deeply imbedded in the whole question of colonialism?

ES: Absolutely. I felt, first coming across Conrad when I was a teenager, that in a certain sense I was reading, not so much my own story, but a story written out of bits of my life and put together in a haunting and fantastically obsessive way. I've been hooked on it ever since. I think that he's not just a great writer of stories, but a great writer of parables. He has a particular kind of vision which increases in intensity every time I read him, so that now it's almost unbearable for me to read him.

IS: Do projects like *The Question of Palestine* and *Covering Islam* represent a kind of endeavor which, in your mind, is kept separate from your more strictly literary-critical enterprise?

ES: Less and less. There was a time when I would do things like *The Question of Palestine* and *Covering Islam* with an eye almost exclusively directed to an audience that had nothing to do with literary matters. But as you know, if you've read them, I draw on certain literary texts, literary techniques, matters of interpretation, which have taught me a lot about the way ideas are transmitted, formed, and institutionalized.

There is no doubt that, until about five years ago, I was leading a very schizophrenic life. I was still confined, or self-confined, to the academic study of English to such a degree that I was routinely teaching courses on the English novel, or the eighteenth century, in a way that had very little to do with my real intellectual concerns. I think that, in the last three or four years, I've devised both courses and ways in which, while I'm not doing overtly political things, my interest in comparative literature has made it possible for me to deal with matters that are closer to my actual concerns: for example, the question of the intellectual; the relationships between culture and imperialism; world literature; and the interrelationships of history, society and literature. In these respects, I feel a lot better and feel that what I'm doing is more integrated.

IS: I want to pick up some of those things in just a moment. But a project like *Covering Islam* reveals that side of you which is influenced and affected by Chomsky. Could you describe the relation of your work to Chomsky's?

ES: I've known Chomsky for almost two decades now. He's a man I admire a great deal. There are a number of differences between us, but I think his kind of intellectual commitment, his relentless erudition, and his capacity for not being put off by professionalism of any sort – whether it's philosophical or mathematical or journalistic – have really encouraged me and a lot of other people not to be defused and put off by disciplinary barriers. And I think he's a very moral man. In many respects, he's a man whose courage and willingness to speak precisely on those issues that affect him most directly – as an American, as a Jew, and so on – have been very important to me.

There are differences between us, but they're not very interesting or important. They have to do, principally, with the need for a certain kind of relationship with a critical mass, in the sense of a people or a cause. Chomsky has always been a solitary worker. He writes out of some sense of solidarity with oppressed people, but his direct involvement in the ongoing political activity of a group of people or a community – partly because of his many interests and the demands on his time – has been different from mine. The second, and perhaps most important, difference is that he's not really interested in theorizing whatever it is that he does – and I really am.

IS: In that sense, Foucault and Chomsky represent the two poles in your mind and practice.

ES: I think so, partly. I suppose, in the final analysis, one has to choose between them, but I've always felt that one in fact could incorporate both of them. In the end, I think that Chomsky's is the more consistently honorable and admirable position, though it may not be the most emulatable position. It's certainly a less cynical position than Foucault's. By the end of his life, I think, Foucault was simply uninterested in any direct political involvement of any sort.

IS: The first book of yours to make any impact was *Beginnings*. If one reads that now, and then immediately reads *Orientalism*, it seems that in *Beginnings* you had not found your voice in the way that *Orientalism* has found it: a much stronger, more individual, more theoretically concentrated voice.

ES: I actually think that *Beginnings* is much more theoretically concentrated. But it may be still ventriloquistic: I felt it important to work through a number of genres, critics, voices. I've always been very taken with choruses, with polyphonic kinds of writing as well as singing. I think there is a kind of consistency through the book, which isn't as relentlessly and ruthlessly concentrated on a particular demystification as *Orientalism*. *Orientalism* was really a very programmatic book in one sense, but in another it allowed a tremendous amount of latitude. It was a great subject, and I felt it could make a greater effect, but *Beginnings* is a book I still feel very close to. There are a lot of things in it that I haven't completely worked out and that are still, for me, very rich – Vico, obviously, being one of them.

IS: Here's a question which you formulate near the beginning of *Beginnings*: "Is there a privileged beginning for a literary study – that is, an especially suitable or important beginning – that is wholly different from a historical, psychological, or cultural one?" (p. 6). Would it be fair to say that your subsequent work – and most especially *Orientalism* – has answered that question in the negative?

ES: I think that's probably true. I would say that the shift from *Beginnings* to *Orientalism* isn't so much the literary point of view, but the textual point of view. I was impressed in *Orientalism* by the extent to which, simply by reading something, people could then go out and look for it. That is what I call a "textual attitude," and it's related to the question I framed in *Beginnings*. Now I'm coming around to change my mind a bit. I have felt, for several years now, in a flat-footed and quite naive way, that, given the enormous amount of bad faith and ideological obfuscation that goes on in social science writing of a certain kind, as well as in historical writing, there's something refreshing and immensely appealing about writing – like that Stevens poem you've been quoting – that is purely literary. The literary grace, if you want to call it that, is different. I certainly think it can be *found* in social science writing: certainly, in *Orientalism*, I found that when people like Massignon were not only great scholars but also great writers, it made all the difference, even if their attitudes were completely peculiar. I think I'm coming to a more temperate view of the relationship between literary and other forms of writing.

IS: Something that is there in *Beginnings* and then becomes stronger, and is very surprising in you, is the Vichian element. How did Vico, of all people, come to get a grip on you?

ES: The tremendous impact which *The New Science* had on me when I read it as a graduate student was, first, probably due to the scene that he paints at the beginning: of a feral and Gentile man; the giants; the period right after the flood, with people wandering all over the face of the earth, and gradually disciplining themselves, partly out of fear and partly out of providence. That kind of self-making struck me as being really at the heart of all genuinely powerful and interesting historical visions (you see it in Marx, obviously, and in Ibn Khaldun): the way in which a body forms itself into a mind and a body, and then into a society. That is so compelling, and so powerful; and he uses texts that have been discussed as ornamental or philosophical in a literary way, to inform this extraordinary vision of development and education. That struck me as tremendously powerful and poetic.

Second, he was always doing it by skirting around religious notions, of the creation and so on. That oppositional quality to his work – his being anti-Cartesian, anti-rationalistic and anti-Catholic – was incredibly powerful. I've read him many, many times since then, and always find him enriching and amusing and informative.

IS: Something that is important to *Beginnings* is the Vichian opposition between Gentile beginnings and theological origins. This sounds like a question formulated by the American Jewish Committee, but did the resonance of that opposition, for you, have anything to do with the fact that Israel is a society founded, perhaps uniquely, on theological origins?

ES: I don't think that Israel is unique in that respect. Don't forget that the world I grew up in was a world in which the local product was the manufacture of religions. Certainly it's true of Islam, certainly it's true of Christianity, and certainly it's true of Judaism: they're all related, they're all monotheistic, they all come out of the same "Abrahamanic" (as Massignon calls it) promise or covenant. That distinction I make in *Beginnings*, which Vico makes so strongly, strikes me as absolutely just. If there is to be any kind of history, it has to be led away from these origins. In that respect, Vico is very Lucretian: Lucretius says, in the first book of *De Rerum Natura*, that the worst ills really come out of the suasions of religion. I think that's certainly true, and I was trying as much as possible to register this. But, as I say, I wouldn't confine it to Israel. My own background includes a rather heavy dose, in my mother's family, of Lebanese, right-wing Christians who are as bloody-minded as Kahane. That whole thing is something that I have no use for at all; what I was trying to do was to pull myself out of it.

IS: A big part of the transition from *Beginnings* to *Orientalism* is the more powerful influence of Foucault in the second book. Did you know Foucault?

ES: Not really. I got to know him afterwards, after I wrote *Orientalism*. We corresponded a bit. What I was always impressed with in Foucault was the method. It seemed to me that like Foucault and Chomsky – I don't really want to compare myself with them – I had amassed a great deal of information and knowledge, and that I was also interested in the way in which these are deployed. I think that both of them share a kind of strategic sense of knowledge: a strategic and geographical sense, as opposed to a *temporal* sense, which is what characterizes the Hegelian and, later, the deconstructive modes. Foucault's and Chomsky's is more spatial, and I think Gramsci was terribly important there too, as a mediator for the other two. I was looking for a way to do it effectively, rhetorically, and to organize a large body of information which I had amassed in almost twenty years of reading in the subject.

In *that* respect, Foucault came to the fore. But I was already aware of the problems of Foucault's determinism, his Spinoza quality, where everything is always assimilated and acculturated. You can already see it at the end of *Discipline and Punish*. *Orientalism* is theoretically inconsistent, and I designed it that way: I didn't want Foucault's method, or anybody's method, to override what I was trying to put forward. The notion of a kind of non-coercive knowledge, which I come to at the end of the book, was deliberately anti-Foucault.

IS: In the book, you say that the phenomenon of Orientalism calls into question "the possibility of non-political scholarship" (p. 326). Does that apply as much to scholarship that remains strictly within its own cultural domain or tradition? That is, scholarship which – unlike Orientalism – is not trying to appropriate another culture.

ES: It's the whole question of displacement, which is a Fryean idea: that everything is a displacement from something else. I think it's probably true that all knowledge is a displacement from something, but I think there are degrees. I think that certainly the most malignant is the kind that's doing the most displacing while denying it the most strongly. *That* you find in societies and cultures and moments that are explicitly imperial. You certainly see it in America; you certainly see it in the nineteenth century in England and France. On the other hand, I think it's possible to say that there are relatively benign forms of displacement that occur internally within a culture and within a discipline, of a sort that are variously pleasing and harmless and benign. Somehow, one isn't really concerned about them at this point. I always feel the pressure on me to describe the other kind.

IS: In *Orientalism*, you say that fields of learning, *and* art, are constrained by social and cultural conditions, worldly circumstance, and stabilizing influences like schools, libraries, and governments. You say that learned *and* imaginative writings are never free, but are "limited in their imagery, assumptions and intentions" (pp. 201–2). Let's come back to what you were saying before about your recent rethinking of whether literature has a specificity within discourse. Is literature necessarily as constrained as, say, fields of learning like Orientalism?

ES: I think that, in fact, one would have to say "yes." The problem with a lot of recent literary criticism, partly under the influence of people like de Man – whom I admired a great deal, and thought was very clever and impressively acute – and Bloom, Frye and the others, is that a great deal of unnecessary effort goes into defining what is purely literary. I don't understand the need constantly to do that. It's like saying that something is American, and the opposite to it is un-American: that whole field seems to me quite boring. What is interesting about literature, and everything else, is the degree to which it's mixed with other things, not its purity. That's just a temperamental view of mine.

Everything one does is constrained by physical circumstance. One of the things I was always immensely taken with in Vico was the fact that the body is always there. If you read a lot of the critics you've talked with, the body doesn't matter at all. But in fact it *does* matter: we aren't disembodied brains or poetry-machines. We're involved in the circumstances of physical existence, and that is very important to me. (I like to play tennis, and squash, and a lot of other physical things.) So those strike me as the more fruitful directions in which to go: outward from the pure, to the mixed and the impure. The constraints are there, but when I say they're "not free" I just mean "free" in an ideological sense. People say "It's a free country": well, of course it's not a free country. That's common sense – I'm not urging some tremendous ideological message. We're in the world, no matter how many times we scream that we're really in the tower.

IS: One aspect in which *The World, the Text, and the Critic* differs from, say, *Beginnings*, is the strength of the critique of Derrida. You say that Derrida's criticism "moves us *into* the text, Foucault's *in* and *out*" (p. 183). I wonder if something like the recent deconstructive interest in legal texts could qualify that. In legal judgments, in common law, we seem to be in an area where we can't talk about moving *out* of the text back into society, because the text and social power are identified.

ES: That is a later development in deconstructive thought. Christopher Norris, in his first book on deconstruction, considers Foucault a deconstructionist. If you're saying that everything that is effectively demystifying or disenchanting – where certain kinds of ideological blinkers are removed, and certain involvements and complicities are revealed – is deconstruction, then I'm for it. But

there is another kind of deconstruction, which I would call
"dogmatic" or "theoretical" deconstruction, which urges a kind
of purity. I don't think that Derrida has been very guilty of it,
incidentally – he's too resourceful. But a lot of his disciples seem
to argue that way. I remember once giving a lecture in which I
talked about Derrida, and one of his disciples came up to me and
said: "You made a mistake: you can't use the word 'reality' when
you talk about Derrida." Anyway, I think the kinds of distinctions
that are made between texts and non-texts are infantile and
uninteresting.

IS: Were you attracted to Derrida much, at the beginning?

ES: I met him when he first came to this country in 1966. I've
always found him an amiable and extremely genuine person. At
times, his work has interested me. But things like *Glas* (although
he and I shared a common friendship with Genet) and *La Carte
postale* I just found not that interesting. I think he's probably a
much better essayist than he is a systematic philosopher, and it's
the kind of sporty quality of his work – which you find in some of
the essays in *Dissemination* – that I've always thought is quite
brilliant. I never really cared for the *Grammatology*. It struck me as
a ponderous and ineffective book. I thought that his earliest work,
on Husserl's *The Origin of Geometry*, was really quite brilliant.

IS: But finally you think that the general influence of his work has
been too much to separate textuality from its surrounding
contexts?

ES: He clarified a certain *Zeitgeist*, which is that we ought to be able
to talk about texts in a way rather more philosophically than the
New Critics did, but fundamentally in the same way, and we
needn't feel silly and irrelevant doing it: in fact, we are dealing
with logocentrism and apocalypse and phallo-this and phallo-that.
You know what I'm trying to say. It gave it a kind of armature that
was important for the American academy if it was to think of itself
as serious and as dealing with fundamental questions.

IS: But remaining within its own fundamental preconceptions.

ES: That's obviously the case. The attempts to link deconstruction
with Marxism and all these other things are interesting, but
they're more lab experiments than they are major steps in the
evolution of a certain type of thinking.

IS: Another figure within this present series to whom there are many
references in your books is Harold Bloom. To my surprise, most
of these references are benign. What positive things have you
taken from Bloom?

ES: The notion of struggle. That's been the most important thing:
the vision he has of everyone quarreling over territory and turf is

incredibly persuasive. I don't think there is any doubt about that – that everybody talks both against and with other people, whether it's poetry or not. That's what I found, and how it relates to questions of influence and what is now called "intertextuality." His other stuff, the proliferation of terms like "clinamen," and the gnostic aspects, and the mysterious and prophetic: I find that amusing and charming – because he has great panache – but it's hard for me to take it as doctrine in any way.

IS: The stuff in his interview about criticism being totally personal and without social context . . . .

ES: That's obvious nonsense. It sounds clever and brilliant. He's quite rightly taken Oscar Wilde as a model, and if you can pull it off, then you do it. But he's obviously in great need of all kinds of institutional supports, as we all are: he needs an office, he needs workers, he needs grants . . . .

IS: Until he won the McArthur Award . . . .

ES: But there you are! He didn't turn it down. He didn't say, "Well, I'm just doing it on my own!" He gladly took the money and off he went: he became an institution himself. Obviously, overstatement is very much a part of Harold's arsenal, but there is a difference between overstatement for effect and overstatement as doctrine – such as saying that all criticism is personal. I suppose that on one level it's true: we are ourselves, and we write what we think and not what somebody else tells us to. But that's like saying "Today is Friday": it's a truism.

IS: In *The World, the Text, and the Critic*, you begin with a discursus on "secular criticism" and end with one on "religious criticism." You give a list of titles which, you say, illustrate the drift towards a new religiosity in criticism (p. 291). Most of those titles are by the critics who precede you in this series of interviews. However, neither Bloom nor Frye nor Frank Kermode – even though they write books with those sorts of titles – is proposing to make literature the object of some kind of institutionalized religious worship. Are we *really* talking about "secular" versus "religious," or are we talking more about "historicist" versus something that continues to believe in a supra-historical aesthetic effect?

ES: You can turn it any way you wish, but I think that it's not an accident that the three critics you just mentioned all write about the Bible.

IS: But one can't take exception to that.

ES: No, I don't agree. I think that it is, precisely, exceptional that the Bible should emerge in certain types of, shall we say, "theological" thought, or thought that can be traced back to a God of some sort, to the divine. I think you're absolutely wrong

– I think it's central to their view. Gnosticism, preciosity of language, obscurity of language – everything that comes out of modernism, which is now crystallized in biblical work – the privacy of interpretation, privileged or hierophantic language: all of these things are part of a clerical attitude.

IS: Hartman's point was that we cannot get away from the element of enchantment that literature contains, and that the attempt to purify that . . .

ES: Who's interested in purifying it? That's the last thing I want to do. Precisely what they're trying to do is to purify it. I'm interested in illuminating it, or putting it in conjunction. What I'm interested in is exactly the opposite of purification: not, as in Frye, literature as some kind of separate, total system, but literature as involved with many other things – in, you might say, an enchanting way.

For instance, one of the things which Frye doesn't develop, but which I've always wished he had, is the relationship between the scheme of the *Anatomy* and tonal music. Music is the great passion of my life. The relationship between literature and certain types of music is a fascinating one. Those are the sorts of things I'm interested in; not the extent to which one can isolate literature from everything else. It's a question of emphasis. Nobody would deny that there is a literary quality to, say, an ode by Keats or a poem by Stevens; but is that interesting in and of itself, past one's enchantment and one's enjoyment of it? Maybe it's enough just to enjoy it, but if one wants to talk about it, I think one can increase one's enjoyment by connecting it to other things. I take that to be what we're all about.

IS: I still don't know exactly what you feel about historicism, as far as literary criticism goes. Do we not sacrifice something as soon as we collapse literature back into any kind of a historicism?

ES: Why is it collapsing? What you're doing all the time is adding words to it that encourage one in thinking of it as a rather impoverishing and reductive method. I would have thought exactly the opposite. Take the example of a critic whom I really respect and enjoy, Raymond Williams, in *The Country and the City*. Now, I suppose that if you were to read one of the country-house poems that he discusses there – one by Jonson, or Marvell – you might say that he is reducing it to its historical circumstances, but I don't think that you could justify saying that. In fact, just as Keats in "Ode on a Grecian Urn" is talking about the way in which a village has to be emptied to appear on the urn, Williams is enlarging the field in which we see a country-house poem. And that seems to me to be anything but reductive. If you're simply saying that a class analysis of "The Wife of Bath's Tale" or "Penshurst"

– where all you do is try to show the level of class awareness which comes through in those poems – is reductive, well, it is reductive: but that doesn't seem to me to be a historicist reading in the Vichian sense of the word, or the Auerbachian sense of the word.

IS: As you've become more interested in the Foucauldian type of historicism, isn't it true to say that you've written less about literature, and more about cultural history – things like Orientalism, appropriative structures?

ES: That's sort of tough to answer. I find it very hard, now, to separate out literature from other things, except in the curricular sense. If you say that I write less about literature in the sense of things that appear on English Department lists, then that's probably true. I may have written less about Dickens than about, say, Renan. I've probably written about a wider range of literature, including a lot of Third World writers who are not curricular in the English sense of the word. I suppose that uncanonical works are what I'm writing more about. But I find it rather disturbing to be constantly asked to make distinctions between literature and other things. I mean, I really do believe – Kermode makes this point, too – that some works are greater than others. A Dickens novel is better than a Harold Robbins novel, and it's silly to argue about that. But that doesn't mean that reading a Dickens novel and then writing appreciations of it are actions that are going to satisfy me, in terms of what I'm interested in.

IS: Could you talk for a moment about the connotations of the word "worldliness," as you apply it to literature and criticism?

ES: On one level, it obviously connotes a certain *savoir faire*: I'm interested in the way that great works *make their way*, the way that, in Proust, Charlus can make his way in the world – he's worldly in that sense. That's a rather resonant and deep meaning for me. The second is the extent to which works reach out and hold on to other works, in institutions, in historical moments, in society. Third is a fantastically anti-metaphysical quality that I find in the most compelling written works, whether they are what you would call works of literature, or what I would call, say, New Journalism, or essay-writing. In the sense that they really are about some form of engagement, I'm very interested in them. You find that even in Hopkins's poems, for example, where he's really reaching out and trying to get hold of things in an almost tactile way.

IS: You having said that, I wonder if we could choose this moment to look at the Stevens poem. A poem like this, which seems intensely personal: in what sense is it worldly?

ES: I'll tell you immediately: the word "scrawny," the "scrawny cry." Unlike almost all of the people whom you've interviewed,

I've never made a great thing out of Stevens. I've always thought of him as a kind of amusing, tinkly poet, who was full of word-play. He's a failed metaphysical poet, in some way; and very home-made and American.

IS: So what about "scrawny"?

ES: I mean the incongruity of the "scrawny cry" and "Not Ideas about the Thing but the Thing Itself." That kind of Platonic or classically metaphysical statement, and then this poem which slowly unfolds and in the end gives you the "scrawny cry" in a context that is obviously taken straight out of the first chorus in Haydn's *The Creation*. "Let there be light!": and then instead of a great C-major chord you get this little toot. It's a fantastically funny poem, and I think that all of Stevens's poems do this kind of thing. It's a carnival poem; but to see in it some metaphysical parable is impossible, because I *hear* poetry, I don't really read it, and there's always a tinkly, "Asides on the Oboe" quality about Stevens. It's like an orchestra tuning up, but never actually playing a piece.

As Kermode says – and I agree with him – it's not as powerful or moving a poem as "Of Mere Being." Stevens is full of "likes" and "almosts" and "as ifs" and very approximative things of that sort: "It was *like* a new knowledge of reality." It's difficult for me to see it in the kind of grandiose, metaphysical light that I think you feel that it sheds on itself. You know: "a battered panache above snow"; that rather awkward Francophonic quality; the relentless repetition of "scrawny." It's rather Hardyesque, in a way. It doesn't have the stately quality of some of Hardy's late lyrics, but that contrast between the sun and the power of the ending of winter, and the scrawny cry, and the chorister "whose c preceded the choir" like an instrument played out of turn, are reminiscent of Hardy.

IS: You haven't talked much about lyric poetry, in your work.

ES: No, I tend to be a plot and narrative person.

IS: Is that anything to do with the fact that lyric is *most* resistant to a historicist analysis, and most insistent on its own peculiarity, its mystery, its isolation, its purity?

ES: I don't think so. It's just that there's a certain privacy to it, which has always meant a great deal to me. For instance, Eliot's "Ariel" poems have always meant a great deal to me, G. M. Hopkins, those kinds of lyrics. There's a certain privacy in them, and in my experience of them, which has made it difficult for me to write about them. A lot of what I write about is not meditative, but quite the opposite: proclamatory. One of the most compelling pieces that I've ever read on lyrics and lyricism is Adorno's piece

on lyric and society. It seems to me perfectly possible to read it as
a kind of monad, the way he analyzes a late Schoenberg piece, in
which all the effort to resist is nevertheless confirming something
that is being resisted. I've always found that to be true: it just
requires a skillful unlocking.

IS: There are two more critics whom you admire and who seem to
me to be antithetical in you, the way Foucault and Chomsky are.
I mean Gramsci and Benda, though obviously Gramsci is much
more important to you than Benda. Gramsci's idea is that there
are organic intellectuals, who emerge from and continue to identify with an oppressed class, and traditional intellectuals, who try
to be Platonic and withdrawn but end up simply justifying
whatever power is in power. To me, you seem in a sense to be both
. . .

ES: That's a great compliment!

IS: No, well, I mean that you write, as a Palestinian, about
Palestine, and in that sense are an organic intellectual. The only
sense in which I mean that you are also traditional is that you work
in a university. And Benda is really a defender of the traditional
or abstracted intellectual.

ES: What I admire in Benda isn't his traditional pose, or the affirmations of the importance of distance. It is his almost clumsy way
of saying: "Look, you've got to tell the truth." It's presented in
the most unattractive way possible: the attitudes are essentially
conservative; the language is deliberately a language of orthodoxy
and distance. But still, in all, what one feels is somebody saying:
"You've got to tell the truth" – that paternal admonition that we
all heard from our fathers. I find it incredibly tonic and refreshing
to read him, precisely because of that. With Gramsci, it's not so
much that organic and traditional intellectual opposition, but the
fact that he was interested in everything. Even though he was very
tightly constrained both in his own body and, later, in jail, he
seemed to be able to experience a fantastic number of things. The
correspondence with his wife and his sister-in-law; all the immense
reading and writing he did, on his own, in prison: that's really one
of the great adventures of human experience. But all of that was
contained within a fairly disciplined commitment to the world in
which he lived.

IS: Everything you've just said has made me think of Nelson
Mandela.

ES: There are some people like that. That's what I found in
Gramsci. Plus the fact that he had an incredibly refined mind. You
don't get a sense of being clubbed over the head – partly because
of the fact that he was writing for himself, and under censorship.

That one could manage *that* is something that I've always tried to emulate. To be interested in as many things as possible: I think that's really what we're best at doing.

IS: Can the university avoid being simply the institutionalization of what Gramsci speaks of as the traditional intellectuals?

ES: Oh yes. I think that the American university is really without precedent. It's difficult to find analogies or predecessors for the strange and incongruous and totally contradictory institution which the American university is. On the one hand, I think it's a very benign institution, as institutions go. Of course, it has its coercive aspects.

IS: But you've shown, again and again, how social scientists, and others within the university, work to legitimize social power.

ES: Yes, but the fact is that people like myself and Chomsky and others *also* exist within the universities.

IS: Without being compromised?

ES: I wouldn't say we've been terribly compromised. I mean, everybody's compromised by affiliation: if a university is taking secret CIA money, as Harvard seems to have done, I suppose everybody is affected in some way. But there's no question that, in some ways, neither Chomsky nor myself would have had the audiences we've had without the university. A lot of the people who listen to us when we speak – it's certainly true in his case – are university students. The university provides one with a forum to do certain kinds of things . . .

IS: But aren't you and Chomsky incredible exceptions, in the way you use that forum?

ES: The exceptions certainly appear from somewhere; they are not out of the blue. And in that respect, I think the university is benign. It can, obviously, co-opt or tame: so what institution doesn't? The most pernicious aspects of the university are not that. The more pernicious aspects of the university – which we're still not quite clear about – are in the way the university is associated with certain social processes. Ethnography, nuclear sciences, etcetera, etcetera: those things are quite clear. But the relationship between the university and the corporation, the relationship between the university and the media: all of these things are complex and troubled matters. Those are much more formidable than mere co-optation. You don't *have* to be co-opted. It happens, but in some cases it could be without consequences that a certain doctrine is co-opted by the university. Like deconstruction: it's entirely a university doctrine, but that it is of the university doesn't make any difference.

IS: What about the pedagogic role? Something that Bloom said struck me very much: all we can hope to do, in the university, is to produce human beings who are capable of sounding like themselves. I interpret that to mean that, within the university, teachers like you have a genuine opportunity to produce human beings who are intellectually strong and independent enough not to be pushed around like pieces on an ideological chessboard – and who are therefore resistant to, for example, Orientalism, or the synonymity of "Palestinian" and "terrorist." Do you feel that function strongly?

ES: Yes, I do: very much so. But again, if one is working with the texts of English Literature, then one feels a great constraint. The problem there is that you have a responsibility to the material, which is a real one; but the main goal is to create in your students a critical consciousness. The last thing I'm interested in is disciples. Any kind of overt communication of a message or method is the last thing I want to do. In that respect, it's very difficult to be a teacher, because in a certain sense you ought always to be undercutting yourself. You're teaching, performing, doing the kinds of things that students can learn from, but at the same time cutting them off and saying "Don't try to do this." You're telling them to do it, and not to do it.

IS: Can't a "critical consciousness" very easily become simply an ethic of individualism – that is, as against "class consciousness?"

ES: Yes, you're absolutely right, and I think that in a certain sense the American university is really a breeding-ground for that kind of individualism – at its best. It's a great paradox that the best thing you can do is to promote an individualism in a student.

IS: Which is what the system wants.

ES: Which is what the system wants, but in a sense the system doesn't want that: it says that that's what it wants, but really it wants a commodity which is called "individualism." So that's where you are: short-changing both sides of that equation. You're not allowing individualism to get too far out of hand, as an ideological thing; nor are you allowing the ideology of the commodity to take over everything. As I grow older – I've been teaching for twenty-five years now – I find that teaching is really impossible, in a funny sort of way. At best, you can read with students. It's important, every so often, to bring in a book that you totally admire, and yet completely understand in its limitations. You can just tell your students, "Look, here is something," or "This is a wonderful poem," or just read it and see what happens.

IS: I was reading a comment recently by someone who said that all this stuff about the politicization of English teaching was beside the point, and that what we should do is to be political, to engage in political praxis the same as any other group, and then go on doing our professional work as normal. The reason I mention this is that they said that in this sense Edward Said is exemplary, because he *does* engage in praxis instead of just going on endlessly about the politicization of English studies. Anyway, that sounded like quite a good position to me. I'm even thinking of adopting it.

ES: Why not? The late-1960s notion of the politicization of pedagogical discourse has spent itself, really. For one, you either can do it, or you can't do it. And then, if you want to be political there's nothing to prevent you: there are millions of issues with which you can connect yourself, and there's no reason always just to make a big harangue of it. That's why I like words like "worldly": they are simple, and do the trick, and get you involved, but you don't have to create a whole complicated apparatus to help you make your points. I think that the important things are competence, interest and, above all, a critical sense.

IS: The objection to this, likely to be made by one's Marxist colleagues, is that it's simply naive to think that one can separate one's professional life from one's political views.

ES: But you're not separating it: you're just leading it in different ways. It's like the voices of a fugue. A fugue can contain two, three, four or five voices: they're all part of the same composition, but they're each distinct. They operate together, and it's a question of how you conceive of the togetherness: if you think that it's got to be this *or* that, then you're paralyzed; then you're either Mallarmé or Bakunin, which is an absurd opposition.

IS: The opposite version of the fallacy of splitting one's professional work from one's political commitment belongs to those Marxists who think that the revolutionary task ends with a radical re-reading of *Finnegans Wake*: as if Marxism were a literary theory.

ES: I just came back from England, where I did a day-long conference with Raymond Williams, and we were talking together about the different social contexts in which we did our work. It's very striking that within an English context one *can* talk about Marxism, or at least socialism, as a tradition having a real presence. You cannot talk about that in America, where there is no socialist tradition of any consequence. So the sudden appearance of the most refined and most learned kinds of theoretical Marxism in people like Jameson – whom I tremendously admire – is an extraordinary anomaly. It partakes of the same personal intellectual brilliance – as opposed to its social and political insights – as in Harold Bloom's work. Now, if *that's* Marxism, it's a traveling variety of Marxism which is quite different to what we were talking about.

IS: Reading Lukács and Gramsci, they still talk about the bourgeoisie as being always on the defensive, and as having to elicit an always reluctant submission from the proletariat. Their great blind-spot is America. They really could not have foreseen American capitalism. They could not have foreseen that a form of social control would spring up in which, far from being defensive, the bourgeoisie would elicit from the proletariat, not submission, but an entire identification with its own interests. I think that the reasons for that are primarily technological.

ES: But you find similar conjunctions in late nineteenth-century England, with regard to the empire. There's always a mediating mechanism. In that case it's empire, and empire works here too. And then there's the electronic media that gives everybody, whether a Wall Street financier or a middle-western housewife or a Californian surfer, the sense that they are participants in a gigantic polity, which is all going to the funeral of these poor astronauts who were killed a couple of days ago.[2] It really is an extrapolation from the nineteenth-century idea of nationalism, but it's an imagination that does all the imagining for you, in a strange kind of way. I don't think that Gramsci and Lukács had any idea of that. Plus, in Lukács's case, his idea of the bourgeoisie was that it was the last class in history: it was Austro-Hungarian, it understood aesthetic forms like tragedy and lyric, and it was passing from the scene. That was what the bourgeoisie meant to him, and the proletariat was a great blank. Gramsci, I think, is more eclectic than that. But neither of them could have foreseen the enormous and sudden growth of the American empire as a going and quite profitable enterprise. I remember, a couple of years ago, a senior UN civil servant saying, "The Third World leaders speak about Moscow, but in their hearts they all want to go to California." The images are very powerful.

---

2 A reference to the explosion, two days before the interview was recorded, of the US space-shuttle Challenger.

Barbara Johnson

7

Barbara Johnson

"It seems to me that women are all trained, to some extent, to be deconstructors. There's always a double message, and there's always a double response. The difficulty, for women, is unlearning self-repression and ambiguation and conciliation, and reaching affirmation."

Barbara Johnson was born in Boston in 1947. She was educated at Oberlin College, in Ohio, and at Yale, where she studied with Paul de Man. She now teaches French and Comparative Literature at Harvard, where this interview was recorded at the end of February, 1986. Although not yet 40, Johnson has already established herself as one of the best-known of the second-generation deconstructors, and has been a lucid yet uncompromising mediator of deconstruction for the North American critical audience. She is the translator of Derrida's *Dissemination*, but, more importantly, has in her own work *applied* the insights of deconstruction in ways that have made it more difficult for Anglo-American critics to ignore. This is because, in the first place, she is a resourceful reader, and her close readings have been undeniably productive in the traditional sense of generating convincing new meanings for old texts. Second, while de Man and Derrida very often deal with texts which are as difficult and foreign as the mode of analysis brought to them, Johnson has tended to take up examples which are familiar, accessible and, above all, recognizably literary. And as well as being a reliable *mediator* of the ideas of de Man and Derrida, she has made major contributions to deconstructive theory itself by foregrounding the question of sexual difference within the general terrain of *différance*.

At the beginning of her book of essays, *The Critical Difference* (1980), Johnson describes what is in effect a technique for reading *différance*. Her account is worth quoting at length:

> Reading, here, proceeds by identifying and dismantling differences by means of other differences that cannot be fully identified or dismantled. The starting point is often a binary difference that is subsequently shown to be an illusion created by the workings of differences much harder to pin down. The differences *between* entities (prose and poetry, man and woman, literature and theory, guilt and innocence) are shown to be based on a repression of differences *within* entities, ways in which an entity differs from itself. But the way in which a text thus differs from itself is never simple: it has a certain rigorous, contradictory logic whose effects can, up to a certain point, be read. The "deconstruction" of a binary opposition is thus not an annihilation of all values and differences; it is an attempt to follow the subtle, powerful effects of differences already at work within the illusion of a binary opposition . . . If, however, binary oppositions in this book thus play the role of the critical fall guy, it is not because one must try at all costs to go beyond them. The very impulse to "go beyond" is an impulse structured by a binary opposition between oneself and what one attempts to leave behind. Far from eliminating binary oppositions from the critical vocabulary, one can only show that binary difference does not function as one thinks it does and that certain subversions that seem to befall it in the critical narrative are logically prior to it and necessary in its very construction. Difference is a form of *work* to the extent that it *plays* beyond the control of any subject: it is, in fact, that without which no subject could ever be constituted.
>
> (pp. x–xi)

Johnson's reading of Melville's famous story *Billy Budd* is as good an example as we will find of this method in operation. When it was first published in 1979 – at the height of the perplexity engendered by deconstruction – the essay functioned for many as an avenue of entry. As an example of deconstructive close reading, it must itself be read closely.

Melville's Billy Budd is a handsome but simple young sailor who strikes down and kills the evil and ugly master-at-arms, John Claggart, after Claggart has falsely accused him of incipient mutineering in front of their captain, the intellectual Edward Vere. Johnson's reading of the story, in *The Critical Difference*, begins by teasing out the usual binary oppositions within Melville's text. This is the point at which traditional criticism usually *does* try to "go beyond" binary

opposition, by halting the play of difference and *resolving* the oppositions around some central meaning.

Johnson's reading moves in the opposite direction, showing how
the differences between entities, far from being easily resolvable,
reproduce themselves endlessly as differences within. In the first
place, the fact that the innocent Billy ends up a killer, and the evil
Claggart dies a helpless victim, "indicates that the real opposition
with which Melville is preoccupied here is less the static opposition
between evil and good than the dynamic opposition between a man's
'nature' and his acts . . . the relation between human 'being' and
human 'doing'" (p. 83). This opposition may also be regarded as a
contrast between two styles of reading. Billy Budd takes all language
at face value, assuming a complete identity between signifier and
signified. Claggart, the ultimate ironist, mistrusts every utterance
completely and assumes a disjunction between signifier and signified,
as between being and doing. And here, again, a series of crossings
occurs: "Claggart, whose accusations of incipient mutiny are
apparently false and therefore illustrate the very double-facedness
that they attribute to Billy, is negated for proclaiming the lie about
Billy which Billy's act of negation paradoxically proves to be the
truth" (p. 86). Billy's act of striking Claggart dead, which is
supposed to negate Claggart's contention that there is, in Billy, a
disjunction between signifier and signified, proves it; and it proves
it in just such a way that the contender is prevented from
appreciating the proof of his contention: "The knowledge that being
and doing are incompatible cannot know the ultimate performance
of its own confirmation" (p. 87).

The gaps between Billy and Claggart, between action and language, between doing and being, are also gaps *within* language.
Whenever Melville reaches a point where he really tries to *explain*
Billy, or Claggart, or Vere, the language of the story collapses into
mere tautology or mechanical repetition. An internal example of the
same affect is that convictions about Claggart's "evil nature" all
arise from a *lack* of prior information about him:

> Evil, then, is essentially the misreading of discontinuity through
> the attribution of meaning to a space or division in language . . .
> The entire plot of *Billy Budd* could conceivably be seen as a conse-
> quence not of what Claggart does but of what he does not say.
>
> It is thus by means of the misreading of gaps in knowledge
> and of discontinuities in action that the plot of *Billy Budd* takes
> shape.
>
> (p. 95)

But what of the most sophisticated reader in *Billy Budd*, the source of truly "authoritative" interpretations, the supposed closer of all gaps and disjunctions in language: Captain Vere? It is at this point of reading Vere's reading that Johnson's own reading becomes most impressive, in that it does *not* function to separate the story from wider social and political concerns by turning it into a mere "language game." Billy accepts the identity between signifier and signified, but internally censors any signifier that contradicts his *a priori* view of how things should be. Claggart supposedly doubts every signifier, except that he naively accepts all those which confirm *his* pre-existing beliefs. Vere, in his reading, tries to get outside of the *a priori* altogether, by anchoring his reading in history, and by subordinating any "personal" or "arbitrary" reading to the need to preserve political order. For him, signs are to be neither motivated *nor* arbitrary, but rather conventional and social. He searches for the right conventional context – legal, naval, or "natural" – in which to judge Billy. The only problem is that the *choice* of context – which *is* personal – will already contain the judgment itself, since each context carries an automatic verdict with it.

Vere's role is to serve the interests of political and military authority by supposedly stabilizing all divisions within and turning them back into divisions between. So *Billy Budd* finally situates itself in the space of the relation between differences within and differences between: a space which is "the fundamental question of all human politics" (p. 106). Like all authority, Vere is in the impossible position of having to consider the consequences of his judgment as part of the act of judging; and among those consequences are the consequences of the judgments that will be made about his judgment. His final decision is anything but final, and is caught up in an endless play of displacement, deferral and, in fact, difference within. As a political allegory,

> *Billy Budd* is . . . much more than a study of good and evil, justice and injustice. It is a dramatization of the twisted relations between knowing and doing, speaking and killing, reading and judging, which make political understanding and action so problematic . . . The "deadly space" or "difference" that runs through *Billy Budd* is not located between knowledge and action, performance and cognition. It is that which, within cognition, functions as an act; it is that which, within action, prevents us from ever knowing whether what we hit coincides with what we understand.
>
> (pp. 108–9)

Since the first evening on which Penelope unwove the pure surface of her shroud, in a duplicitous performance of fidelity, the place of woman and the play of *différance* have been inseparable in Western literature and philosophy. And yet the Yale School, as Johnson says in a recent essay on "Gender Theory and the Yale School," "has always been a Male School" (p. 101). The drift of all of her own recent work has been towards a feminist deconstruction. She has been articulating the relation between woman and *différance*, and the curious "centrality" of both repressed terms, in numerous ways. Her article on "Teaching Ignorance," for example, discusses Molière's play *L'Ecole des Femmes*, where two men try to teach a woman contradictory lessons, though both are teaching her a kind of ignorance. Molière's Agnes may, in fact, not be in the unique or peculiar situation she seems – either as woman *or* as student. The founding texts of Western pedagogy, Plato's dialogues, already suggest that the relation between learning and ignorance may not simply be one of difference between. These texts often function by setting up contradictory teachers; and what Socrates teaches people, after all, is that they *don't* know what they think they know – that is, ignorance:

> just as the existence of more than one sex problematizes the universality of any human subject of knowledge, so contradiction suspends and questions the centering of Western pedagogical paradigms around the single authoritative teacher. In this sense, paradoxically enough, it could be said that Plato's belief in Socrates' pedagogical mastery is an attempt to repress the inherent "feminism" of Socrates' ignorance. And it is out of this repression of Socrates' feminism that Western pedagogy springs.
>
> (p. 182)

In fact, this paradoxical relation between ignorance and knowledge is already very much present in the view of literature put forward in *The Critical Difference*. Literature, we are told there, is what shows us that the "unknown" is not some ineffable realm beyond knowledge, but lies rather in the "oversights and slip-ups that structure our lives." It shows us that "It is not, in the final analysis, what you don't know that can or cannot hurt you. It is what you don't *know* you don't know that spins out and entangles 'that perpetual error we call life'" (p. xii). The question of sexual difference, too, is present in *The Critical Difference*, but almost always in a curiously implicit way. In her essay on "Gender Theory," Johnson addresses this curiosity:

> It would not be easy to assert that the existence and knowledge of the female subject could simply be produced, without difficulty or epistemological damage, within the existing patterns of culture and language. *The Critical Difference* may here be unwittingly

pointing to "woman" as one of the things "we do not know we
do not know."

(p. 111)

Imre Salusinszky: I want to begin by talking about the "Yale
School," partly because it now seems to be disintegrating – you
were an early defector. Were you a graduate student at Yale?

Barbara Johnson: Yes, in the French Department, from 1969 to
1977. Then I taught there, from 1977 to 1982.

IS: Can you describe the early effect of Derrida in the United States?
How did that influence begin to take its hold?

BJ: As I remember, there was a course by Jacques Ehrmann on *Tel
Quel*, the year I was a first-year graduate student in the French
Department at Yale. That was a course in which Derrida was one
among several French theorists being studied. Derrida didn't
stand out from the *Tel Quel* group at that point, and people were
more interested in Barthes or Mauron or even Lacan (this was just
a little bit before Foucault came to seem so important). The sense
was that interesting things were happening in Paris. My recollection of the situation at Yale is that theory was coming from France,
and being channeled into the French Department, only through
Ehrmann; and that he was somewhat isolated in the department,
because theory was something very abstruse and very faddish, and
it divided students into the in-group and the old-fashioned group.
(As a first-year graduate student, I was intimidated by the in-
group and didn't take Ehrmann's course.) After de Man arrived,
it didn't take very long for the center of theoretical gravity to shift
to de Man, especially after Ehrmann's death, and to Comparative
Literature as opposed to French, so that the "Frenchness" of the
thing became diluted. The first year that de Man came, he gave
a course on Nietzsche, which a lot of people audited, including
Bloom and Hartman. That, I think, was where the "Yale School"
officially began.

IS: Hartman says, in his interview, that he and de Man and Derrida
all discovered that they had been reading similar things in the
1960s – things like Nietzsche and Rousseau – and he suggests that
the origins of the "Yale School" are in that, rather than in some
kind of simple "pollination" by Derrida.

BJ: That strikes me as correct. I remember hearing Hartman give
a lecture, before he actually returned as a professor, which was
later to become the essay "The Voice of the Shuttle," and which
I found fascinating. So there was Hartman, there was de Man,
there was Ehrmann: there were all these people doing various
things, and obviously being influenced by something that was in

the air. It was by no means all summed up under the rubric of deconstruction: that came much later. Nor was it called anything like a ''Yale School'' until much later.

IS: Did Bloom say much at those de Man seminars?

BJ: I remember one discussion, in particular, of the image of the tiger in ''On Truth and Lie in an Extra-Moral Sense.'' The sentence says that man is ''hanging in dreams, as it were, upon the back of a tiger.''[1] Bloom had a lot to say about that tiger.

IS: How did you eventually come to translate Derrida?

BJ: One year, he was coming to Yale to give a lecture that had to be given in English. They needed someone to translate it very quickly – some graduate student/slave. It ended up in my mailbox, and after Derrida saw the translation he recommended me to do *Dissemination*.

IS: Is that what drew you into his work?

BJ: No, I was already very interested in his work, and was already working on Derrida and Lacan. In fact, I was more interested in Lacan, in the beginning.

IS: Really? The influence of Derrida seems much stronger, in your ''mature work.''

BJ: I think that's because Derrida is a reader, and that's what I aspire to be. Lacan is a writer, and probably a listener, and certainly a ''reader'' of the unconscious. But you don't see the activity that Lacan performs as a reader: you see intuitions and you see results and you see transformations of the act of reading.

IS: It has often been said of Derrida – he says it himself, in the interview – that he became more influential here than he ever was in France. What might be the causes of that?

BJ: There is a way in which Derrida's approach to reading – if you restrict it to a theory of the textual production of meaning and of the suspension of meaning – joins up with very deep existing roots in American literature departments. So there is constantly a danger of falling into a New-Critical understanding of Derrida. I'm not sure that that is ultimately a bad thing for literary studies, but it is certainly not what a French person would understand from Derrida's work. In many ways, the fact that deconstruction has found such propitious soil in this country is due to its similarity to the kinds of questions which were asked in Reuben Brower's course here, or in New Criticism generally.

IS: This is precisely the point that Said was making: that the American ''lit. crit.'' establishment could embrace deconstruction

1 ''On Truth and Lie in an Extra-Moral Sense,'' in *The Portable Nietzsche*, edited by Walter Kaufmann (New York: Viking, 1954), p. 44.

without having to depart from any of its most fundamental para-
digms of textual self-containment, aesthetic autonomy and non-
reference. You'd clearly want to challenge Said's implication that
deconstruction is just New Criticism revisited.

BJ: I would challenge it only on a very "Platonic form" level,
because I think that a lot of deconstructive readings that exist are
not very different from New-Critical readings, and *don't* really
challenge the assumptions of the isolatability of the text, or the love
of ambiguity for its own sake – as if, once you have reached a feeling of satisfactory exhaustion of a certain kind of problematic, you
have something and can stop.

IS: As if deconstruction were some kind of tragic counterpart to New
Criticism, where you look for the lacuna or the *mise-en-abyme*
instead of the creative ambiguity. But how, then, do we distinguish
deconstruction at the level of "Platonic form"?

BJ: It's paradoxical to talk about deconstruction "at the level of
Platonic form," but certainly one of the things that is essential to
it is to put in question exactly where it is you're standing, to be
doing the activity you're doing: what are the boundaries you are
assuming for your activity; what are those boundaries safe-
guarding, and what are they opening? In order to be truly
deconstructive, you would have constantly to move the locus of
your questions, not just move on to another text. You'd have to
say: "What am I doing, sitting and talking like this, in this institution?" And: "Why am I reading *this* text?" Instead of just, "This
text is a given, now let me read it."

IS: That kind of relentless questioning is where you continually
situate the pedagogic effect of deconstruction – and where Derrida
does too, in his interview. But then it comes back to something
which came up, in a different way, with Said: whether critical
consciousness, and the relentless questioning of every foundation,
does not collapse back into the standard academic individualism,
or liberalism.

BJ: Well, it depends on what kinds of questions you ask about your
foundations. If you say, each time, "In what way is the thing I'm
questioning actually being presupposed by my act?" you can get
into a very sterile form of self-reflection, where all you do is
become better and better at avoiding the kinds of criticisms that
you can anticipate. I don't think there is a very interesting future
for such an inquiry. But if you, for example, ask: "In what way
do any of the questions I ask imply that I am taking something *other*
than the individual questioner or writer into consideration as a
subject of this inquiry?" it would mean you'd have to leave room
for something other than your own critical consciousness to be

participating in your inquiry. There is a tendency in a deconstructive training to make you feel that if you are just critical *enough* – if you're watchful in all directions and constantly enlarge the boundary in order to include a question about the gesture you've just made – then that is somehow sufficient. I don't think it is: that leaves no room for a surprise; it leaves no room for someone or something to surprise you and say "Stand aside, *I* want to speak." And you're no longer thinking as a response; you're thinking as a self-protection.

IS: On the subject of the history of deconstruction in America, I want to ask you a little bit more about de Man. Bloom tells an anecdote in which de Man says to him, "You don't care about the 'troot,' Harold," and Bloom replies "There is no 'troot,' Paul, there is only yourself." That's the first part of the anecdote. The second part – I'm sure that Bloom has conflated different meetings into this one – is where Bloom goes on to tell de Man that he *clones* his students, whereas none of Bloom's own students resemble each other in the slightest. Now, if de Man did clone his students, then obviously your own name would be one that would come up as a candidate, since you're always one of those spoken of as being most influenced by him in your practical criticism. Did de Man's influence work as a kind of cloning?

BJ: When you said that Bloom said that there is only the self, did he mean only de Man's self, or only his self?

IS: He means that there is no critical method, but only the critic's own self. It's like Pater: the criticism you write is the record of the adventures of your own self among masterpieces. As soon as you fall into method – as de Man presumably did – then instead of producing students who are capable of being themselves and having their own adventures among masterpieces, you produce people who simply are replicas of yourself.

BJ: I think that what de Man taught was *resistance* to self. It might look, from the outside, as if all resistances to self have something in common, or are more similar than all selves, but I'm not sure that's true. In other words, I'm not sure that Bloom's interest in his own mind, his self-absorption, *doesn't* resemble that of a student who might learn from him. I don't think that Bloom is particularly interested in having students, or in helping students, or in being a teacher, in quite the same way that de Man was – which doesn't mean that de Man was interested in making people resemble him. He was interested in making people not misunderstand, and in becoming an ally of their self-resistance.

IS: What exactly do you mean by "self-resistance" here?

BJ: Every time you feel yourself tempted to conclude what seems

natural, or what seems satisfying, or what seems commonsen-
sically true, you arrest your movement towards that for a moment,
and examine what you are putting together. So it's more a way of
suspending satisfaction, even to the point of asking yourself,
"Could the opposite also be true?" Very often, de Man's reason-
ing goes something like this: it looks as if a text is produced to
express the desire of a subject; but, since the only desire we *know*
has been expressed is that of the text's own self-constitution, what
legitimates our belief that the text is the product of a subject's
desire, rather than, let's say, the subject being an effect of the
text's desire? Not that he's substituting the second for the first, but
he's saying, "*What prevents us* from seeing this as equally possible?"

Speaking of cloning, let me tell you another anecdote about the
relation between Bloom and de Man. I was walking my dog
Nietzsche one day, and ran into Bloom. He said, "What is this
dog's name?" I said, "Nietzsche," and he said: "Ah yes, I knew
it was either Nietzsche or Rousseau!"

IS: How would you describe de Man's influence on you – not
personally, but on your writing?

BJ: Well, I think that the personal does have something to do with
it, because de Man was one of the few teachers I've ever met whose
integrity in the pedagogical enterprise was equal to his integrity in
the writing enterprise: there was absolutely no discrepancy
between his commitment to his research and to the kinds of questions that he felt were essential, and his commitment to promises
that he made, or support for people whom he thought were valuable, or time he would give to students. He was never slighting a
student in order to gain glory for himself, or anything for himself.
He was not looking in the mirror; he wasn't after an image of himself at the expense of anybody. That's very rare in the academic
establishment.

That was the most impressive thing, so it seemed to me paradoxical that people would accuse him of anti-humanistic beliefs, or
anti-people beliefs, when he was the most pro-people person that
I had ever met – in ways that were truly effective, and not in ways
that merely made people feel good, or made people believe that he
was on their side when he wasn't: he never failed people.

IS: One thing that strikes me if I read an essay of yours and then
an essay of de Man's is that, in both cases, there is a relentlessly
close-up textual analysis, an insistence on staying on the back of
the text right up to the end, together with a hesitancy towards
making sweeping theoretical generalizations. Is that something
that de Man promulgated?

BJ: I would say that he did, although he certainly does not avoid generalization altogether. That was what he did in classes: used a text that you could hold in your hand to expand or exfoliate a set of questions. But the questions were always *also* coming from elsewhere. The inspiration in that was that you can afford to spend this much time on a crux that interests you: you have the right to stay with it; you're not in a hurry to get on to the next generalization. It was good for me, as a student, to see someone else take the time to stick with something that might look like a detail, for as long as it took.

IS: What you've described, though, does sound like the kind of leisure that only an élite institution can afford. Kermode says that this is something he always disagreed with de Man on: the idea that literary studies should be severely restricted in terms of numbers. Obviously they would have to be, if you were going to spend hours and hours on each particularly complicated crux.

BJ: I would use a therapeutic model as an analogy here. Let's say that you are a family therapist. You are treating a child with anorexia, and you have the whole family come in to a room once a week. You decide to focus on table manners, and you and the family spend six months focusing on table manners in the most minute detail. One day, something happens, and the whole power structure of the family reorganizes. Now, you might say that, in order to decide to spend that much time on table manners, you had to have the financial conditions that made such a thing possible. Certainly. But the investment you make in a detail does not necessarily exhaust itself with that detail. It may absolutely make something else much more efficient; it may amount to a shift, in a huge sense, of the whole. You can't know, but, if the detail interests you, you can try to believe that it is because it is a path to something much larger than itself, which you won't find out until later, if ever. I don't think that the belief that the size of the material is proportionate to the size of the significance of the inquiry is correct: the material doesn't have to be of a size proportionate to the impact of the results.

This is not to say that I think that a class or an institution should be a series of discontinuous, in-depth investigations of very minor or small textual nodes. When, for example, de Man would teach a course on Proust and he would focus on two paragraphs, a reading of the whole of *Remembrance of Things Past* was implicit in the choice of the paragraphs. He's a diamond-cutter who decides that *this* is the place he's going to cut. It may be that the actual reading is the tip of an iceberg, and you may want to know more about the iceberg, and you might want to know how he, as a teacher, was communicating the acquisition of the iceberg to the

students – instead of just the cut. That's the big question I had
about his teaching. He made it look as if all you had to do was cut
here, but he didn't tell you how to pick the "here." That's
something which everybody would have to learn for themselves:
finding the passage where all the questions you might have about
the text come together in some way.

IS: As you say in an essay on de Man, "Rigorous Unreliability,"
the point at which deconstruction chooses to cut is often a reflexive
moment, a moment where the text seems to comment on itself or
on its own process of composition (p. 74). I used that as a cue
recently in teaching *The Inferno*, and as an experiment concentrated
on the passage where the pursuit of usury is condemned by being
distinguished from the pursuit of – in the broad sense – art.[2]
Now, I was surprised at how much resistance there still is in
students – even Yale students – to that kind of a deconstructive
approach to teaching: a feeling that it destroys the point of reading,
elides the difference between texts, and is finally a version of
nihilism.

BJ: In teaching, there are certain forms of satisfaction that students
expect, and one can be too hasty in frustrating those expectations,
which amounts to a form of dogmatism: "You have that satisfaction? Here: I'll take it away." This is something that can always
happen, but doesn't seem to me to be an effective way of teaching
self-resistance.

IS: It is bad faith too, in a way. Most of us have arrived at the point
of being university teachers of literature because we fell in love
with literature as children, and because we became mystified by it.
If we had all struck demystifying teachers of the facile type you've
just described when we were 15 or 16, it's quite possible that we
would never have gone on to build our lives around literature. So
to have a sense of oneself as demystifying one's students' pleasures
is bad faith at the deepest level.

BJ: Yes, and I don't think that was at all the effect of de Man's
pedagogical presence. Rather, the effect he had was that the text
was incredibly more rich than you expected, and its author and its
language were revealed as extremely clever. The kind of truth that
the text was conveying was much more complex and profound
than a *simple* determination of meaning could possibly suggest. It
seems to me that the most effective teaching that would derive from
deconstruction would begin by emphasizing how much more
meaningful the text might potentially be, rather than how much
less meaningful it could be, by deciding to respect its silences, or

2 Canto XI, 97–111.

respect its forking paths (instead of starting immediately on moments of self-reflection, which I also find attractive and tempting, but where the circle remains too small).

IS: Hartman was saying that deconstruction isn't a movement from mystification to demystification, but a fall from one mystification into another that is richer and deeper. The very notion of reaching some point of absolute demystification would have to be the most anti-de Manian, anti-Derridean notion I've ever heard.

BJ: Yes, but once you've said that, it implies that the trick would then be to try to avoid seeming to have reached a belief in demystification. Whereas there has to be an equal desire to reach something. You have to desire to get to meaning or to truth or to satisfaction, somewhere along the line, in order for the demystification to have an organic relation to anything other than your own narcissistic desire for it to be as complicated as possible. Something outside of yourself has to be calling you, or else the desire merely to be right or to be smart is going to take over.

IS: Another moment worth picking up in the Bloom interview is where he refers to Geoffrey Hartman as one of the "American casualties" of the influence of Derrida and de Man. In Bloom's current polemic against deconstruction, this notion of its being a foreign import – some kind of "Japanese car" of criticism – is very strong. What do you think of that critique of deconstruction as a purely foreign import that's been brought over here wholesale from the Continent?

BJ: I don't think that it has remained foreign *enough*. I think it's become Americanized so fast that that criticism doesn't apply to it, in its current form, at all. I don't think that in Europe – and particularly not in France – a movement called "deconstruction" could ever have lasted so long and become so codified. As far as deconstruction being Hartman's downfall goes, I think that Hartman's powerful relation to Wordsworth among others existed before deconstruction, and exists after the period in which Hartman was most interested in deconstruction. One of the things that appealed to Hartman in deconstruction was the liberation of his own playful linguistic tendencies. It's probably advantageous for someone with that propensity to have more limits, rather than more freedom, to work against, but I think that a lot came out of his encounter with deconstruction.

IS: I wanted to ask Derrida a question which, finally, I didn't really have the guts to ask him, so I'll ask you. Deconstruction has been much talked about. Now we even have articles in the *New York Times* which try to explain it. So you must often be asked, by people in other departments of the university, or people you meet outside the university, what deconstruction is. Can we formulate a lay-person's definition of deconstruction? Can we communicate it to people who don't have a training in either literature or philosophy, without becoming overly reductive? Are you ever asked about this?

BJ: All the time. One thing I could say is that the training most people get from the beginning, in school and through all of the cultural pressures on us, is to answer the question: "What's the bottom line?" What deconstruction does is to teach you to ask: "What does the construction of the bottom line leave out? What does it repress? What does it disregard? What does it consider unimportant? What does it put in the margins?" So that it's a double process. You have to have some sense of what someone's conception of what the bottom line would be, is, in order to organize the "noise" that's being disregarded.

IS: By the way, the concept of the "bottom line" is a very American one. I'm not even sure that I understand what Americans mean when they talk about the "bottom line."

BJ: Well, suppose you ask somebody for advice about where you should get your mortgage, and they give you twenty pages of computer printout about worst-case scenarios, best-case scenarios, rates, qualification-ratios. You say: "What's the bottom line?" In other words: "Where should I go, and what should I say?"

IS: You must, of course, be asked to define deconstruction quite a lot, being the resident guru here at Harvard.

BJ: I'm the only person at Harvard who is specifically known as a deconstructor, and that's as much a liability as it is anything else. People don't know what they mean by that, so people come expecting me to know things and advise things and believe things that I don't recognize at all. My tendency is to assume that no one here has any idea of what deconstruction is, and also to indicate the extent to which I don't think it's an interesting question to identify whether something is deconstructive or not, or to define the boundaries or the procedures of deconstruction, or to answer such questions as "Can you do it to the Bible? Can you do it to this?"

IS: In other words, it's not useful to say what the deconstructive "bottom line" is. In *The Critical Difference*, you say that

> *deconstruction* is not synonymous with *destruction*. . . . It is in fact much closer to the original meaning of the word *analysis*, which etymologically means "to undo" – a virtual synonym for "to de-construct." The de-construction of a text does not proceed by random doubt or arbitrary subversion, but by the careful teasing

out of warring forces of signification within the text itself.
(p. 5)

This quotation, and its analogy with "analysis," allows us to consolidate, and meet head on, a variety of the objections which are commonly raised against deconstruction.

There is, of course, a debate, which long precedes deconstruction, about whether analytical knowledge, leaving aside the special case of mathematics, is really knowledge at all; about whether analytical or deductive knowledge tells us anything about the world. The objection, then, would be to say that deconstruction *is* analysis in that sense. In every text we look at, we find that the same thing has happened. We can describe it in various ways, and a common de Manian way would be to say that we find that the rhetoric of the text has subverted its grammar; that the propositions in the text are undone by the very rhetorical form in which they are framed. The "logical positivist" objection to this – and I think that it *does* comprehend a lot of the objections to deconstruction – is that you've said nothing there, but simply made a comment about the way *you* use the words "grammar" and "rhetoric"; and, in every text you come up against, you reiterate this peculiarity about the way you use the words "grammar" and "rhetoric." The objection, then, is that analytical knowledge of the text – this sense that we "undo" the text and get inside it – is really not a form of knowledge at all.

It all comes back to de Man's discussion in *Allegories of Reading* of the passage in Proust where Marcel's grandmother wants him to leave his books and go outside, which is like the continuous moral imperative that says that any kind of formalism like deconstruction is, finally, too reductive, too "inside."

BJ: If people turn to literature in order to learn something about the world, which they have and do, then the analytical knowledge that one is able to reach is a knowledge about the relation between how the text functions and the desire behind the act of reading, the expectation that literature should say something about the world: it's not knowledge directly about the world.

Suppose a person were to read Rousseau's *Confessions* in order to learn what kind of a person Rousseau was. A deconstructive analysis would show that in fact what you can learn is the way Rousseau's story-telling desire fulfills itself, and frustrates itself. This is a way of returning to the original question – "What kind of a man was Rousseau?" – through a respect for the interest the medium has in itself, and the opacity of the medium with respect to its avowed function as a mirror. It is because we turn to literature and philosophy with a desire for truth and for referentiality that an analysis of the text's rhetoric's subversion of grammar makes sense. If there were no such desire then, indeed, analytical knowledge would be completely sterile. But if it is indeed the case that people approach literature with the desire to learn something about the world, and if it is indeed the case that the literary medium is not transparent, then a study of its nontransparency is crucial in order to deal with the desire one has to know something about the world by reading literature.

IS: Another variety of deconstruction often talked about by its opponents is what Kermode calls "ludic" deconstruction. He feels, and many agree with him, that deconstruction – and particularly the later Derrida – pays a terrible price for its "ludic" temper, which is really a form of sterile showing-off that finally alienates people.

BJ: I think that watching someone else at play can always be irritating. But what is going on in Derrida's ludic elaborations is a very careful expansion of the notion that relations among signifying chains really cover, in a much more closely woven way, problematics that one thinks of more in terms of the referent; that, in fact, the closeness of certain terms, or the way in which the mind travels from one signifier to another, really does operate more than one is usually aware of. One of the things that people get irritated at is when Derrida will give a title, and then spend the whole time talking about how clever his title is. If one doesn't think that he chose the title because it was a condensation of what he wanted to talk about, or that it actually comes from elsewhere and is not the origin of the discussion of it, then one has a right to think that it's really self-enclosed. That's certainly always the danger, because there *is* a notion of a network, or a closure, or an overdetermined linkage at work that might at first sight make one feel that some freedom is being curtailed, or that the mind is somehow being constrained and forced to look at this as opposed to relating freely to an object or an idea. That perception of overdetermination is, of course, precisely the point.

It's precisely the way Derrida resists seeming to forget himself and speak only truth that people see as a concentration on self. But the voice that seems to speak out of nowhere and point only to an object is no less grounded in its own self-sufficiency and self-satisfaction – it is simply abiding by a convention of self-erasure that is so in place that you don't see it. By foregrounding the very words, or the material, or the standpoint that he himself is occupying, Derrida is not really calling more attention to himself, and not really giving more importance to the place he's standing than people who background that question: it's probably about equal.

IS: We were talking before about the dangers of deconstruction becoming a new kind of New Criticism, a purely self-involved textual practice of "close reading." This was Edward Said's claim against it. I guess that there really isn't any form of political engagement implied by deconstructive criticism – as against, say, Marxist criticism.

BJ: There's no political program, but I think there's a political attitude, which is to examine authority in language, and the pronouncements of any self-constituted authority for what it is repressing or what it is not saying. Even the training in sensitivity to ambiguity can be a training in avoiding ambiguity when necessary, so that if *you* have to draw up demands, then you, as a person trained in deconstruction, would be much better, supposedly, at using ambiguity when it suited your purposes and not using ambiguity when it didn't suit your purposes, rather than doing it in a wild way and not controlling it. It certainly is no less likely to enable you to take a political position than any other approach.

IS: You don't see any necessary connection between deconstruction and Marxism?

BJ: Well, I think that Marx was as close to deconstruction as a lot of deconstructors are. The fundamental analytical-critical attitude is, or should be, cultivated in both approaches. To bring to the surface the hidden inscriptions of the economic system is really not an operation different in kind, although it's different in location, from a deconstructive opening up of, not just a text, but a whole textual configuration and a whole sense of what it means to talk about the relation between a text and its context. Much of what Marx does is very much uncovering hidden presuppositions and showing contradictions, and this is not at all foreign to the concentration on actual formulations.

But both of them can end up being reduced and dogmatized by emphasizing their conclusions rather than their procedures. In polemical situations, or in politically revolutionary situations, you might not choose to avoid dogmatism. But a lot of what passes for Marxist criticism is not similar to Marx's own procedures – obviously, since he was not really a literary critic. Derrida is not primarily a literary critic either. That's really the interesting thing: why is Marxism such a focal position in American literary criticism, and not really as important in any other discipline or domain in this country?

IS: Partly, I guess, because literary scholars are more used than other people to sifting through Continental ideas; and partly because literary criticism is one of the only areas of endeavor in the United States where Marxism can be practiced harmlessly. The imperial ideology is stunningly solid here, and to try to extend Marxism beyond its application to literary texts could be very personally costly.

BJ: Or you would be simply dismissed as ineffectual or marginal. In this country, it's very easy to isolate and neutralize ideas, or incorporate them into and make them part of the establishment.

IS: Another question I wanted to ask Derrida – in this case there wasn't time – is whether we could ever have such a thing as a "deconstruction of everyday life." This all comes out of a passage near the beginning of the *Grammatology*, where Derrida says that we *could* examine things like "military writing" and "athletic writing" (p. 9). I could give you many examples of the kind of thing I have in mind: the way that certain types of cultural practice seem to hinge on binary oppositions – on keeping certain things apart from other things – in ways that in their very nature cannot be sustained. Take the extraordinary culinary prohibitions of certain ultra-orthodox Jewish communities: the obsession with keeping any product which has any porcine connection whatever out of the system is bound, eventually, to fail – and *that* might be its fascination. To take another example, this time of "athletic writing": where I come from we play a type of football – more like a religion, really – in which there are two rules – against "holding the ball" or "holding the man" – which, at a certain moment, align themselves in a type of contradiction or mutual cancellation which is strictly deconstructive, and which I think has a lot to do with making the game compelling. One can see a similarly deconstructive moment, or gap, in the rules of many sports, which is what makes the ball "electric" – like a signifier – and keeps it moving through the game. Do you think that we can write a "deconstruction of everyday life," looking at things like sports, religions, road law?

BJ: Yes. For instance, you could look at the way that "nothing" is packaged and marketed, in the form let's say of soft drinks for dieters: the whole emphasis on consuming things that have less. Why is less more? This certainly seems related to the functioning of blanks, let's say, in a Mallarmé text. Huge industries are created to package and market blanks, nothings.

IS: Do you find yourself using very much of what you've learned from Derrida and de Man as you move through the extra-university world?

BJ: I think it's really part of me – not always to my advantage. Once you are trained to look at things in a certain way, you get into a habit of hearing *everything* that people are saying, and not just what they think they're saying. Of course, it's a grand delusion to think that you do hear everything that people are saying, or everything that you say. But the tendency you have to take in more than you can use, and to be particularly interested in contradictory relations between body-language and verbal language, for example, increases, the more deconstructive you are.

IS: One point at which deconstruction, everyday life, and politics converge is at the point of sexual difference. I want to talk a little about deconstruction and feminism. Sexual difference – without which, as you say in *The Critical Difference*, there would probably be neither literature nor criticism (p. 13) – is the difference beneath the difference beneath the difference. Is it at the point of a deconstruction of sexual difference that feminism and deconstruction have things to say to each other?

BJ· Within feminism, there have always been arguments about whether there is really a difference between the sexes or not – in other words, whether it makes sense to argue in favor of disregarding differences on any question in which differences are at issue, or whether it's better to argue for respecting differences and reducing their hierarchization. I think that what deconstruction can help with in this is how to deal with a situation in which you need to articulate the relation between equality and difference, or between disregarding difference and re-articulating it: a system in which things both are different and are not different. That sort of logic is one that Derrida develops. The non-either/or kind of logic is very useful. So it's not simply a deconstruction of a binary opposition in which you end up showing that in fact the postulate of sexual difference doesn't hold – you can certainly do that, but then you don't have access to some of the questions that are really urgent. If you do that on the one hand, but on the other hand try to analyze what is happening when questions of urgency are associated with a postulate of difference, you get into a much more complex logic, and deconstruction can really be helpful.

IS: People talk of you first as a deconstructive critic, not as a feminist critic – although the question of sexual difference comes up constantly in your work. How is your mode of deconstruction affected by your being a woman?

BJ: I think women are socialized to see more than one point of view at a time, and certainly to see more than their own point of view. It seems to me that women are all trained, to some extent, to be deconstructors. There's always a double message, and there's always a double response. The difficulty, for women, is unlearning self-repression and ambiguation and conciliation, and reaching affirmation.

For me, there are two things going on in the place I am at, right now, in criticism. One is definitely that I've gone as far as I want to go with opening up ambiguities. I need to attach that kind of consideration to questions whose answer cannot simply be, "It's undecidable." At the same time, I find that a lot of feminist criticism is very shy of ambiguity, not interested in undecidability, even as a provisional exploratory situation. So my tendency would be to inject more suspension of answer into feminist criticism, rather than less. But I realize that that goes along with female socialization, rather than against it.

IS: What do you have in mind as the sorts of question which cannot *be* undecidable?

BJ: Places where it begs the question to say "It's undecidable." If you were reading a text like, say, Zora Neale Hurston's "How it Feels to be Colored Me," at the end you can say that the text does not give you an answer to that title; it doesn't tell you; it really shows that the whole thing is undecidable and cannot be formulated in that way. But you know that you've only gone so far, by saying that. You have not, at all, accounted for the fact of racism, the fact of disadvantageous conditions of life. So that's not a satisfying place to stop with such an investigation. What you would have to figure out is how to ask questions that would *take* the impossibility of answering a question like that, alongside the social system that acts as if there is an answer, and then analyze the relation between those two.

IS: Women working within literary criticism at least have the advantage that there are canonical women writers – increasingly, thanks to feminist criticism. And there are an increasing number of canonical women critics, too. But you are also in philosophy, to some extent. There, the situation is very different, and we have to come to terms with the extraordinary fact that there is not a single canonical woman philosopher. I've always wanted to know why women have made such inroads into the literary canon and the critical canon, when there is a whole history of Western metaphysics from Plato to Jacques Derrida which doesn't contain a woman.

BJ: I don't think it's that there are no women philosophers – you can certainly cite Simone Weil, or Simone de Beauvoir. In order to ask the question, you don't necessarily have to stick to the canon. It could be that the canon has been more rigid than the facts would lead you to believe. I think that the questions that philosophy has traditionally asked have been questions that mask the question of sexual difference. They have always assumed a universal subject as the issue, and it has not been – but I think will be – the case that philosophy has opened up the question of the non-universal subject. That is, obviously, a philosophical question, but ever since Aristotle it's been answered: "Woman is a deviation from man, so let's stick to the real thing."

IS: I want to ask you a little about the relation of criticism to literature. Following de Man, in *The Critical Difference* you say that "the difference between literature and criticism consists perhaps only in the fact that criticism is more likely to be blind to the way in which its own critical difference from itself makes it, in the final analysis, literary" (p. 12). That's a fairly representative "Johnsonian" remark. If there's one thing that many of those who are hostile to whatever Hartman, de Man and Bloom all represent dislike, it is the tendency they have to elide this distinction between literature and criticism. What does your own formulation, of criticism as blind literature, say about the social function of criticism? How do you answer people who say, "When you say that, you've thrown away any possibility of criticism as a system of knowledge that deals with a body of data"? Isn't it to pull the rug out from under ourselves, as far as any kind of social mission goes?

BJ: To say that there is ultimately no difference between literature and criticism is to say that you would not be able to find standards by which you could evaluate, objectively, the truth value or the moral value of criticism, any more than you could do so for literature; that, although literature and criticism conventionally make different claims about their own truth value, and obey different constraints, the lack of any real criterion or standard by which they could be measured is the same in both cases. Criticism offers no more proof of its validity than literature of its truth. When people feel that there is something hubristic about calling criticism literature, they are responding to the lifting of a constraint – or what they perceive to be the lifting of a constraint – upon the critic. I think this is wrong: it is not that people like Hartman or Bloom are lifting a constraint upon themselves, necessarily. It's rather that they are perceiving that, even with the constraint to attempt to be as valid as possible, you still end up with something for which no test of validity can be conclusive.

IS: We can obviously separate criticism and literature in one sense, though, which is that criticism is institutionalized. In your essay on Molière's *School for Wives*, called "Teaching Ignorance," you ask some very pertinent questions about the pedagogic institution:

Are our ways of teaching to ask *some* questions always correlative with our ways of teaching students *not to ask* – indeed, to be unconscious of – others? Does the educational system exist in order to promulgate knowledge, or is its main function rather to universalize a society's tacit agreement about what it has decided it does not and cannot know?

(p. 173)

That raises what is really the big question of this little series of interviews: whether the university can ever get outside of ideology, or whether it will always be some kind of ideological finishing-school. What limit is there to the kinds of question we can ask in the university?

BJ: The kinds of question that you could immediately – not gradually – get to, about privilege, are repressed. Your own complicity in a system that keeps certain forms of privilege in place is undeniable. Any institution would put certain constraints on you, and one like this is certainly at the top of the list of complicities. It seems to be hypocritical to teach in a place like this and act as if you're not complicitous. So you would have to deal with the contradiction between your desire to put the institution in question and your desire to remain a member of it: that would have to be something you would think through. I'm not necessarily saying that you would therefore have to decide that you didn't have the right to speak out against the way the institution functions, or even against your own participation – but it doesn't seem to me that you can have it both ways. On the other hand, you say, "But where, except in the institution, could you effectively question and change it?" If your object is to change it, and *keep* it, you're obviously in a compromised position anyway. If your object is to get rid of it, you would not remain inside it for long – if it disappeared – and you probably would be able to get rid of it more easily from the inside than the outside.

Simply saying what's wrong with something is not a vision of a better alternative, and it can be that you take a facile position and sit in the middle of something, receive all the benefits that it confers, and act as if seeing its flaws is a sufficient way of distancing yourself from the bad conscience that goes along with it. There are a lot of different ways you could go. You could say that this institution is not going to be substantially changed by me, or by anything that I will do, enough to cease to be influential in shaping people who will probably become leaders in this country. Therefore, how should I contribute to the training of leaders in this country, to bring about a better understanding on their part of justice, or reading, or whatever you want to call it? This certainly seems to be what I tend to do, but I'm glad that there are people who think that more drastic measures are needed. It just seems like that's what I'm equipped to do.

IS: How has deconstruction affected your practice as a teacher in the classroom?

BJ: I'm less likely, by temperament as well as by training, to give a discourse of knowledge. I'm much more likely to give a discourse of hesitation. This is also laziness on my part, so I don't hold up my teaching style as a constituted art: it is as much an accident as it is chosen.

IS: I spoke to Derrida about some of these things, and he said that deconstruction should never become reified into a school. Deconstruction should simply ''insinuate'' itself. Do you think it has become a school – or has it only insinuated itself?

BJ: I think that where it is named isn't where it is actually operative. There is not, necessarily, a correspondence between something which, within a school, is called deconstruction, and an activity which is actually having deconstructive effects. You're imprisoned within some sense of dogmatism if you say ''Now I am going to be deconstructive,'' because you can't deal with every question equally. I don't like feeling required to be a deconstructor, to represent deconstruction, to act like a deconstructor. When I give a talk that is asking certain questions, and I'm asked after it ''Was that deconstructive?'' I always have to answer ''Yes, and no, and I don't know.'' I don't think it's as clear to me as it used to be what is or is not deconstructive about my work.

IS: Still on teaching, you say in your Editor's Preface to the special volume of *Yale French Studies* on pedagogy that ''teaching is a compulsion to repeat what one has not yet understood'' (p. vii). This casts deconstructive teaching very much into the interrogative mode you were just talking about – where you present your students not with answers, but with a new set of questions. This came up with Derrida, too, when I asked him whether deconstruction was a purely interrogative mode of philosophic inquiry. He said that he saw it as affirmative, but as a kind of affirmation which has passed through a heavily interrogative phase. You've depicted deconstructive pedagogy as an interrogative activity: do you agree with Derrida that there is an affirmation at the end of deconstruction?

BJ: It doesn't have to be at the end. If you take the Ancient Mariner as an example – as I do in that preface – he's certainly affirmative, but it's also clear that there is, at the base, a compulsive desire to repeat his lack of understanding of this experience – that's why he has to tell the story.

IS: And what's affirmative about him?

BJ: That he grabs the Wedding Guest by the neck and says: "You'd better listen to me, or else!" That the text says, "'There was a ship,' quoth he": this is affirmative, this is a story, this happened. And the Wedding Guest responds both by being "of sense forlorn" – a loss of meaning – and by being "sadder and wiser" – something has been affirmed.[3]

IS: Let's turn, finally, to one of Stevens's final poems. Let me tell you why I chose "Not Ideas about the Thing but the Thing Itself." It struck me as a poem that I could very fruitfully talk to Derrida about, because it reminds me uncannily of the ending to "Plato's Pharmacy." As you put it in your Translator's Introduction to *Dissemination*, Plato is "working after hours in his pharmacy" (p. xvii). He hears a sound, and the question posed by that ending – I've never fully understood it, but have always been haunted by it – is whether the sound is coming from outside, or whether it is a sound in his mind, the residue of a dream. It is precisely the same question of inside and outside – whether we *can* get outside – that structures this poem, and with just the same figurations. Anyway, I then discovered that Derrida refuses to discuss English poetry, or to comment on intellectual areas with which he's not closely acquainted – something which could not be said about all of his critics.

So the object of this exercise – which now exists only as the residue or trace of an original intention, or dream – is to try to ascertain what the consequences are, at the level of practical criticism, of very different theoretical positions. What would be a "Johnsonian" reading of this poem? Lyric, by the way, has proved pretty difficult for deconstruction.

BJ: It may be difficult for deconstruction because lyric is so inherently deconstructive. I find it somewhat of a double-bind to be asked to represent one's natural tendency, because it then becomes unnatural.

IS: Of course: I know I can't really get a "Johnsonian" reading. But, confronted with this text, what sort of things would Barbara Johnson look for; what sort of things would catch her eye as she began to think of writing about it? I think that's a fair question, even though I know we can't duplicate a "natural" process here in front of a tape recorder.

BJ: What catches my eye is: why is the poem expressed in terms of

3 Samuel Taylor Coleridge, "The Rime of the Ancient Mariner," in *Selected Poetry and Prose*, edited by Stephen Potter (New York: Random House, 1933), pp. 19, 57.

a "he," and in the past tense? What tense is the title implicitly in, and what's the rest of the assertion? What does the word "It" mean, in the last sentence? What's the relation of the word "like" – at the end of the second-last line – to the word "like" in the third line of the poem? Is the letter "c" the "thing itself," or the most thing-like thing in the poem? Or the least? Why is this told as a story, since it is as if making a claim about the capacity of this poem's language to represent reality? Why does such a claim have to be made in the form of an anecdote?

IS: So you don't look for binary oppositions: here, for example, inside versus outside?

BJ: The outside/inside opposition is a thematic one: it's part of the poem's dialectic; it's part of the way the poem is suspending its question about whether you get reality or whether you only get words, or mind – or whatever the alternative is. In other words, it's very thematic. Certainly, the inside/outside opposition struc-tures the poem's thematic preoccupations, but it doesn't really structure the poem. The poem reaches outside itself with these suspension-points – the dots – and you could ask why it is saying that it, itself, *has* an outside at these two points. Is the "c" its inside? Or, again, is it something which has no inside? I guess that, at this point, the theme of inside and outside would not be what would attract me.

IS: So what do you think we really *are* supposed to take those final words of "Plato's Pharmacy" to "mean?" (I ask the question within all the requisite quotation marks, under erasure, and everything else.) You are the translator.

BJ: It's very smart of you to have thought of the end of "Plato's Pharmacy" in connection with this poem: they really do go together. If Plato is thought of as the originator of the dialogue form of philosophy, and of some sort of notion of dialectical think-ing, then how are you going to represent the genesis of the dialogue, or of the dialectical? Suppose you say that it happens in and to language when a subject is inserted in language and can no longer tell where his place is, in it. How would you depict such a scene – of a subject coming to grips with the comings and goings of language, both his own and not his own (and he can't tell the difference)? So that this scene of muttering and having the bits of language break up and seem to form a dialogue is, I think, a scene of the genesis of the philosophical dialogue. The fact that it takes place in a pharmacy means that the philosophical dialogue does not have nothing to do with death.

IS: I'll study those words closely when I come to transcribe this dialogue.

Frank Lentricchia

8

Frank Lentricchia

"The only serious site of Marxist struggle in the United States is in the university. That's not a reason to disparage that site of struggle, it is not a reason cynically to evaluate this as a kind of idealistic jerk-off. It is to say that if Marxism finds itself in struggle in the university . . . then that's where it is at the moment, and it should pursue its project *there*."

Frank Lentricchia is Professor of English at Duke University, in Durham, North Carolina. The following interview was recorded at his home in Hillsborough, near Durham, at the earliest ending of winter: March 21, 1986.

By training, Lentricchia is an Americanist and a student of modernism, with a special interest in Frost and Stevens. His first two books explore those interests and, although affected by the critical currents of their time, do not display a particular concern with contemporary literary theory. Lentricchia's major impact came with his third book, *After the New Criticism* (1980). In terms of polemical intent, the book might just as easily – though, at that stage, more wishfully – have been called *After Deconstruction*. It is a closely argued critique of the major strands in the contemporary scene of American literary criticism. The argument is that a variety of influential critics – including, by the way, most of those interviewed in this book – have forgotten about, or willfully repressed, history. They thus continue the aestheticizing and autonomizing approach to literature of the tradition they had pretended to rupture: the New Criticism of Brooks, Eliot, Tate, and Ransom. Frye, Kermode, Miller, Bloom,

Hartman, and de Man all come *after* the New Criticism alright, but
they do not get beyond it.

The New Critics, Kermode, Frye, and poststructuralists like Hartman and Miller, are all identified by Lentricchia as parts of a larger
formalist tradition: "the formalist critic is concerned to demonstrate
the history-transcending qualities of the text, and whether he wields
the textual cleaver of difference or that of irony, he portrays the
writer as a type of Houdini, a great escape artist whose deepest theme
is freedom, whose great and repetitious feat is the defeat of history's
manacles" (p. 185). *After the New Criticism* was also one of the first
books to devote extended attention to the work of Harold Bloom.
Although Bloom would see himself as anything but a formalist,
Lentricchia presents him as not at all having evaded New-Critical
aestheticism:

> The principle of continuity in the tetralogy is precisely an
> aestheticist impulse. Poems are created by the poetic faculty; the
> poetic identity is somehow ontologically severed from human iden-
> tity. And so all those forces outside of poetic history, as Bloom
> narrowly conceives it, have no bearing upon the discourse of
> poetry. The psychic and social life of the poet as a man in the world
> count for nothing; history in a big, exclusive sense cannot touch
> the sacred being of intrapoetic relations, those dyads which taken
> together constitute an élite and inviolably autonomous body of
> discourse.
>
> (p. 331)

Bloom's notion of criticism as poetry, says Lentricchia, "invites an
interpretive anarchy: a programmatic subjectivism that can only lead
to the purest of relativisms" (p. 339).

Despite the tone of that rebuke, the model of historical consciousness lurking behind *After the New Criticism* is drawn less from Marx
than from Foucault. Lentricchia, like Said, follows Foucault in defining discourse not as a passive medium of representation, but as an
act of power. Such a definition would

> take away the option from critical theorists of closing off a literary
> realm from its practical and diacritical relations with other realms.
> Literary discourse in the wake of Foucault no longer needs to be
> forced into contact with political and social discourses, as if these
> were realms outside of literature which writers must be dragged
> into by well-meaning critics. For as an act of power marked and
> engaged by other discursive acts of power, the intertextuality of
> literary discourse is a sign not only of the necessary historicity of
> literature but, more importantly, of its fundamental entanglement

with all discourses. In its refusal to center power either in a dominant discourse or in a subversive discourse that belongs only to
poets and madmen, Foucault's later work gives us a picture of
power-in-discourse that may move critical theory beyond its
currently paralyzed debates.

(p. 351)

Lentricchia recognized Paul de Man as the most influential of the
deconstructive critics, and it is towards him that the strongest
polemics are directed. This even includes drawing an extended
parallel (as Bloom, in fact, has done) between de Man and Cleanth
Brooks, both of whom try to free literary texts from "declarative
statement." They both dismiss any straightforward referential function for literature, but only in order to reintroduce referentiality on
a bigger, super-historical scale. In Brooks's case, the non-
referentiality of poetry is what allows it, paradoxically, to refer to the
real – that is, complex and ambiguous – texture of experience; for de
Man, the non-referentiality of literature is what reveals to us that *no*
language can speak about anything but itself with authority
(pp. 312–13). Within a de Manian realm of "wall-to-wall
discourse," visions of *aporia* confront us everywhere, so we must

> resist being pushed there, unless we wish to find ourselves with de
> Man and other avant-garde critics in the realm of the thoroughly
> predictable linguistic transcendental, where all literature speaks
> synchronically and endlessly the same tale. In the rarefied region
> of the undecidable, what is called literature is emptied of all
> linguistic force except the force of its own duplicitous self-
> consciousness. In this realm the discourse of literature would
> suppress the powerfully situating and coercive discourses of
> politics, economics, and other languages of social manipulation.
> (p. 317)

Since *After the New Criticism*, Lentricchia has continued his polemic
against de Man with increasing vigor. In a 1982 essay, for example,
he says that "the political fruit of de Man's bottomless self-irony is
not caution and care . . . but timidity, indifference and impotence –
qualities which pass in the academy in the guise of sophistication and
wisdom" ("Reading Foucault," pp. 57–8). The polemic is extended
in Lentricchia's most recent book, *Criticism and Social Change*, where
Foucault is replaced by a more local antagonist to deconstruction:
Kenneth Burke. The overriding premise of the book is that society
is a function of education, and not vice versa; its primary inquiry is
into whether literary intellectuals can have a radical effect *as* intellectuals. Lentricchia traces the progress in Burke himself from formalist

to critical consciousness: that is, to historical and class consciousness. Burke joins Foucault in "his concept of intellection as rhetorico-political activity" (p. 150). Like Foucault, Burke shows the way that literature and criticism are formed by broader historical/institutional discourses; more than Foucault, he suggests ways in which literature and criticism can *resist* them. Both writers show us that "our potentially most powerful political work as university humanists must be carried out in what we do, what we are trained for" (p. 7). What Burke, especially, suggests is the way that critics have a *power of rhetoric* which may be used for *or* against ruling-class hegemony:

> Burke insists that art conceived as rhetoric opens up radically divergent social functions for the writer. He may work, as in the writer's classical vocation, on behalf of a dominant hegemony by reinforcing habits of thought and feeling that help to sustain ruling power . . . Or he may work counter-hegemonically as a violator, in an effort to dominate and to re-educate (*in*form), to pin us to the wall, in order to assist in the birth of a critical mind by peeling off, one by one, and thus revealing to us for what they are, all bourgeois encrustations of consciousness. In the widest sense of the word, he would encourage cultural revolution.
>
> (p. 147–8)

After the New Criticism was not only engagingly polemical, but also perspicacious: there *has* been a historicist reaction against deconstruction since around 1980. In terms of polemic and prognosis, it seems to me that the truest precursor of the author of *After the New Criticism* is neither Burke *nor* Foucault, but, fittingly, the author of *The New Criticism*, John Crowe Ransom. Ransom, too, was a gifted polemicist, whose polemics were directed at overturning what *he* saw as the reigning bloc in American literary studies; and he, too, was centrally concerned with the relation of literature to history. Of course, Ransom's polemic came from the opposite direction. In *The New Criticism* (1941) and *The World's Body* (1938), Ransom's argument was that history had been allowed to *dominate* literary studies in the United States, to the impoverishment of any understanding of the specifically literary/linguistic qualities of poetry. It is the *historical* approach which has despecified literature, telling "endlessly the same tale" about it. Ransom's polemics are not less pointed than Lentricchia's, nor less conscious of their own "outsider" status. In *The World's Body*, he complains that most of the incumbents of the "old and reputable" English departments in the United States are still historical scholars. It is not so, he says,

in economics, chemistry, sociology, theology, and architecture. In

these branches it is taken for granted that criticism of the performance is the prerogative of the men who have had formal training
in its theory and technique. The historical method is useful, and
may be applied readily to any human performance whatever. But
the exercise does not become an obsession with the university men
working in the other branches; only the literary scholars wish to
convert themselves into pure historians.[1]

Of course, Lentricchia himself is only too well aware that there was
an "old" or "lay" historicism governing English studies in America
before the New Critics ever came along. My citing of Ransom is
intended neither to refute Lentricchia, nor to suggest that there is no
progress in criticism. But the fact that Lentricchia and Ransom do
represent the same kind of rhetorical moment, albeit from different
sides, suggests that the *kind* of progress made by criticism may
involve a necessary and continuing shuttle-movement between the
linguistic and historical approaches. One side will always be waiting
to inform the other that it has forgotten or repressed some affect or
feature that is specific to language; the other side will already have
begun formulating its demonstration of how that affect is itself
historically determined.

Imre Salusinszky: Near the beginning of your latest book, *Criticism
and Social Change*, you talk about the effect of your personal
background on your writing – the fact that your grandparents were
Southern Italian peasants, and so on. Within the sense that these
things do have something to do with intellectual productions, could
you give a brief rundown of your life-history?
Frank Lentricchia: I was born in Utica, New York, on May 23,
1940. My parents are second-generation Italian-American. All
four of my grandparents were born in the South – I mention the
South because it was in the South that there was the harshest
poverty and exploitation. My mother's father used to tell me,
when I asked him what he did in Italy: "Shovel shit." He wasn't
speaking in metaphor. They came here at the turn of the century,
individually: my grandparents didn't meet – on either side – until
they got here. To say that they were working people would be to
say the obvious. My grand*mothers* were also working people. They
worked in factories; they were not "ladies," or homemakers in the
ladies' magazine sense of the word. My mother worked in a factory
– for General Electric – for years: she was not a "lady." I

1 *The World's Body* (Baton Rouge: Louisiana State University Press, [1938] 1968), pp. 334–5, 327.

remember standing near her, by the sink, while she washed dishes. I was under 10, and remember her saying: "You must go to college no matter what." No one in our family had gone to college. My parents stopped school after the eighth grade because they had to work. And I remember my mother showing me her hands. She worked on an assembly line, and she handled metal parts eight hours a day. She would say, "Look at these hands: they're a man's hands." And they were: heavily calloused, strong, rough. My father worked two and three jobs all the time. He and my mother raised us in her parents' home. My father bought his first car when he was in his thirties. They bought their first house when I was in college.

The grandparents are very important because I really grew up with them, my mother's parents. On my father's side, my grand-father – whom I did not get to know till very late, because they had moved to Florida – I found out was a poet. He wrote volumes of stuff. He was a socialist, an atheist, and a very silent and inward man: a man I really did not get to know until after his death, through his writing. My grandfather on my mother's side was and still is a powerful presence, a man who would say: "What this country needs is a Mussolini." A man who cheerfully voted for Eisenhower. A man of the earth and a great story-teller: I came into literature *there*, with that grandfather.

You asked me how this sort of thing made an impact on me, and I'm not sure what the answer is. I have told you something of what I think about, when I think about my past – and I think always about my past in these senses. It's a typical story, in certain ways. Now, when it comes down to the question of how this stuff relates to my own literary-critical productions: who knows what the relationships are, what the underground forces really are? But when I write, I'm aware, at some level – not always, but inter-mittently – that I'm writing from a position as a critic who is not in a typical position in the American academy. That fact some-times weighs heavily upon me. I can't say that it's shaped all of my work: if you read some of my early stuff, you'll see no relation-ship with my Italian-American working-class background. But, these days, I have to say that one of the things I'm aware of is that I'm not a gentleman scholar. And, especially in my last two books, this has made me wary of theories of literature that avoid the kinds of differences you can't avoid.

I think it's very easy to become sentimental about what I'm talk-ing about, and that's one of the reasons why I don't talk about it very much. I feel impelled to write an autobiographical essay once in a while about this stuff, and I've always held back, because I fear this goddam sentimentality about it. There are many negative things I could tell you about my background, about being an Italian-American. It's not wonderful, in many ways: but it's real to me, it's how I came into the world; and I can't help but see that this sort of thing makes a difference. I can't help but see these differences in people, in writers. What I'm working on right now depends very heavily on making such differences count, not in the so-called background of a writer – as if the text had some sort of identity which we could accept as an autonomous thing – but in the foreground. If that means not talking about literature as literature, well, for me that's just fine.

This has something to do with American feminist criticism. This is why I stressed that my grandmothers worked, and my mother worked. One of the great things about feminist criticism is that it has brought this whole issue of gender to the front-burner. But one of the great problems of American feminist criticism is that many American literary feminists can't tell the difference between Nancy Reagan and my mother: the difference between a woman of privilege, a "lady," and a working woman. It seems to me that mainstream feminist literary categories have trouble with that, can't even get close to making that distinction count for something. So while I'm sympathetic to the impetus of the feminist project, I can't be sympathetic totally until it begins to be able to distinguish and differentiate those kinds of experiences.

IS: One finds the same tensions between the radical left and, for example, the Gay Rights Movement, which is, even more than feminism, primarily a bourgeois oppositional group.

FL: I've said to very close gay friends of mine that they're very radical on one issue, and they're with Reagan on most of the other issues. They don't much disagree.

IS: But the "one issue" of feminism is an all-embracing one, in a way that the issue of gay rights is not.

FL: Well, the one issue of feminism *may* be an all-embracing one, if it doesn't conceive of female sexual identity and the socialization of females as some sort of isolatable territory for Elaine Showalter and Sandra Gilbert to examine. I think that they haven't begun to examine the fact that female sexual identity and male sexual identity are interdependent, for one thing. It's impossible to talk convincingly about one without the other. Second, they run away from the contextualization of sexuality within economic realities.

Stevens, in a letter, says to his wife that he's been writing poems, that it's something that gives him a great deal of pleasure, but that she mustn't tell anybody about it and must keep it a great secret. At the end of the letter he says: "So that, you see, my habits are positively lady-like.''[2] His poetry was conceived in sexual and economic self-consciousness. The traces of that conception are all over the poems, there are more than traces of it in the letters, and it's substantially there in certain of the essays. But this is not the kind of story that American feminists and other literary traditionalists seem interested in, whether the subject is Stevens or Stein, maybe because poetic modernists have been taken at their word when they say that they're really writing poems that come from the imagination, which is situated on Mars. So that we can have all this material – the Stevens letters, the Stevens journals – and Harold Bloom and Helen Vendler will surely read all of it, but it will never get into their work. I think that the poetic project of modernism is the real last bastion of formalism: you can get your dirty materialist hands on the novel or the drama or the essay, or do it with philosophy, but you can't do it with ''Not Ideas about the Thing but the Thing Itself'' or ''Notes toward a Supreme Fiction.'' But that's where the project of historicizing really must take aim. What I'm really talking about is what I'm doing right now, and what I hope to be doing over the next several years.

IS: In a recent essay called ''On Behalf of Theory,'' you talk about the ''most interesting, productive and . . . human moment in our work'' as being the moment of ''unrestrained doubt, when we feel utterly *unjustified* in doing anything, when we question everything, when what we do seems to us to have unacceptable consequences or (horribly) no consequences at all for our lives as social beings'' (p. 107). Did this moment, in your own work, occur sometime between your book on Robert Frost and the beginning of the material which became *After the New Criticism*?

FL: No, it's much before that. The book on Frost was 1975, and it was an effort to get out of another crisis which followed the publication of my book on Yeats and Stevens, *The Gaiety of Language*. This has been a pattern in my life: I have a very difficult time living with what I wrote yesterday. I felt a certain emptiness about *The Gaiety of Language*, which was a work in an extreme formalist mode.

IS: It was an empty gaiety?

FL: It was. And desperate. I had the feeling that somehow the human beings who had written these poems were not evident in my pages in any way. The Frost book was some effort to resolve that. The beginnings of it went back to the mid 1960s, when I was reading a good bit of Poulet, the so-called phenomenological or "consciousness" critics and Hillis Miller's early work (which I still think of as his great work). The whole effort that this group made to restore the human presence in literature was very attractive to me as an antidote to this formalist thing that I had created in *The Gaiety of Language*. The Frost book was part of that.

Then something happened after the Frost book, which is what you're getting at. What happened was not so much a personal crisis as a kind of institutional crisis. By the mid 1970s, literary theory had completely exploded in this country. It was simply the most exciting time to be in the profession. I was then at Irvine, at the University of California, where Murray Krieger and Hazard Adams established the School of Criticism and Theory and brought interesting critics out to the West Coast. At that time, I began to get a sense of what my project was going to be for the next decade. I'm just now beginning to move towards finishing that project up. I thought at that time that there was amazing historical ignorance about what was going on. We had one book after another on structuralism and Derrida, as if there were no other games in town, as it were; as if these recent movements did not have a history. It seemed to me that I had a project in trying to situate this stuff, and in trying to say that there are many things happening. Now, clearly there was more than an objective "mapping" intention there – there was also a polemical project involved, a sense that one game after another was repeating a certain maybe inescapable impulse in literary criticism.

IS: The impulse to separate literature off from everything else?

FL: Yes, the segregating impulse. That formed the polemical object of *After the New Criticism*, which was then turned against the book by the Derrideans and the de Manians, who responded to the effect that you can't talk about history naively – as if I had – and that history is textual and problematic – as if the terms "textual" and "problematic" were enough to silence any move in the direction that I wanted to go. But despite some of the whippings that the book took in certain quarters, it wasn't long after it came out in 1980 that even the deconstructors wanted to say that they were politically responsible and were interested in history. The political and historicist rhetoric that you now see in deconstruction and all over the place was not there prior to 1980. The intention behind the book was to write a kind of *German Ideology*. It was an attempt to say: "We've got 'Young Hegelianism' again, and the materialist moment of criticism has to arrive."

IS: You're quite right about the forgetting of genealogy in each succeeding critical movement. For example, it was quite common when deconstruction "hit" to see descriptions of the transition from the New Criticism to deconstruction which pretended that Frye had never happened. In fact, one of the things that struck me first about *After the New Criticism* was that it did not commit that mistake.

FL: You touch there upon another intention of the book. If your intention is in some way critical and satirical – if you say you want to write a *German Ideology* – one of your styles has to be the style of debunking. When I wrote the Frye thing, I wasn't innocent of that, but I tried to point up the structuralist and poststructuralist moment already in Frye.

I don't know where the forgetting you describe comes from. There is what one can only call, in literary types, an avant-gardeist impulse. This impulse can be full of historical consciousness: no one was more brilliant than de Man in showing that to be the case. But the sons and daughters of de Man have forgotten this part of it, and the ignoring of Frye is a sign of this desire to rupture oneself and to feel that one is at the real cutting edge, that one's thought represents a real progress, that one has left behind all naiveties. The problem with the avant-garde is that it can only exist by saying that everyone else is a traditionalist (including yesterday's avant-garde).

IS: Still worrying at the important early transitions in your work, here is a typical quotation from *The Gaiety of Language*:

> With the knowledge that poetry is an "adult make believe," as Stevens said, and with the greater knowledge that it does not matter, the mind immerses itself in the joy of the poetic medium. It is a necessity for many of us.

> (p. 192)

That is a terrifically Bloomian kind of quotation.

FL: Yes, I wrote that: I believed it passionately when I wrote it; I do not believe it any more. It represents something, and there it is. What else can I say about it?

IS: Well, in *After the New Criticism* there are chapters on "Versions of Phenomenology" and "Versions of Existentialism," and in a way this seems to be more about a working-out of your relationship to your own previous work than it is about the people it discusses. One could easily talk about your first two books as versions of phenomenology and existentialism.

FL: I didn't think of it that way, but it has been pointed out to me, by you and by others, that there is certainly an autobiographical theme being worked out. It was not intentional, but that is only to say that this is the way my criticism unfolds, the way my writing unfolds: I am always working it out with respect to my past. I can change my mind.

Let's go back to that quotation. In fact, Barbara Johnson shrewdly quoted that to me at a conference we were involved in – to the great amusement of considerable portions of the audience. Given where I stand now, that quotation is often offered as the skeleton in my critical closet. That's fine: I don't think that one gets away from formalism; I don't think that one should; I don't think I want to. The idea that one wants to or should suggests that history is outside the text again. If you believe that history is within the text and that the clean distinction between text and history is absolute garbage, then the key task of formalism remains to describe those subtle moves in language that we associate with literariness, *with any eye towards* the history which they contain and express and evoke. This is a different task from the formalist task, a different task from saying that "it does not matter" and that "the mind immerses itself in the joy of the poetic medium."

IS: In *Criticism and Social Change*, this is what you say about American intellectuals who share your type of background:

> This kind of intellectual, who has been confirmed "traditionally" in the educational process and who more and more is becoming a presence in American universities, will need to retrieve his outsider's experience; but having done that, he will find that his desire for radical social action – assuming that he feels such desire – will have to work through the mediation of the peasant origins of his immigrant . . . grandparents.
>
> (p. 8)

I'm still thinking about what the moment of critical self-doubt in your work might be, and in this passage it seems to comprise moving from the role that you have discovered yourself in – that of a "traditional" intellectual – and trying to recoup, to become an "organic" intellectual. But can one have one's cake and eat it too, in the sense of one's institutional position? Is the university not so completely the institution of the traditional intelligentsia as to make the move you describe impossible? Can such a recoup be performed inside the university?

FL: I'll put my answer in religious terms, which I do not intend literally: God's work is everywhere. We're not questioning the fact that the university is an especially sensitive institution, a place where, as a professor, one meets and teaches God knows how many students. One's personal impact, one's shaping political and moral influence, is enormous, so the question can't be: "Do we have the opportunity, as educators, to make a difference?" Clearly, we have it every day of the week, as teachers – not to mention as writers. The bleak, Foucauldian sub-text to what you're saying is: isn't it true that the institution will somehow recoup and translate your efforts into these traditional molds? I don't understand why that necessarily has to be the case. It assumes that institutions, and institutional discourses, exert a kind of totalitarian control over the individual – something like in the paranoid visions of *Discipline and Punish*.

Have you seen this movie *Brazil*, by the way? I don't know if those guys read *Discipline and Punish* (clearly they've read Orwell), but it strikes me as a wonderful dramatization of that entire vision of Foucault's, although harsher than Foucault. I think that Foucault really does have a sentiment for the aesthetic, and the pastoral, as a kind of anarchic moment of release and resistance which is not only possible, but effective, in a kind of long-term way. But the movie really subverts that. So that the question about the institution is Foucauldian and, finally, worse than Foucauldian, because it's from the sort of perspective of these people who made *Brazil*, where *everything* is saturated by coercive power and there is no escape.

That just doesn't make sense to me, in my experience. Who's going to stop me from doing the things I do in the classroom? Who's going to stop me from teaching Wallace Stevens, for example, in the way that I teach Wallace Stevens, which for some literary types may seem unliterary? Who's going to stop me from telling students about Stevens's early career, when he was living in New York and hanging around the bums in the Bowery and the Italians in the Village – and writing things about them, and responding to them? Who's going to stop me from delineating Wallace Stevens as a middle-class American: a privileged, upper-middle-class kid who, when he gets out of Harvard, starts acting like a character in a Theodore Dreiser novel who achieves an economic self-consciousness in his middle twenties? Who's going to stop me from doing that?

IS: I don't think anybody's going to stop you doing any of those things. For some reason, with everyone I've spoken to, I've come at this question without ever being quite sure what I *am* asking. Of course, the reason for asking it is that a large part of the impetus for this series is "the question of the university": the question of criticism *in* the university; whether that is where criticism properly belongs; and what compromises criticism – in the broadest sense – is required to make by virtue of its *being* in the university.

Supppose we accept the Newman/Platonic notion that there *is* an "idea of the university." If there is such a thing (with which the modern institution that we call "the university" could not fail to be infected) then surely that idea of the university – right back to its medieval origins – has something to do with the belief that there are some things – or some *thing* – which can be discussed in isolation from political or ideological preferences or difference. Now, such an idea is clearly a fiction: but it may be what Stevens calls a "supreme fiction," a necessary fiction; a fiction which, knowing it's a fiction, we have to continue to believe in because, if we abandon it, everything we think of as the university will collapse around it. And if it *were* close to the "idea of the university" that something could be discussed without reference to politics or ideology, then it *would* always end up by capturing you as a "traditional" intellectual.

FL: Well, the "idea of the university" remains alive and well among humanist scholars, and it's alive and well in the mind and publications of William Bennett.[3] It's alive and well in many of our colleagues. That traditional idea of the university is a powerful one. It does precisely the kind of work that you describe: it forcibly separates literature from difference – sexual, political, and social. On the other hand, diversity in the university is more and more the case. Us "pigs" are getting in, you know. Michael Novak, a sociologist of much repute on the right, wrote an article in *Harper's* magazine in the late 1960s describing the exclusion from intellectual circles of the "pigs," the "invisible" minorities, the Poles, the Italians, the Greeks, and the Slavs. But us "pigs" are getting in now. And the entry of women and Blacks has been eased in recent years, and their impact is also diversifying the university.

Of course, we can be recuperated; of course, we can want to imitate the masters: that was the point, by the way, of my reference to my Southern Italian origins. It is not for nothing that I tell you that my grandfather voted for Eisenhower and told me that what this country needs is a Mussolini. There was their experience shoveling the shit, and then there was the experience of the *padrone*: one or the other. There was no middle ground, and if you wanted to get away from where you were, the best thing would be to be where the *padrone* was. Right? Absolutely. And to be where the *padrone* is, in intellectual terms, is to be where this "idea of the university" is: to become a traditional humanist intellectual. By so becoming, one is trapped within a situation in which one's roots and one's awareness of difference and the impact of difference on literature are forgotten or repressed. This can happen. I think a good part of my education witnessed that happening in myself.

3 US Secretary for Education.

IS: It's like two verbal formulations which, perhaps, describe the same phenomenon. One of them would be: "The university, after all, has provided the main haven for Marxism in the United States." The other is: "The university has *contained* Marxism in the United States."

FL: I really distrust that second formulation, because it comes from certain kinds of Marxist, and it also come from certain kinds of poststructuralist who don't like Marxism. And it comes from certain traditionalists, who like to mock the efforts of a Marxist project. It's a reactionary position, because it says that ideas don't count. It's a completely undialectical position, and has nothing to do with historical materialism. It's a mechanical materialist position, and it really says that the action is in the factories, or what have you, and certainly not in the classroom.

IS: Yes, well, you say in the essay "On Behalf of Theory" that "those who scourge academic Marxism might remember that Marx saw struggles against ideas as struggles against political, material forces" (pp. 109–10). But he didn't see that as the end of struggle, or the only side of struggle.

FL: But *a* side of struggle.

IS: But isn't it the only side of Marxist struggle in this country?

FL: Absolutely. But so what? The only serious site of Marxist struggle in the United States is in the university. That's not a reason to disparage that site of struggle; it is not a reason cynically to evaluate this as a kind of idealistic jerk-off. It is to say that if Marxism finds itself in struggle in the university – in the world of ideas – then that's where it is at the moment, and it should pursue its project *there*. Because there is not now (nor ever will be) a serious Communist Party in this country, because Marxist intellectuals are mainly professors, should not in itself be a source of corrosive irony towards left intellectuals. When it is – and it *is* a source of corrosive irony – then those who speak cynically of left intellectuals should examine the implications of suggesting that the university is not a good place to pursue social change. What the fuck are they doing? If they believe that, they should resign their jobs. I myself have no hang-up with that. I know people have said it about my work, and I hear people talk about this, but I have never felt that I ought to be someplace else. I'm happy to be where I am. There is no greater opportunity than the opportunity of perverting the young. Isn't that it?

IS: If, as you say, Marx saw struggles against ideas as struggles against material and political forces, and if such ideas include ideas about literature and criticism – the sorts of ideas that you pursue – then how come Marx, himself, gave only the scantest attention to literature?

FL: He had other interests. He had other things to do.

IS: That's for sure! Do you mean he was going to come to it?

FL: No, I doubt it. I don't believe that there would have been an aesthetics. I think it's almost not an interesting question. Marx was theorizing history, society and social change. Literature is within that, and because he didn't do it is no strike against him: others would and did.

IS: There are two writers central to your work, and I'd like you to describe how you came to them, and how they affected you: Marx, and Kenneth Burke.

FL: I read them both a long time ago. I can't say that there was any substantial impact of either for a very long time. In the middle 1970s, in an effort to contextualize my own discontent with the drift of literary theory, I had to go back to Marx, and shortly thereafter I went back to Kenneth Burke. Kenneth Burke, it struck me, was one of those rare figures who had never made any of the mistakes – if we can call them that – that were made in contemporary literary theory.

Now, one might say that *After the New Criticism* was a negative book, in many ways. As Terry Hawkes said, it had one "messianic" moment: the Foucauldian chapter. I think that the Foucauldian pages in *After the New Criticism* were overstated by the context in which they operated. I did feel the need for a breath of air; for something to hold on to in the contemporary scene, on to and against what I had been reading: Foucault struck me as the great antidote, at that moment. But after that publication, I felt the need to say something, in a more positive vein, about where literary theory might go, and that led to the writing of *Criticism and Social Change*. The actual biographical incident was that I had been aware that I had done precisely what I would say others had done in *Criticism and Social Change*: I had left Burke out of the picture, when I felt that Burke was everywhere in the picture (he's in a footnote, I think, in *After the New Criticism*). Feeling those feelings, along came Hayden White who said "Would you do an essay for this volume on Kenneth Burke that I'm putting together?" I thought that was a terrific idea. I had just finished this other book, and I was thinking about Burke. That's what launched *Criticism and Social Change*: the re-reading of Burke. My feeling was that here was a story that surely had to be told, because it was the story of contemporary theory before the fact. The point was not to say merely that Burke had gotten there before – although I think that that's an interesting historical point – but that he had done it without falling into these formalizing, divisive tactics.

You just have to look at the books of Burke – just peruse their contents – and then peruse the contents of Paul de Man's work and then ask yourself: "Which man is engaging something beyond the realms of literature?" The answer is quite clear. Then the next question will become: "Is the man who is engaging the various discourses of culture and their social ground doing it in a persuasive way?" Again, the answer is quite clear. All of this inter-disciplinary drift which we've experienced recently – which I think is wholly positive – all of this anti-formalist mood of the last five years – which I think is positive – is all there in Burke, without denigrating the formalist moment. It's important to say that: certain of the Derrideans and de Manians have assumed that the move to history is necessarily a naive move which wants to by-pass the formal moment. It does not, and you see that in Burke.

To do the Burke book, I also began seriously teaching Marx, at Irvine. But I think that it's not a Marxist book. The latest review I got said it was a manifesto for the Marxist academic. I don't see it that way, and I don't call myself a Marxist. Clearly, great parts of my recent work have a good deal of sympathy with that, but I don't fit myself very well into that group, and that group hasn't been particularly interested in my work, aside from Fred Jameson. And Perry Anderson has been warm. And Terry Eagleton, to a certain extent (although he seems to have conveniently forgotten that he stayed up all night – as he told me – to read *After the New Criticism*: you would not know that that experience occurred from *Literary Theory: An Introduction*. But let that pass!)

IS: Talking of Marxism, when the Reverend Jerry Falwell heard that I was going to interview you, he said to me: "Ask Lentricchia, the ingrate, why he, of all people (with Southern Italian immigrants as his grandparents, and having experienced all the benefits of the New World that they came here to bring him) now attacks precisely those values that make this country a place where Southern Italian immigrants' grandchildren can be professors at Duke."

FL: Wonderful. If only my grandparents could respond to this! The benefits of the New World! Nobody gave them anything. They broke their backs. So did my parents. I like teaching at Duke and making the salary I make. I don't have the theory of Marxism that what Marx wants for the world is for everyone to be poor. I like Garcia Marquez's notion of Marx much better: what we need is for everybody to be able to drink good wine, to drive a decent car, and so on.

IS: Besides: how come Marxists – to be genuine – always have to be poor, when no one demands that reactionaries be rich?

FL: But your question touches a bigger point. I'll answer it by saying that these dreams of America have been *very* difficult to make come true and for many they never came true. The game was rigged, and we know that the game was rigged, and that one of the key ways of rigging the game has been the invoking and the utilization of certain notions of self-determination.

IS: It's interesting, though, that the only way you can get into a position of demonstrating that the game is rigged is by being an example of the fact that it's not absolutely rigged.

FL: It's not absolutely rigged: that's why I'm an optimist. My grandparents and parents *made* life better. If I thought it was absolutely rigged it would be another reason to slit our collective Foucauldian throats. I don't think the game is absolutely rigged. I'm pleased to be living here. I think people have at least minimal opportunity here to change their lives, in an individual and a collective way. I'm not one of these people who thinks that this is the worst place on earth, despite our inhumanities and stupidities. Would I rather be living in El Salvador? In El Salvador, in Guatemala, professors get their heads shot off: not here. Not yet. That's not a sign that professors here are inauthentic, but that the level of decency is much greater.

We ought to talk about the middle class, too, in America. That's where I have problems with literary Marxists. This category barely exists in Marxist theory, as you know. That's one of the reasons I'm not comfortable with the tag ''Marxism.'' I don't see an interesting or sympathetic analysis of the position of middle-class people in this country. And I think that one of the projects of literary critics who do American literature from these sociological angles might be to situate a number of our writers precisely within those confines. Because that's where they come from, and that's where the great social contradictions in American literature come from: from that funny place.

IS: Let me read you some sentences from my interview with someone who does not resemble the Reverend Falwell to any degree, the great Bloom:

> What I understand least about the current academy, and the current literary scene of criticism, is this lust for social enlightenment; this extraordinary and, I believe, mindless movement towards proclaiming our way out of all introspections, our way out of guilt and sorrow, by proclaiming that the poet is a slumlord. . . . This is clap-trap. The poet is not a slum-lord; the critic is not a hireling of the stock exchange. . . . If they wish to alleviate the sufferings of the exploited classes, let them live

up to their pretensions, let them abandon the academy and go out there and work politically and economically and in a humanitarian spirit. They are the hypocrites: the so-called Marxist critics, and all of this rabblement that follows them now in the academies. They are the charlatans, they are the self-deceivers and the deceivers of others.

FL: You know, I love Harold, but that statement is so far off the wall that I don't know how to begin to respond to it. The poet *might* be a slum-lord: it's possible. The critic *might* be a hireling. But the point is not that they are or are not. The point is how the poet's identity as a poet is constituted: what interests it expresses; what social positions it grows from; what it bears upon; what it hides and doesn't hide. These are not matters of self-congratulation. One of the things that is bad about Harold's comment is that he assumes that critics who are interested in the social and political identity of literary writing are necessarily out to show the things that he suggests – that the writers whom he would consider to be great are really repressive bastards and voices of the ruling class.

IS: But you *can hear* that at the Marxist sessions of any MLA Convention.

FL: Well that's another reason why I don't have particular sympathy with the Marxist literary rhetoric in this country. Look, I'm a great fan of Wallace Stevens and Robert Frost, two of the more reactionary literary figures of our century. But it's not even important what their explicit political opinions are, which is not to say that their deepest vision is liberationist or socialist – that's not true at all. What is interesting about these writers is the social richness and complexity of their literary existence. These people express and reflect upon and mediate where we are and where we've come from. That is the reason for doing this kind of work: not to beat your breast, not to put yourself over these people and say "Look how horrible they are." That is an absurd position to take. A number of literary Marxists take it and, as you say, you can hear it articulated at the MLA. But I have no sympathy with it, since it assumes that *they* know where we should be, that *they* have the right and decent values and the rest of us do not.

Now, the other point that Harold makes is that if these people were authentic and humane they would get into the streets. Does this mean that Harold is suggesting that all those who remain in the academy – including himself – are not humane, are "charlatans"? Or is it only if you remain in the academy and speak this way that you are a charlatan? Whereas you are not a charlatan if you remain in the academy and have interests that are

Bloomian and so forth, and have no concern with the fact that Stevens was a man who had to worry about earning a living, for example; who made it in a certain way; who liked to collect *objets d'art* from all over the world and who believed that you weren't really living unless you paid five dollars a pound for Viennese chocolate. Does he believe that only those within the academy who are not concerned with those facts and with how such biographical facts feed into a larger social scene are doing authentic work? He paints himself into a kind of irrelevancy, it seems to me.

IS: Well, I think he would say that the authentic thing is to stay within the academy and admit that criticism, like literature, is a form of self-exploration, self-discovery and self-exfoliation.

FL: Whose self? Where is this self? The reader's self? Harold's self? My self? Where did this self come from? Was Harold self-born? Was he self-originated? This is the problem with Harold's theory: with all of its historical, self-conscious sophistication, it carries buried within itself a radical desire for self-origination. I wish that Harold would pursue his sense of himself as the only proletarian at Yale.

IS: Both you and Said admit to having learnt from Bloom. What has been your relation to him? He doesn't get as bad a run in *After the New Criticism* as some.

FL: Harold? *He* thought so: he was very upset about it. But I thought that his was an "exemplary career" in the sense of exemplary for what criticism ought to be doing. First, there is the historicist character of his project. Then the sense that writing and literary life comes from struggle is very important: that is what distinguishes him from so many of the people he is generally associated with, and what makes him distinctive. I also like his stress on the voice, by the way. But I think he overdoes that. He isolates the subject from structure (to use Marxist jargon that he'll hate) and he has no interest in seeing how structure flows into or constrains the subject – especially social structure.

IS: But the subject for him is the same absolute that language is for the deconstructors.

FL: That's right. But it seems to me that a little Bloom can go a long way in the struggle against structuralism and structuralist, Althusserian Marxisms. I'm interested, in my current work, in moving through the biographical individual *into* social structure. I'm interested in starting with the fundamental sexual, economic, social and familial givens about the writer, and moving from these, as unavoidables, to the larger structure – without making the mistake of thinking that the structure stands outside the subject, but recognizing that different subjects move into history through their bodies, through their families, through their social locale and so forth. We mustn't elide these differences. This is a point that I find attractive in Harold: the stress on voice. Of course, all of his stress on voice, on struggle and historicity seems to me absolutely, and by intention, contained by his sense of literariness as a kind of domain that we can consider apart from its social setting: I find that a problem.

Another element of this problem is that Harold says he's interested in the relations of "strong" writers to one another. Where this really comes from is that Harold's education – like a lot of our educations – ignores the fact that writers at 18 or 19 (especially modern writers) don't necessarily think of their relationship to Milton and Aristotle: they exist within a visible and palpable market of contemporary writers. That level of struggle has also to be taken care of. To come at this another way: it won't do to try to take the measure of literature and society rather directly, as if literature doesn't have its history. The relationship of a writer to his or her literary past is *one* dimension of the historical project, and one that cannot be ignored by a criticism that would be socially relevant. Often, social and political struggles are encoded in very specific and apparently antiquarian jargons and languages. That's the currency for a writer: his or her struggle with that literariness.

IS: Regarding your treatment of Bloom in *After the New Criticism*, his response to that in *Agon* is humorous. He says that you should stop deceiving yourself: you are not a son of Marx and Foucault, but of James and Emerson and Frost (p. 42). Then, in *Criticism and Social Change*, there is a demonstration near the beginning of how much a weak pragmatism resembles Reaganism (p. 3). Is that a response to Bloom's characterization of you as a pragmatist?

FL: I don't know that I was responding to Bloom's remarks. What I would say is that he's on the right track when he says that I'm a son of Emerson and James more than Foucault and Marx. What he's saying is that some American literary critics, who've been socialized in the American literary-philosophical tradition, have certain values deeply imbedded in themselves. They have a kind of anti-systematic strain that's always working itself through their prose. It's very distrustful of generalization of all sorts, including social generalization. I suspect that one of the reasons I don't call myself a Marxist is that I don't call myself anything. I feel terrifically uncomfortable with labels, and I also feel terrifically uncomfortable when some of the things I deeply want to see happen start becoming merely popular things at MLA. Slogans. Bandwagons. Christ! To put it bluntly: everyone (except Harold)

wants to be a political critic; everyone wants to be political; every
other word is "politics this" and "politics that," "history this"
and "history that." It makes me want to say I'm not interested in
that any more.

IS: But isn't the desire to be "an original theorist" what is "most
retrograde and anti-intellectual" in contemporary criticism (*After
the New Criticism*, p. 346)?

FL: Yes, and I am subject to that retrograde impulse. But it's not
that I want to be original, it's that I feel that these sudden professional appropriations are without real commitment. There seems
to be something empty there. It's a fashion: let's face it, one of the
ways to get noticed, to get published, to become important in
literary-critical circles in this country is to be perceived as being on
the avant-garde edge of certain movements. Right now, the thing
everywhere is politics and history, with a strong dash of Marxism
and feminism. I just distrust that whole enterprise, because I guess
I think it *is* an enterprise: there's a kind of business going on here.

IS: In the United States, questions of "truth" very quickly become
coterminous with professional questions, in a way that is not
necessarily in the service of "truth." There is an almost instant
intermixing of any new idea or approach with professional ends,
professional rivalries, professional battles for power.

FL: You're using "professionalism" in its horrid sense. The horrid
sense – which is a powerful sense – is that, since this is what we
do, we need a certain language and terminology to do it, we need
to publish our stuff, we need to further our careers . . .

IS: On the other hand, you only have to spend ten minutes in a
major British university to see what fantastic senses there are to
American "professionalism." There, there is no professionalism.
One effect of that, for example, is that jobs can still be handed out
on an "old boy" network, without regard to publication or
productivity – not to say brains.

FL: Professionalism in a democratic context (in a US context) has
one fantastic sense for me. To go back to Michael Novak's little
word, it allows the "pigs" in. The pigs have a chance. In other
social contexts, the pigs may never have a chance. But the old boy
network is strong here, too. Very strong.

IS: Now, the other writer who's been crucial to your development
of a historicist approach has been Foucault. This is an extraordinarily vulgar question, but when you insist that we place the
literary work not only in literary history, but in the mesh of all
human experience or history or discourse, is it primarily a matter
of history *then* or history *now*?

FL: I would never say the placement of the work in "all human

experience,'' but we'll leave that aside. I think that the answer to
your question is "both." Foucault was very strong on emphasizing
what he calls the "malice" of those historians who have these
projects that are full of passion but are masked with the language
of objectivity. After Foucault, one cannot go back to that very
easily. I don't think, however, that one's work as a literary
historian has to be prefaced by fifty-page analyses and intermittent
meditations on "Who I Am" or "Where I Come From" and all
the rest of it. There may be a place for that sort of thing, but it
doesn't seem to me to be absolutely necessary. It seems to me that
"Who I Am" is constantly expressed in the kinds of work I do.
The liberating message of Foucault, for me, is a message he never
intended, since he had such disdain for phenomenology, existentialism, and the subject: my own sense of myself, as a subject, has
to get more and more into my work. That's where I see my opportunity: to break down this myth of objectivity, which permits
people to read one as if one were writing from the perspective of
eternity, as if one had this transcendental perch. So the message
is probably a message which Harold would like: one's writing – at
the level of style, rhythm, voice, diction, the whole shebang – has
to be shaped by one's self. Of course, as William James points out,
it's very nice to say that, but a self is a very hard thing to have.
The self that we think we have is very often this very conventional
thing that sounds like everybody else.

IS: Much of what you say, in *After the New Criticism*, about Foucault
and the entanglement of literature with other discourses, is
reminiscent of what Said has been saying, in *The World, the Text
and the Critic*, in his interview, and elsewhere. What is your relation
to the critic who is, with yourself, one of the truly signal mediations
of Foucault for the American literary audience? Has Said
influenced you?

FL: In the middle 1970s, with that story I told you about the context
of coming to write *After the New Criticism*, Edward's work and Fred
Jameson's work were instances of what I found to be healthy
criticism that didn't fall into the traps that I saw in other theorists.
So there's just no question that they influenced me, whatever we
mean by influence: I read their work and was impressed with their
work. Certain general things that Said has worked out strike me
as inescapable orientations among the many orientations which
undergird my work. I can't say that I've been as interested in his
literary work as in his political work. I've had trouble making the
connection, often. But at the level of its political project, and at the
level of its general theoretical orientation for literature, I think it's
as admirable a project as I know.

IS: Let's address, for a few moments, the central polemical thrust of *After the New Criticism*, which is clearly still tied up with Foucault: the critical consciousness you bring to bear on the notion of the aesthetic realm, or literary history, as isolatable things. According to the book, this is the mistake into which – just as it seemed as though he might be a way out of it – Frye fell. It is the trap into which – just as it seemed as if he might be a way out of it – Frank Kermode fell (via Stevens's idea of the "fiction"). This is the recurring story of *After the New Criticism*, like the succession of captivities of Israel in the Old Testament. People seem to be perpetually close to breaking out of the neo-Kantian dualism, but the ferris wheel always catches them again on the downswing. This notion of being able to talk about literature and the aesthetic as a separate thing is, of course, not a contemporary disease, nor does it begin with Kant. How can we hope, here in the late bourgeois world, to undo something so basic to our intellections?

FL: I don't think we should try, in a certain sense; and were I to revise *After the New Criticism* – which I have no desire to do – I would have a slightly kinder description of what you call the fall into the aesthetic, that moment of being recaptured and isolated and frozen out of the flow of time. *Slightly* kinder. My sense is that you can't help that, in a certain way. Literature always orients itself with relation to other literature, so that the critical moment which wishes to describe that is inevitably going to sound as if it were falling into the formalist trap. Even Fred Jameson's work has been described, by hostile critics, as rarefied (Said has said things of that sort, and has included me in the rarefaction project). I think this is always the case, but is not necessarily a reason for despairing of carrying on with a project that is more than that. The literariness of literature has to be a part of the project of describing the involvement of literature in the world. If it doesn't go through that, I don't think it's going to be a convincing project, because it's going to say things that are simply not true. It's going to say that what writers have on their minds is responding to Reagan, or some other thing: sometimes they do, but the fact is that I don't think that culture works that way, or that politics works quite that way within culture. The examples of these direct political confrontations are often not particularly interesting. The more complicated responses to society come through in mediated ways.

I'll give you an example, from what I'm working on. The context of early modernism in this country is, politically speaking, an imperialist context. We can see that reflected overtly in certain areas of culture, and what we then have to ask ourselves is: how is it, at the same time, that there is an attack on canonicity evolving, parallel to the imperialistic moment and parallel to the development of modernist poetic discourse? What is the relationship of certain clearly irrationalist procedures and pragmatist procedures, in writing, to that imperialist moment? These are not questions which have easy answers, but I think that one of the things you see in literature at that point is a kind of response that is not a direct response to the American imperial adventure. You see direct responses in figures like William James and Mark Twain, but you see it displaced in Stevens or Pound or Frost, having its effects on other areas of culture and thinking. So you see a kind of spread of this anti-imperialist passion, through writers who, if you asked them directly about it, might not have any qualms about overt American political imperialism: at another level in their work, they are articulating principles that feed an attitude that is antithetical to an imperialist political project.

IS: I suppose that the real question, raised by *After the New Criticism*, is whether we should have a category of aesthetic or literary effect, but then not try to keep it pure of other discourses, or whether we shouldn't have an aesthetic category at all.

FL: The concept of the "Literary" and the "Aesthetic" is a kind of fact of modernist history that we live with. A notion that it is a "mistake," or isn't a "mistake," is probably irrelevant. The question becomes: what are the contexts of the growth of that idea? What is the matrix of that? Why do people have thoughts like that about their art? That strikes me as an important question. It's a question that's been raised and probed by Raymond Williams, throughout his work, but the Williams project is by no means completed. The work of materializing modernist literature is mainly one that lies ahead of us.

IS: The problem is not that it is a project that still lies ahead of us, but whether anything of what we presently think of – or, perhaps, even love – as "poetry" can survive the project. The question is whether dialectical materialism and poetry are not, always, in some sense constituted as the Other of each other.

FL: That's been the history of the idea of the modern. In effect, that's one way of summarizing, in one sentence, the history of literary theory.

IS: Well, we've always known that we've constituted poetry as the Other of materialism. The question I'm asking is: isn't it possible that materialism has constituted itself as the Other of poetry?

FL: That's not how Marx originated his project. But literary materialists have often talked that way: as if the real enemy were the aesthetic; as if attention to history and social responsibility entailed the turning of one's back on poetry – "Send poetry to

Siberia!'' But, again, that strikes me as an odd move, because it
says that there *is* an area of culture that stands outside history.
Since when? On the other hand, you have to say to the Blooms that
to materialize Stevens's poetry and the economic and sexual
context personal to him, his family and his time is *not* necessarily
to treat the poetry in a dreary, uninteresting way; it is not
necessarily to ignore the erotic fullness of Stevens's language; it is
not to ignore the play of his language. It is not to ignore any of
these things: it is to see them speak in a different way. It's stun-
ning, isn't it, Imre, how this argument – we're saying that Bloom
represents it, tonight – keeps repeating itself on the side of the
poets?

IS: But that is one of the things that makes me suspect that the relation between poetry and dialectical materialism *is* deeply
antithetical, in a way that could be thought about even more
seriously than it has been by people as distinguished as you and
Said.

FL: We can't ignore it. One of the aspects of that rhetoric has been
a daemonizing, by each, of the other. A daemonizing of poetry as
what is irresponsible and inhumane – which is what Harold is
referring to in the poet as ''slum-lord.'' And then a daemonizing
of materialism as removing all spirit, all generosity and all
difference: this gray, dreary, socio-economic monolith. That's
been the history, especially since Marx, of this debate. All of
Harold's favorite Romantic poets were involved in precisely that
kind of struggle. So don't we have to say that there is a certain
specific, historical narrative that we have to unfold in order to
understand this?

IS: The question being whether the narrative we unfold it within can
stand outside of the antithesis itself.

FL: I think it can, and I don't think it will happen very easily,
because of many literary institutions, including the institution of
publishing anthologies of poetry. You read Wallace Stevens, for
example, in this book called *Collected Poems of Wallace Stevens*. You
don't read anything with it: you don't read any other Stevens; you
can't tell from reading these poems that anything else ever
happened. To get that other stuff into this volume seems
technically unfeasible. So if you ask me about this poem ''Not
Ideas about the Thing but the Thing Itself,'' as the poem that
finishes off the *Collected Poems*, I have to respond to it ''on the
page,'' ''in itself'': I'm forced into precisely the kind of formalist
procedure that gives me the willies.

This touches on the re-imagining of the teaching of literature,
and the literature curriculum. This re-imagining will get down to

material realities in the brute sense of this book that I have before me. It can no longer be a book in the class, as such. We're going to have to become *bricoleurs* of the curriculum; we're going to have to find ways to put together things so that when we read a poem like "Not Ideas about the Thing but the Thing Itself" we're not forced into the banalities of modernism, or of 1960s experimentalism – where we talk about Stevens as the great "meta-writer" who is aware of the perilous relationship between fictions and things in themselves, and who knows that you can't really get outside, and who indicates his sophistication with "like" and "as." What a thundering banality, to say that about that poem! The poem, by itself, seems to force you to say it. The title of the poem is not even Derridean: it's Kantian. What is this desire: to get *behind* Kant; to get *outside* Kant; to get outside the critical tradition in philosophy? We can say those things, and to say them to undergraduates is a revelation to many of the undergraduates. But when we get to *our* stage, Imre, how can we live with that? I'm bored by that kind of stuff.

IS: So how *should* we talk about the poem?

FL: Under ideal circumstances? Had I the opportunity to have all the materials, with this poem? If I could show how the discourse of this poem was coterminous with other kinds of discourses, including earlier Stevens poems, and stuff that's not in his poetry?

IS: Before what you said before, I was going to suggest that we take as our motto, in discussing the poem, a line from *Criticism and Social Change*: "That inside/outside distinction is killing us" (p. 7). A line which, of course, has nothing to do with the issue here.

FL: It has a lot to do with it. Stevens has been *the* poet of the "inside" of "literature." This is a place where it's very hard to open the poem up to the flow of his larger social existence. The first thing to say is that the title is not to be understood as a response to Kant or some sort of philosophical problem. I'm interested in the fact that Stevens expresses here something that Yeats, for example, expresses in a number of his last poems: the feeling that he's been living an unreal existence, that he's been somehow cut off from real life. It's not a Yeatsian problem, but there's certainly an echo of that there.

There is another level of the poem which might be approached by asking ourselves about these ellipses. For one thing, they occur often in Stevens, and in crucial places, as in "On the Road Home":

It was when I said
"There is no such thing as the truth,"
That the grapes seemed fatter.
The fox ran out of his hole.

You . . . You said,
"There are many truths,
But they are not parts of a truth."[4]

The ellipsis functions there similarly to how it functions here. This
is not a moment in which words have been left out: it's a moment
in which words do not exist for what Stevens is trying to signify;
in which language disappears; and in which, somehow, one is experi-
encing unmediated, full presence – a contact outside discourse. This
is the trick of the ellipsis, and that's part of the maneuver of this
poem: to suggest that one is at the verge of a stunned reception,
a breakthrough-moment in which something has been finally
cracked. It's a moment in which language ceases to suffice – though,
of course, he's manipulating language to do this. What he wants
is to give the sense of an awe-full reception: an intransitive, ecstatic
moment of fullness. The ellipses suggest a radically anti-literary
impulse, a poetry of silence, where nothing will do but naked
confrontation.

Another thing that is clearly discussable is the "colossal sun."
That particular metaphor is a great force in Stevens's work,
including in such early poems as "Sunday Morning" and "Plough-
ing on Sunday." In "Sunday Morning" it figures, again, the breakthrough: "Supple and turbulent, a ring of men/Shall chant in orgy
on a summer morn/Their boisterous devotion to the sun."[5] I've
always thought of this in connection with Section 11 of "Song of
Myself," where the twenty-eight young men are bathing in the
ocean, and a woman who is the grandmother of the female presence
in "Sunday Morning" is viewing these guys through the drapes.
One would want also to notice that the vision of the turbulent men
is a utopian moment, a vision of the future: it's very carefully
projected as a vision of paradise, and one would want to say, "Where
are the women, in this chant; what kind of a utopia is this anyway?"
Thinking that thought, one will think thoughts of a recurrent, all-
male society that is constituted in several of the great moments of
American literature, from Rip Van Winkle through wonderful chapters in *Moby Dick*, through Whitman and all the way to Norman
Mailer.

IS: But, you see, there is another utopia *in* "Sunday Morning,"

4 "On the Road Home," in *Collected Poems* (New York: Alfred A. Knopf, 1954), p. 203.
5 "Sunday Morning," op. cit., pp. 69–70.

which is the woman's bedroom. The great question of the poem, for me, is: why is she getting up so late?

FL: Well, because she's a leisured lady. She doesn't say to somebody: "Look at my hands: they're a man's hands." This is a leisured and "peignoired" female who can sleep in.

IS: I think it is also, though, because the poem is addressed to her by a lover, and is partly a seduction poem. But we are getting too far from "Not Ideas."

FL: No we're not. That's the point: to leave "Not Ideas" strategically. One of the other things one will have to examine is Stevens's early journals: those long walks on weekends. Now, when did Stevens experience the pleasures of the sun, or of the trees, or of the birds and the bees? Not on Monday through Friday, because Monday through Friday he was working at the office. He's very clear on this, in the journals. There are naked statements about how he feels unreal, Mondays through Fridays, and feels himself a physical, sensuous human being on these weekend excursions. The whole experience that he is talking about in "Not Ideas" – this experience of breakthrough – is an experience that occurs outside the office, as it were, and at a specific time of the morning: "The sun was rising at six . . ." If you read Stevens's letters, you find that that's when he got up: to have his shave, take his bath, and so on; and, as he says, to think about supreme fictions. The sun rises at six, whether Stevens gets up at six or not, but the fact is that Stevens gets up at six to get ready to go to work. So, again, this moment is isolated in the way that the weekend is isolated. Another issue here is the weekend as a therapeutic and aesthetic experience of the bourgeois life.

IS: So, in your thinking at the moment, it is primarily the poet's body or experience which allows us, at last, to grab the poem from the isolated world of "Great Books" and reinscribe it on to history?

FL: There are many ways to do it: I prefer to do it that way, to proceed through the poet's "body" (as you put it).

IS: You know, Stevens talks about the relation between poetry and materialism in his essay "Imagination as Value." He says that there will always be those who say that the imagination is of no use to those who live in solitude and misery and terror, but answers: "Of what value is anything to the solitary and those that live in misery and terror, except the imagination?"[6]

FL: He also says that poetry is that which gives life its "savor."[7]

6 "Imagination as Value," in *The Necessary Angel* (New York: Alfred A. Knopf, 1951), p. 155.
7 "The Noble Rider and the Sound of Words," op. cit., p. 30.

When Stevens uses a word like that, you have to take him
seriously, and the hedonistic sense of that word is relevant. It
restores a kind of physical sensation and contact. He's constantly
into that, to go back to "Not Ideas." That's what that poem is
moving around.

IS: Lastly, the question of deconstruction. One of the signs under
which your texts move through the academic world is: "Opponent
of Deconstruction." I've sometimes wondered whether your
unambivalent criticism of de Man is not a displacement of your
very ambivalent relation to Derrida. You're not really sure what
you want to do with Derrida, so you bracket that and deal with de
Man instead, because you *do* seem to know what you want to do
with him.

FL: I'm sure that *After the New Criticism* carries that sign you
mentioned: "Opponent of Deconstruction," but not of Derrida.
And there is a kind of misreading of *Criticism and Social Change* that
suggests that I have created Paul de Man as a villain in the book.
This is incredible to me, because most of the book, after that initial
posing of an impulse in de Man against an impulse of Burke, is
to bring the two together. I don't think that you can understand
what I do with Burke, in the rest of the book, without understanding the accommodation of de Man and Burke.

But, rhetorically, I needed to say something to differentiate the
two in an unambiguous way. There is a certain war on de Man
and de Manians in my work: there is no question about that.
Burke doesn't seem to me to be trapped into those moments that
I describe de Man as being. The thing that the de Manians have
never done – when they wail and whine over this – is to confront
the reading of de Man that's done point by point, blow by blow,
in that opening section of *Criticism and Social Change*. They say I
melodramatize the issue; they say I create a villain: but they never
engage the argument. If I'm wrong about de Man: well, show me.
I've shown you mine, now you show me yours.

IS: What saves Derrida from the fate of American deconstruction?
What do you think the historical use of Derrida boils down to?

FL: His work as a whole has always been concerned with much more
than literariness in the enervated sense. He has globalized
literariness, and his particular strategies for understanding writing
may be useful in understanding political issues. I don't see that
worked out in Derrida's work, but it seems to me that the tools are
there. There is an arsenal of things in Derrida that are useful for
doing work that the Yale group and their students have not yet
done. The students of the Yale group are beginning to be
interested in doing these things, but in so far as they do them they

will do things that de Man not only didn't do, but that his work does not allow.

IS: Barbara Johnson said that the political use of deconstruction was in the analysis of the rhetoric of authority. You would say that it's not enough to analyze the rhetoric of authority, because there is also the question of authority of rhetoric: our rhetoric.

FL: The power of rhetoric. To what end do deconstructors wish to analyze the rhetoric of authority? To show its internal fissures, its slippages, the quicksand on which it stands. What deconstruction does there is what it's been doing with Dickens and whatever. I'm not impressed with that. All it says is: "We can do to this what we do to literary texts." The end of this stuff is the analytical moment when it shows the fissured foundation, and the awe at its own capacity to demonstrate it. The showing of that strikes me as irrelevant from the point of view of praxis and social life. You have to say: "It may be very true that authority stands on an abyss, but in the meanwhile the woman at the A & P is making two dollars an hour and has six kids to feed, and her boss doesn't know that the authority of his rhetoric stands on an abyss and probably wouldn't give a shit if one of us told him so."

IS: But can't Foucault also function as a Marxist analysis, or critical consciousness, washed clean of all need for praxis?

FL: The Foucauldian "New Historicists" do their best to elide the terms "ideology," "class" and "praxis" from their own discourse. They're concerned to show the basis of power or authority in a society, and the way that that power or authority flows through all relations and all discourses. So you get the sense that in any given social formation there is a kind of monolith of power that crushes and makes irrelevant all intention. The political end of *that* kind of criticism strikes me as being madness, if the makers of *Brazil* are right. The possibility of change never arises in the New Historicists. That's where they depart from Foucault. For me to ignore the possibility and reality of change is for me to betray who I am and where I've come from. I'm not going to do that.

J. Hillis Miller

9

J. Hillis Miller

"It is arming people with the power to read, which I see as an absolutely fundamental necessity in order for them to make their way in the present world: this is what I think the study of literature can really do."

J. Hillis Miller was born in Virginia in 1928, and educated at Oberlin College, Ohio, and at Harvard. He is now University Professor in the University of California at Irvine, but until 1986 was Fredrick W. Hilles Professor of English and Comparative Literature at Yale, where this interview was recorded in the middle of April, 1986. During 1986, Miller also served as President of the Modern Language Association of America.

As in the case of Geoffrey Hartman, the important development in Miller's intellectual career was a move from phenomenology to deconstruction, the crucial period was the late 1960s, and the main cause was Derrida. Unlike Hartman, however, the early influence on Miller was not Hegelian phenomenology but the "criticism of consciousness" practiced by Georges Poulet (who was Miller's colleague at Johns Hopkins in the early 1960s).

Also, Miller's attachment to *both* movements has been less qualified than Hartman's, and more systematic. Miller is that which seems contradictory: a systematic deconstructor. His deconstructive method is far from the "ludic" extreme, and it is in all likelihood his clarity as a thinker and writer which has made him as important as anyone – including Derrida – in *disseminating* deconstruction in the United States, over the last two decades. The source of this clarity – and Miller certainly has his difficult moments – is twofold. Most importantly – and Miller's undergraduate degree was not in literature but in science – all of his books on literature and language are attempts to understand and explain an aberrant phenomenon in systematic terms. Second, Miller's field is Victorian literature (with a strong secondary interest in nineteenth- and twentieth-century poetry), and his own work has picked up a good deal of Victorian methodological orderliness, not to say bulk: he prefers to publish long studies at regular intervals and has never, interestingly enough, published a collection of essays. The most impressive parts of his books are often the passages of theoretical exposition (contrary, again, to Hartman, who is best known as a close reader). It is probably this expository leaning that has made Miller the leading polemicist for the Yale School.

In his first three books, Miller combined Poulet's methodology with his own theological preoccupation. *The Disappearance of God* (1963) is a study of De Quincey, Browning, Brontë, Arnold, and Hopkins in their separate struggles to overcome, through explorations of immanence, an increasingly transcendentalizing Christian tradition. These writers do not, on the whole, succeed, but they *do* open the way for the modernist "poets of reality" – Conrad, Yeats, Eliot, Dylan Thomas, and Stevens – who follow them and, according to Miller's account, decide that "if there is to be a God in the new world it must be a presence within things and not beyond them" (*Poets of Reality*, p. 10). Facing the nihilism that is the terminus of any absolute transcendentalism, these writers

> are in the end poets not of absence but of proximity. In their work, reality comes to be present to the senses, present to the mind which possesses it through the senses, and present in the words of the poems which ratify their possession.
>
> (p. 11)

A major focus of interest in these two books, as well as in *Charles Dickens: The World of His Novels* (1965), is on the consciousness of the writer as immanent in his or her texts. In *The Disappearance of God*, literature is defined as "a form of consciousness, and literary criticism is the analysis of this form in all its varieties" (p. vii). In *Charles Dickens*, Miller advises us to reverse the usual causal sequence between an author's psychology and his works, and see those works as *the means by which* the writer apprehends and re-creates himself. Taken together, all of the passages in a novel will reveal a

> profound harmony. Taken all together, all the unit passages form the imaginative universe of the writer. Through the analysis of all the passages, as they reveal the persistence of certain obsessions,

problems, and attitudes, the critic can hope to glimpse the original unity of a creative mind. For all the works of a single writer form a unity, a unity in which a thousand paths radiate from the same center. At the heart of a writer's successive works, revealed in glimpses through each event and image, is an impalpable organizing form, constantly presiding over the choice of words.

(p. ix)

The passages I have been quoting from Miller's early work sound, of course, at the furthest extreme from deconstruction, but I still wouldn't want to draw too strict a division between the two halves of his career, seeing the progress of his thoughts as being rather dialectical. There are, of course, many passages in Miller's later books which consciously jar against his earlier work. In *Thomas Hardy: Distance and Desire*, for example, he says in a preface that we must "put in question certain habitual metaphors" of criticism, including those which "propose to explain the text by something extra-linguistic which precedes it and which is its generative source – the life or psychology of the author, historical conditions at a certain time, some event" (p. vii). Miller has shifted radically from the search for the consciousness behind words to an awareness that there are only more words there:

> The pre-text of a given text is always another text open in its turn to interpretation. There is never an extra-linguistic "origin" by means of which the critic can escape from his labyrinthine wanderings within the complexities of relationship among words.

(pp. vii–viii)

Miller implicitly sets out the course of his own thinking in a 1971 essay on Poulet. The first half consists of praise and exposition, but the second half is a critique of Poulet from the perspective of Derrida. Poulet is interested in the presence of a writer's consciousness in his works, and "this priority of presence in Poulet's criticism is associated, finally, with a tendency to take language for granted in literature" (p. 212). However, near the close of the essay Poulet's work is salvaged again by virtue of the fact that at a certain point it "challenges its own fundamental assumptions" and so *leads directly into* the issues raised by Derrida. Nothing, in deconstruction, succeeds like failure, and Poulet's very *failure* to discover any stable center of consciousness becomes an antithetical contribution to deconstructive theory.

Miller's latest two books, *Fiction and Repetition* (1982) and *The Linguistic Moment* (1985), repeat the pattern of *The Disappearance of God* and *Poets of Reality* in that they apply the same method, in close

sequence, first to a group of Victorian novelists and then to a group
of Romantic and post-Romantic poets. This strange repetition-
pattern testifies to the ability of a powerful critic to renew his own
canon, for himself and for his readers, by re-reading it. In place of
presence and consciousness, the canon is now everywhere inscribed
with trace and undecidability. And criticism, instead of attempting
to ground texts in consciousness, now involves a constant "questioning of the ground" (*The Linguistic Moment*, p. 423).

Miller's leading role in contemporary American criticism has
developed from his willingness to question his *own* grounds, wherever
that questioning may lead. This has taken him against the grain of
his natural intellectual tendencies: from the orderly, established and
systematic towards that which is formless, chaotic, possibly going
nowhere. In other words, Miller has been consistently prepared to
gamble on the shape of the intellectual future, without being forced
to; and so far he has been winning:

> Interpretation, "literary criticism," is not the detached statement
> of a knowledge objectively gained. It is the desperation of a bet,
> an ungrounded doing things with words: "I bet this is a lyric
> poem," or "I bet this is an elegy," or "I bet this is a parable,"
> followed by the exegesis that is the consequence of the bet.
>
> (*The Linguistic Moment*, p. 26)

Imre Salusinszky: When a tradition of a series of interviews is in its
infancy, it is easy for the interviewer to ask his standard questions
in ingenious new ways every time; and it's easy for the interviewees to make sweeping statements and stake out their own
claim (or their own ground, or their claim to a lack of a ground).
But as a tradition of a series of interviews grows older, things
become crowded, and it becomes much more difficult for the interviewer, who seeks various ratios that will make his old questions
seem interesting. And, of course, things become more difficult for
the subject as well.

In an attempt to make this conversation a little different, I
thought that we would first proceed backwards through your
thematics, from the near future (the forthcoming publication of
The Ethics of Reading), back to the late 1950s and early 1960s. Then
we will pause for a few moments – in a kind of timeless realm –
and think about Stevens, and the Stevens poem. At the end, rather
more quickly, we will come forward again in time – but this time
via your biography.

J. Hillis Miller: So it will be biography on the last page, instead of
the first.

IS: That's exactly the difference I'm looking for.
In *The Ethics of Reading*, which has not been published yet, you
talk about ethics as an effect of language, and as the result of a
failure to read, at the allegorical level. I find this a very difficult
idea, and would ask you to flesh it out.

JHM: One way to talk about that would be to place it in the context
– as all of your interviewees are invited to do – of the relation of
literary study to society. My motive for turning to this topic has
no doubt been a response to what's going on all around in the
United States now. That is to say, a turning back to questions
about the relation of literature to history and society. More
specifically, it's a response to reproaches made to deconstruction,
the sort of thing I do: reproaches from both the right and the left,
claiming that it is élitist, that it is concerned only with language,
and that it detaches language from the real world and from any
questions of ethical or, especially, political responsibility.

The shift from politics to ethics is specifically motivated by a
feeling I've had all along that the question of the relation of literary
studies to politics is a little abstract, in a lot of senses. One sense
is that it tends to assume, a little too easily, that there's a direct
political intervention in the act of, let's say, writing a piece of
criticism, or in the act of teaching, or in the act of reading. I have
no doubt that there is a political facet to everything one does in the
university; there is no question about that. But it does seem to me
to be indirect and mediated: it is not as immediately political as,
for example, voting. When I vote, that has an immediate political
effect, and has something to do with electing the candidate or not
electing him. When I teach Stevens, it has a political effect all
right, but it would be much more difficult to identify what that
really is.

One of my feelings about all this talk about literature and
politics is that it may exaggerate the political effectiveness of the
study of literature. What's really making history at this moment,
in the United States? One would, I think, in all candor have to say
that it doesn't have a heck of a lot to do with the study of Stevens,
in any direct way. It's likely to go, say here at Yale, by way of
indirect and uneasy-making relays, where somebody who is in one
of my undergraduate seminars may ten or fifteen years from now
be the Director of the CIA. The question of how his decisions and
actions, in that situation, are affected by my teaching – it's not that
it's not affected – is very hard to identify. For that reason, I said
to myself that I could be more concrete about this by focusing on
what is more direct, and has more to do with one person face to
face with another: namely, ethics. It's obvious that it's possible

then to reproach me for being, again, abstracted from my real political situation, but I think I have an answer to that now, by saying that I'm talking of that by way of the ethical situation.

The question I've asked myself is: to what degree is what we really do as students of literature – read books, write about them, teach them in the classroom – ethically effective and, therefore, politically effective? The notion about the failure to read – reading allegorically – which you correctly point to as fundamental to the argument, might be phrased in a way that would be easier to understand by saying that what fascinates me is the way in which the act of reading – and therefore these other things – does have a margin or remainder or edge, which is not accounted for by all the presuppositions I bring to it, or by my institutional, political or social situation. In that sense, it is really unpredictable, so that there is no way to know ahead of time what it's going to be, when I read, or when one of my students reads. But it *is* something that, in its turn, makes something happen in the real world, and may therefore be effective. Unless literature has that margin, there's not much point to it. If you can fully account for a piece of literature, or for my act of reading, by social/historical determinants, then it melts into historical forces which you might as well study by studying history. The claim that I'm making is for that margin or edge, which I think you can study best and identify best by actually looking at a text. The failure to read, and the reading allegorically, comes in as the presupposition that this act of reading, with its inaugural novelty – this tiny margin of unpredictability – does have its effects in the real world. As I began by saying, they can be exaggerated, but they are not accountable by some kind of direct causality. It's the indirection that fascinates me, and that's what I was trying to define in this notion that there is an ethical component, but not one that in any direct way follows from what the text seems to mean: "misreading" would be a name for that.

I've been teaching the short stories of Thomas Hardy recently, where there's a very good paradigmatic, textually inscribed example of this. This is the book of stories called *A Group of Noble Dames*. It's a frame-story: a men's outing club, stuck in the rain, is reading these stories, and one of Hardy's points is to show that the response of the men to the stories is always in hilarious incongruity with what the stories seem to say: it's always reductive and repressive. It seems to be one of Hardy's points not that the story doesn't produce something, but that it produces something which is incongruous with the meaning of the story. My notion is that that's probably a law. You begin by saying that literature does not make all that much happen; but it does make some things happen, and what it makes happen is something that university administrators ought not to be too reassured about. One of the ethical things a teacher can do is to choose the syllabus, but you can never know what will happen. Take Gandhi's or Yeats's reading of Thoreau: that was real history, but the relationship in each case to what Thoreau was saying was devious.

IS: And "ethics" is the name you give to this margin or edge?

JHM: I begin by borrowing a definition of ethics from Henry James. James defines writing a book as part of the "conduct of life" – a very Emersonian phrase that should please Harold Bloom – and then defines the conduct of life as "things done, which do other things in their turn."[1] No doubt there is ethics alright – it's the field that has to do with conduct and responsibility and choice and decision. The question is: is there an ethical component to reading? My claim is that the act of reading is a thing done which does other things in its turn.

IS: On the subject of reading, in your message to the profession in the "President's Column" of the latest *MLA Newsletter* you say, of the act of reading:

> I suggest that real reading, when it occurs, which may be not all that often, is outside the institution, allergic to institutionalization, private, solitary. I suggest, finally, that real reading, when it occurs, is characterized primarily by *joy*, the joy of reading.
> (p. 2)

That's a very Bloomian quotation, and it's interesting to hear something like that coming both from someone who styles himself as being at the very margins of the profession, and then from someone who is at the very center of the profession. What does it say about the university if the main enabling act that we perform – reading – is necessarily outside it?

JHM: That was an intentionally hyperbolic formulation of what I've just been saying about that margin. Without in any way denying the enormous multiplicity of determinants in the act of reading – reading is never solitary, in the sense that there are all sorts of things looking over my shoulder that do involve my institutional responsibilities, where I come from, family background, everything of that sort – my claim is that there is a little margin, and *that's* the solitariness I was talking about. It's that surprise, and I was trying to give it a name which corresponds to my experience of reading, which is the name "joy." There's something joyful

1 *The Golden Bowl* (London: Macmillan, [1905] 1923), p. xxviii.

about that: it's an exciting moment. Whereas, simply discovering that Milton means what all the other books say about it is not joyful – not for me, at any rate. One wants to read, therefore, against what other people have said.

My difference from Bloom is easy to specify. It has to do with selfhood, as opposed to language. Bloom wants to say that the thing that is performing that act of solitary reading, which is anti-institutional, is something called the ''strong'' self. And it looks as if he believes that that's intrinsic, essential, given to little Harold Bloom before he started reading Hart Crane: a possession that he had from the beginning, something that's inalienable and absolutely solitary. I don't believe that. What I believe is that the myth of the self is no doubt indispensable, but that the reader is a kind of locus where language takes place. It's play within language that makes it unpredictable more than anything that I can claim comes from my initial, intrinsic self. Nobody would have any trouble saying that Harold has these theories because of certain social, psychological and historical backgrounds in himself. It's vulnerable to that, just as no doubt what I'm saying is vulnerable to somebody saying the same thing about me. Nevertheless, there's a difference between saying that this is a linguistic transaction – in which what I bring to the act of reading is a certain power of reading, which is a linguistic power that makes me a locus or a node of something that occurs within language – and saying that I, the strong self with an absolutely unique personality, make the work mean something that's caused by that.

IS: Nevertheless, Bloom's account of the ''joy'' of reading – tied up, as you say, with the realization and development of selfhood – is translatable in an easy, though limited, way into terms of social usefulness: he teaches others how to experience this joy, and how to struggle towards their own voice or selfhood. In your account of the joy of reading as intersections occurring at a node of language, how do *you* make the translation to the social benefit of teaching it?

JHM: That's a good question. I think the danger of the Bloomian account is that it would reinforce the assumption in students that they already have whatever they are going to have, and that graduating from Yale is simply going to authorize them to go on being what they already were when they came here, or to impose the ideology that they had when they came here. That is, it reinforces what is already *the* ideology of Yale undergraduates – in so far as I have been able to identify it – namely that the value of something lies in my power to give the thing value. Bloom fits that ideology. My evidence for that is a little question I ask my section in Literature 120, way back at the beginning. On the very first day, I ask them to write a one-page paper: "Tell me how you would know that you had it right with a work of literature." In so far as there is anything that pervades the answers, it is the claim that "It's right because I say it's right." I find that interesting: these are not students who've studied with Harold Bloom, but it is already Bloom's idea and I think he's simply reinforcing that.

Now, what do I say? I was thinking about this, and trying to formulate my answer. For me, the study of literature is not so much reinforcing as *apotropaic*. It's a demystifying study; it's the most concentrated area where we might be able to recognize the effects of language and learn, in a way, to protect ourselves from its enormous power in actually making us do things and making us make judgments and making history happen in these ways that are devious. It's not the only place to study that, but it's a very concentrated place to study what you might call the effects of ideology on the materiality of history. It is arming people with the power to read, which I see as an absolutely fundamental necessity in order for them to make their way in the present world: this is what I think the study of literature can really do.

IS: I guess that the reason that the students in your first-year section produce naive Bloomian readings is because it is in line with what is truly *the* American religion: of self-improvement, of there being an inner power which can be realized or not realized in the world. You can see it anytime if you flick on the cable TV. And as Bloom himself points out in his seminars, it is the major strain in the native American religions of the nineteenth century: Mormonism and Christian Science.

JHM: Though I would think that there is another strain in the American religious tradition, which is that side of Protestantism which is critical of graven images. This is the anti-ideological side where, by pushing just a step further, you end up somewhere like where I am. Along with that self-improving side – the Emersonian, strong-self side – there is that "I am from Missouri" side, the side that says "Prove it to me" and that tends to be suspicious of large formulations. The trouble with the strong-self side is that it's very easy for it to become Ronald Reagan saying: "The rest of you guys haven't got any guts, so I'm going to decide on my own to bomb Libya."

IS: Which is to view the world as an arena for the manifestation of your own selfhood.

JHM: That's right: "I, Ronald Reagan, the strong self, make this decision to show how macho I am."

IS: These selfhoods can conglomerate into a national selfhood which can be extraordinarily dangerous in its operations.

JHM: And the response to the bombing, at the moment, is apparently largely positive.

IS: "Let's turn Libya into a parking lot!" was one comment I heard from a view on CNN yesterday (I almost said "CBN," where you'd be even *more* likely to hear it).[2]

JHM: Like trying to bomb Vietnam back into the Stone Age. We didn't succeed in doing that, but that was the instinctive motive: the feeling that the strong self ought to be able to go over there and subdue those people. That's the trouble with the *agonistic* model, which I was interested to see Said responding positively to in Bloom.

IS: We were talking about reading in the university: what are the consequences of deconstruction for the university, particularly in terms of curricula and the division of faculties and departments? These seem to be based on a notion of difference that would be threatened by *différance*.

JHM: The consequences would be considerable. They would be different in different universities.

One of the things that struck me about your series of interviews was the way in which each of the interviewees – no doubt I'm doing it – tended to define himself as against all of the others. It's very striking in Bloom, but it's true also for the others. It's a natural move. "I am criticism, and the others are all deconstruction," says Bloom; then Kermode says that the world is full of little Bloomians, but – the pathos of this! – "There are no Kermodians." Those statements strike me as slightly in bad faith, in the sense that Kermode knows perfectly well that he's had an enormous influence: lots and lots of people have read his books. And Bloom says, "I have no followers, I'm all alone," as if there were not thousands of people out there reading him. On the other hand, the group of people you've taken is necessarily parochial. For example, they're all East Coast people. From some other sort of perspective, there might have been other ways of doing it. The other thing that's striking about them is their diversity. Each one of them says, "I'm not like the others," as though they were in some way at the center.

So what I think will be a salutary aspect of your book of interviews is the evidence of this diversity. It's by no means a single operation, and that's an important fact. One of the things that I have learned, and that Derrida stresses, is the heterogeneity or overdetermination of any social situation, such as a single univer-

2 CNN = Cable News Network; CBN = Christian Broadcasting Network.

sity or, even more, higher education in the United States. So when you ask a question like the one you asked a moment ago, one would have to recognize that any single perspective is going to be very partial, that it's an enormous field, that there are people teaching at the University of Kansas, for example. Deconstruction is a good example since, like Marxism, it's diffused all around the country; it's active here, there and everywhere, in one way or another. So you can't locate it at one single place, at Yale. It's going to have different effects in different places, and they will depend on what the local university is like.

Nevertheless, one can say, I think, that one effect would be clearly to break down traditional divisions among the departments. The simplest way to define that is by way of the difference it makes to study a canonical work in juxtaposition with other works in the same national canon, as opposed to studying that same work juxtaposed to works from a different canon. It's not a matter of overturning the canon. It's the effect of teaching *Great Expectations* not in the context of other Victorian novels, but in the context of Roland Barthes' *S/Z*, Freud's "Dora" and so on. That seems to me the institutional politics of deconstruction, as much as anything. It's a different way of reading, but it's also a different assemblage of texts.

To be concrete about this, one could say that one of the really conservative things about Bloom, in his interview and in his work generally, is that it's deeply rooted in the Yale English Department. His canon *is* the Yale English Department canon. You give him a Stevens poem, and he thinks about Whitman. That's OK: "Father Whitman." He's got a sequence which is not much different from the traditional courses in the English Department here. The big traditional courses in the English Department here are English 125, where you do Chaucer, Spenser, Shakespeare, Milton, Pope, Wordsworth – then the canon goes to pieces, no Victorians, some twentieth-century poets; and English 129 – "World Literature" – which begins in Homer and Aeschylus, and includes mostly works which are the traditional "background" texts for the English canon as traditionally conceived. That's still world culture for Harold Bloom. Something happens when you put Stevens side by side with Paul Celan, or Ponge, or Freud (but Bloom's Freud is primarily Freud as an English writer). I would think that one of the major things that deconstruction, as well as other importations of that sort, has done is to move in the direction of making our humanistic culture more genuinely multilingual.

IS: Well, within this broadened and more simultaneous context – in which we can read a poet next to a philosopher, a philosopher by the lights of a poet, place Barthes next to Stevens – what happens to the divisions between the departments? Would they be retained or jettisoned?

JHM: It depends on the university, and I wouldn't have any prescriptions. Another way to put that would be to say that there's no point in throwing out the traditional demarcations of literary history until you've got something that's pretty clearly better. An enormous number of terrible courses have been conducted in the name of some kind of thematic content: "The Beast Myth Through the Ages." I would rather both take and teach a course in "The Victorian Novel": I understand what that means, and think you might get somewhere with that. On the other hand, there probably is some rearrangement going on now of the way things really happen and take place: that is, reading. That's signaled, for example, by the existence of a large number of departments which are either called departments of "Literature" or of "English and Comparative Literature," and which contain another region which is "Literary Theory": that's different from a traditional department of English, which thinks of itself primarily as teaching the canon of English literature. There would be rearrangements of that sort, as well as more team-taught courses and so on. But one would have to go very slowly in doing that.

It's a manifest fact that a great deal of the real philosophy that's been taught recently has been taught out of Philosophy departments. Philosophy departments, by insulating themselves in the very valuable but somewhat limited region of logic and analytical philosophy, have cut themselves off from doing work which then has been picked up by "amateur" philosophers outside, like Paul de Man teaching Hegel. That's a fact of humanistic studies.

IS: Early on in the history of American deconstruction, your polemics (with M. H. Abrams, for example) engaged an assault from the traditional or, if you like, "logocentric" wing of the American academy. Now, as you were saying right at the beginning of our conversation, you are much more engaged with Marxist and New Historicist criticism. I want to read you something from your response, six years ago, to an article in *Critical Inquiry* about you:

> I do think the conservative aspect of deconstruction needs to be stressed. Its difference from Marxism, which is likely to become more sharply visible as time goes on, is that it views as naive the millennial or revolutionary hopes still in one way or another present even in sophisticated Marxism. This millenarianism believes that a change in the material base or in the class structure

would transform our situation in relation to language or change the human condition generally. Deconstruction, on the other hand, sees the notion of a determining material base as one element in the traditional metaphysical system it wants to put in question.

("Theory and Practice," p. 612)

JHM: Did I say that?

IS: Interestingly, this seems to separate you not only from Marxism, but from the whole tradition of criticism from Matthew Arnold to Northrop Frye, which consistently – like the Marxists – imbues criticism with a millenarian, socially revelatory function. It could be said that, after placing reading outside institutional boundaries, you are there cutting deconstruction off as occurring solely *inside* the institution, because you want to separate it from any work for social change.

JHM: By no means. My target, in those remarks, was the Marxist concept of materiality. It was to say that there is something wrong with the power given to the notion of materiality as determining history, and on the basis of that claiming that a change in the material base would therefore lead to social improvement. That was my target, not the notion that whatever we do ought to be socially effective. I happen to take a dim view about the millennium: if it were about to come, we probably would have it already, and things don't seem conspicuously to be getting better, from the social point of view. My belief in the millennium is, like everybody's, a belief in one that's always tomorrow, and it would be the millennium of good readers. I believe that what actually causes the materiality of history is bad reading: this goes back to that claim I was making that teaching reading might make for social improvement by making people good readers. It's so unlikely that we would have a whole nation of really good readers – good reading is so difficult and unlikely to happen – that it's a millennium I don't think is going to occur. That doesn't mean that we oughtn't to work for it, and that *is* what I'm working for: to make my teaching effective, socially, by making good reading occur.

What I mean by the way in which bad reading creates history is very straightforward. Bad reading is always, as Paul de Man says, ideological in the sense that ideology is mistaking the materiality of the sign for the materiality of the signifier. When you think you've got it in that sense – a straightforward correspondence between one and the other – you are likely to do things which result in the materiality of history. This can be very specifically defined: sure, it's the distribution of food, what's in our bodies, whether we get enough to eat, whether we're warmly clothed. More alarmingly, the *real* materiality of history is who gets killed, bombed and so on. The places where ideology intervenes in history have, alas, tended to take the form of a lot of people getting killed. So that when de Man says that texts at a level of allegorical complexity like the *Social Contract* make history happen, to me that means all those people being guillotined in the French Revolution. And that, I think, is too bad. What one might hope to be able to lessen would be the number of people who get murdered not by viruses, but by some mistaken effect of language – the Holocaust being a fantastic example of that. No doubt there were all sorts of economic, social, historical causes of the Holocaust, but one of them has to be what was going on in the minds of those murderers, and that was a fantastic example of a piece of ideology: "We have to get the final solution." That's so unimaginable that it's very hard to think about it or face it, especially because we may be, ourselves, in complicity, at this very moment, in doing something of the same sort. How could we know? It's easy to condemn them, but can we be sure we are exempt from similar effects of ideology? "Let's turn Libya into a parking lot." Is that so different from the Holocaust?

So I would think that the study of literature might have good social effects in eliminating that process. At the moment, the most appalling fact in our historical situation is to live under the threat of nuclear annihilation. Pushing that button that starts the bombs off cannot occur except through language. Talking about it, studying it, trying in some way to demystify it, might be what the study of literature could do to prevent that from happening.

IS: This is what, nowadays, seems to be taken as the progressive social effect of Derrida's insights: the deconstruction of the rhetoric of all authority. However, your discussions with Derrida himself on this point must surely be affected by the fact that, unlike you, he has had serious engagements and affiliations with the hard left, in France. He wouldn't dismiss Marxism, I think, in quite the same way that you do.

JHM: I wanted to go back to say that, though I was quarreling and would quarrel with that specific point within Marxist doctrine, neither then nor now would I in any way dismiss Marxism. I disagree, therefore, with what Harold Bloom says, because unlike him I would see the current development of an indigenous American Marxist thinking – which is very widespread – as a fundamental feature of American university life. Just as the accommodation or appropriation of deconstruction in the United

States is producing something that is specifically American – as Derrida keeps saying, he has more power and influence here than he does in France; deconstruction is really an American thing – so I would say that something is really happening in the United States to Marxist thought that is neither entirely continuous with Marx himself nor with modern French or German Marxism.

I take American Marxism very seriously now, and I would say that the field of action in humanistic and literary studies in the United States now invites or requires a kind of confrontation or dialogue or negotiation of something that may be non-negotiable in the end: between linguistically oriented studies like deconstruction on the one hand, and Marxism or Foucauldianism on the other. That's one of the reasons I'm interested in going to California. I see that as a place where Foucault has always been much stronger than he is here, and as a place having a slightly different kind of political-institutional arena than here: it's where some of the action in this area is going to be. That's not said in a spirit of hostility – "Stupid Marxist" – but rather out of a feeling that those new sociologists of literature have to be confronted. I hope to do that: my "ethics of reading" work is generated by the beginning of that discussion in myself.

IS: In your engagements with historicisms new and old, there are two different arguments that go on in your work. The major one has to do with our inability to get outside language. I'd like to table a few quotations about this. In *The Form of Victorian Fiction*, which is a transition work for you, we hear that "human culture and the imitation of human culture in a novel have the same structure. Both have the nature of language" (p. 140). Many years later, in the *Deconstruction and Criticism* volume, you say that "language . . . thinks man" (p. 224). In *The Ethics of Reading*, against the New Historicism, you say that "the study of literature . . . remains within the study of language." Finally, and most importantly, in *Fiction and Repetition* in 1982 you say that

> A recent skirmisher in the rarefied atmosphere of pure theory argues that criticism went wrong when it became close reading. This, if I may say so, is a major treason against our profession.
> (p. 21)

Now, these quotations locate what is bound to be one of the main things that deconstruction's opponents on the left are going to say against you and deconstruction: that it is only a more sophisticated version of the old New Criticism, which you wrote your Ph.D. under the influence of.

JHM: The dissertation was steeped in Kenneth Burke, which is not quite the same thing as Brooks and Warren. Burke was already, in his influence on me, interested in those social orientations. It was the notion of a work of literature as a strategy for encompassing a situation by means of language which attracted me in Burke, and which I was applying in the dissertation (which has never been published). That would be one answer to what you've said: that the New Criticism is already diverse and heterogeneous, and different people have gotten different things out of it. My New Criticism all along was much more Burke and Empson and G. Wilson Knight: a weird New Criticism, from the point of view of Yale orthodoxy. The second thing to say is that I'm not at all ashamed of that filiation or lineage. If you really understand Kenneth Burke, you don't need Derrida as much.

I was at a conference the other day at Ohio State University, where I was commenting on a paper by Shoshana Felman on some wonderful new work she's doing on testimony. It was a reading of Camus' *The Plague* as a book about the Holocaust. In my comment on it, I was trying to develop this notion that what's strange about Camus' *Plague* is that what was in fact an effect of the Nazis – that is to say, a deliberate ideological-linguistic horror – is allegorized as the plague. So what in fact was a human cause of history is allegorized as something as inhuman as the bacillus that caused the plague. Now, at a certain moment my good friend Terry Eagleton rose up and denounced me for being an idealist, for saying that language causes history. It's exactly the question you've been asking: and that's what I'm trying to think out.

One way to think it out would be to say that, no doubt, there are all sorts of non-linguistic things that make history happen. If there is a great earthquake in California, that's not caused by human thinking or language. Nor was the plague; nor is the AIDS virus, though the spread of the virus has a socio-linguistic component. So there are lots of things that happen without language. However, I would extend the range of language much further than Eagleton. I would say, for example, that the region of economics that has to do with money and the valuation of things is really linguistic, if you mean by "linguistic" having to do with signs and the power that signs have. That's what Marx says. Money, economics, is in the region of the study of signs, and also of the mystification we get into when we mistake the materiality of the sign for the materiality of the signifier. That's the fetishism Marx talks about. So that my response to Eagleton would be just what I was trying to say in that passage you read about materiality. *He's* being an idealist, by idealizing what are effects of language, in the broad sense, as though they were power structures that had the

nature of earthquakes: they don't. Wall Street is not an earthquake; it's a whole lot of people acting in terms of something that
has the structure of language.

I would then go back to say that the study of literature is not
supposed to be the study of everything: it's the study of literature.
It is not that the study of the historical surrounding of a work of
literature is not very important, but the proof of the pudding
comes when you put that work of literature within that context;
and that means reading the work. My difficulty with some of the
work of the New Historicists – work that I greatly admire for its
life and energy and commitment – is when they come to the actual
work of reading the text that they're talking about. Stephen
Greenblatt, for example, has a marvelous essay about herma-
phroditism in the sixteenth century, and at the end, in a rather
perfunctory way, he says that this explains Shakespeare. I'm
prepared to believe that it explains a lot in Shakespeare, but he
doesn't really show that. Or there is another admirable book, by
Catherine Gallagher, which is about my field, the Victorian novel.
It is absolutely wonderful on the social background of Victorian
novels. My problem comes when she talks about Mrs Gaskell, for
example, and it seems to me that she's prepared simply to
summarize the plot and to talk about the people as if they were real
people. That would be a concrete example of what I meant by
saying that the immediate frontier of literary study is trying to
bring those two things together. What would happen to Catherine
Gallagher's hypotheses about the Victorian novel if she had really
"read" the Elizabeth Gaskell novels that she talks about, in the
sense of the close rhetorical analysis of Gaskell's figures of speech
and so on? Something would happen, but something would also
happen to my reading of Elizabeth Gaskell when it's put in her
context. So I'm going to learn a lot from those people.

IS: You've partly answered my next question, which has to do with
the second locus of your argument with historicism. In *The Ethics
of Reading* you talk about the kinds of connections which the New
Historicists make between literary texts and history as being shot
through with fairly naive and old-fashioned metaphors to do with
mirroring and reflection. Does that connection *have* to be a naive
one, or could we insert a notion of *différance* into the relation
between the text itself and the text of history?

JHM: Yes, that can be done, but I think that it's difficult and
requires much methodological sophistication as well as much
learning. There's no doubt that it's going to remain controversial,
but that will be the life of doing it. What would really happen to
Catherine Gallagher's hypothesis about Mrs Gaskell had she done

a deconstructive reading of the actual text? I've done a little bit of that with *Cranford*: Mrs Gaskell is very interesting from that point of view. I think something would happen, but it would make immensely more complicated the models of the relationship between the text and history. That is what I was talking about: those metaphors of text and context, which are metonymic or synecdochical, or all of those images of reflection. If it isn't that, then what could it be?

It's here, I think, that that notion of heterogeneity and overdetermination might be valuable. The methodological model here might be Freud. One of the things that I've learned from Freud – take one of the great case-histories like "Dora" – is that he's doing something, in a sense, infinitely easier: all he's trying to do is account for pathological symptoms in one patient. Dora's got these problems, symptoms, and comes to see him. By the time you get through, you have this immensely complicated network of details, which he speaks of, specifically, as overdetermined. You have all those footnotes, where he's taken it back to the original thing and then he says, "No, it wasn't that she was in love with Herr K., it was really that she was in love with Frau K.": there is an infinite regression in the identification of the causal thing. All those great images like that of the trains that come to a switching, the place of crossing, and so on. The methodological model is immensely complicated. It recognizes the heterogeneity, the multiple meanings that a given sign or symbol can have. This is just to account for one single person and her problems. If you start trying to do that with history, I think you have to be prepared for something that's even more complicated, and you have to be a little tentative about your account (avoiding the oversimplification, for example, of those institutional histories that say that all English departments are so-and-so).

IS: Back a further step, into your early deconstructive phase. It was concentrated, to a large degree, on the notion of unreadability or undecidability: the impossibility of reading, in the sense of determining a univocal meaning. In *Fiction and Repetition*, you say that your fundamental premise "is that the specific heterogeneity of a given text can be exactly defined, even though a univocal meaning cannot be justified by the text" (p. 231). This is still very much present in your latest book, *The Linguistic Moment*, where you say that "any cultural expression in our tradition, such as a literary text, is undecidable in meaning, though the choices the text offers (among which the reader cannot except arbitrarily decide) may be precisely defined" (p. 54). Here we come up against what is properly a philosophical problem, and could easily slide into fruitless Platonic speculations about whether there is only, really, one thing, or whether there are numerous or multiple things. By which I mean to ask: how can we determine the range of undecidability, if we can't determine any single meaning within that range? Wouldn't that range, taken as a whole, constitute a univocal meaning in itself anyway? And what allows us to determine *any* of the possibilities of meaning?

JHM: I see the problem, but I don't see this as a pointless paradox, or as regressive in the sense that I'm really saying there is only one meaning. My targets in those statements were two. One of them is, in a way, personal to me, or to my situation in criticism: namely, the notion of organic meaning. In the New Criticism that I learned, and especially in relationship to the nineteen-year dialogue with Earl Wasserman that I had at Johns Hopkins, it was the thing that he kept insisting on. So there may be something personal or parochial in my wanting to undo that idea. On the other hand, my target was all of those people who seem to have read one essay by Derrida – the one about "Structure, Sign and Play" – and who have misunderstood what's said there about play. All they know, or think they know, is that deconstruction says you can make the text mean anything you want. What I want to say is very simple, and I don't see how anybody could argue with it: complicated and heterogeneous though the field of a given text is, it nevertheless is finite. For all practical purposes, you can identify what the major components of the possible meanings are, within which any reading would fall.

The only way in which I would modify a little bit, now, what I said there, would be to emphasize the feeling of a kind of virtual infinity in the experience of meaning. It's not that everything is in there, but that you can always return, even to a poem or novel that you've taught over and over again, and find something else there: another way to talk about it that you hadn't really fully talked about before. I say "virtual" because it's not infinite: *Great Expectations* has only so many words, only so many themes; it places itself in a certain way within the repertoire of possible themes in Western literature, but not all of them. It's finite, in that sense. On the other hand, it's big enough so that even the same person can go on teaching it all his or her life and go on finding new things in it. And I think that needs to be emphasized, too. My reading is controlled by the text – it's not a wanton imposition on my part – but at the same time is not easily limitable.

IS: It's interesting that you mentioned Wasserman, because what I meant to say before was, when you say that the specific heterogeneity of a given text can be exactly defined, I want to ask you what separates that from the determination of a univocal meaning, since even the most logocentric of the New Critics never said "This poem means X." They, too, would always define a field of meaning that was heterogeneous. Their point, of course, was that poetry, unlike everyday discourse, was a structure of tensional irony which could contain contradictory meanings. In other words, the argument about undecidability feeds back into the criticism of deconstruction as "just the New Criticism writ large."

JHM: I think I could specify the difference. Empson and Burke are closest to deconstruction, among the New Critics. I have an easier time distinguishing myself from other forms of the notion of organic unity, let's say Wasserman's: he wanted everything to fit into some kind of spatial array. But, however much emphasis there is in Empson – let's say in *The Structure of Complex Words* – on diversity, and even irreconcilability, it's always within a single *structure* of incompatibilities, where all of these things are related to each other in some dialectical way. At least hypothetically, this would allow for a kind of synthesis, even though it would be the bringing together of lots of diversity and irony and so on. The notion in deconstruction is that the meanings between which one cannot decide are asymmetrical. That is to say, there isn't anything you can do to bring them together. They're not open to organic unification; they're not open to dialectical synthesis. The term "heterogeneity" has a different meaning, in the two regions. That's what I see in works of literature and that, I think, is what de Man or Derrida would be saying about works of literature, that differs from the New Criticism.

IS: Another difference between you and the New Critics is that their whole point was to separate this heterogeneity off, not as a language effect, but as a *poetic* effect. Language was divided in two: you had poetry, where this heterogeneity, albeit limited in its free play, was allowed to take place; and then you had the "everyday" or "normal" use of language. That's not a move made in deconstruction. Or is it? After all, you don't read the texts of the world in this way. When you receive a letter from the University of California at Irvine, offering you an endowed Chair and outlining the terms of the offer, you don't determine that *that* text is undecidable.

JHM: I look at it pretty carefully!

IS: Looking for the fissures.

JHM: Looking for the problems and fissures. No, on the one hand you're right: one of the controversial aspects of deconstruction that has been attacked all around is the blurring of that notion of sequestered literature. On the other hand, one of your interviewees attacks de Man because de Man wants to talk about literariness. And he does, but it's obvious that what de Man means is that there is a feature of language which you can call "literariness" – it might be given other names: rhetorical effects, places where figurative language interferes with straightforward grammatical meanings – and that effect of "literariness" *is everywhere*. It is a feature of language in general. One studies literature, as such, because that's a very concentrated place to investigate this. But what you're investigating is a universal feature of language, which would contaminate even that letter from the President of the University of California, in one way or another. I hope not in such a way that they don't pay me.

IS: The criticism that an organicist would bring to bear on your notion of the impossibility of determining univocal meaning would be that it leads to a kind of nihilism (one of the terms, I think, that Abrams used in one of your early engagements with him). What interests me about your treatment of the criticism that deconstruction is a kind of nihilism is that you're there waiting for it: nihilism is one of the most persistent themes of all your work, and is by no means limited to the period after your engagement with Derrida. I'm thinking, particularly, of the first chapter of *Poets of Reality*, which is about nothing if not the question of nihilism. In the "Critic as Host" essay, which is responding to Abrams's criticism on this score, you say that nihilism is not the opposite of metaphysics, but is inherent in metaphysics, and that deconstruction is the untangling of the inherence of nihilism in metaphysics, and vice versa. You say that deconstruction doesn't escape from this inherence, but moves joyfully back and forth within it (pp. 230–1). That's a fascinating description of the activity of deconstruction.

JHM: The context of my remarks is Nietzsche and Heidegger, and their analysis of nihilism as a feature of metaphysics. One might think of passages where Heidegger says that people think that nothing isn't anything, but in fact it's an occulted revelation of being. What I would want to say, however, is simultaneously two things. On the one hand that, although it cannot really do so, deconstruction is an attempt to move as far as possible outside that oscillation within metaphysics between metaphysics and nihilism, and to see it (although it's impossible) from the outside. Or, to put this another way: to demystify the spookiness of those terms. I take it that that's what Derrida means when he talks about the joyful aspect of this: it's not necessary to see the experience of nothing as being apocalyptic.

On the other hand – and this "other hand" is very important – there is an aspect of what happens to me when I read Stevens or Shelley or Dickens, which is the experience of something to which I could give no name; which, in that sense, is nothing, but which at the same time seems to be the encounter with something other than language which is woven into language and causes these effects. It is impossible to talk about this without mystification, without the misleading implication that you're falling back into some kind of religiosity. Nevertheless, that's the way it seems to me. You could say that what I have against the reproach of nihilism is that it's saying that deconstruction is absolutely empty, anti-religious, doesn't take anything except language seriously, and so on: that is so foreign to my actual experience of literature that it makes me angry, both as a mistake about what nihilism is, and as a mistaken understanding of what I try to do.

IS: I want to come back to some of those things in a moment, but not before taking another chronological step back. With Lentricchia, we were talking about the way that everyone has some particularly critical moment of self-doubt in their work, after which a complete change of direction takes place. It wouldn't take a genius to place the crisis, in your case, during the period in which you successively rewrite your important essay on Poulet, producing a final version around 1971 that contains a sort of supplement on Derrida. Over this period, you move from being a Poulet-influenced critic of consciousness, and of the presence of reality in consciousness, to being a Derrida-influenced critic of language, and of the absence of reality in language. Was the influence of Derrida a sudden, revelatory moment in your intellectual life?

JHM: No. I would say two things about that. The greatness of Poulet is to carry his own presuppositions to the point where they almost turn back on themselves. There are important essays in his work where consciousness becomes narrowed down to an infinite point and sort of dissolves. So I was prepared for that. But I was also prepared in another way. The very powerful response, on my part, to Poulet, who was tremendously exciting for me to read – there's no way to account for that, it's very personal – was a response to problems that I found apparent in Burke and Empson during that earlier stage. So that I came to consciousness as a solution to problems that had to do with language. You might say that I never really solved those problems.

The reading of Derrida is a good proof of the point that you can never tell which books are going to be decisive for your life. It wasn't that anybody told me that I should read Derrida, though Eugenio Donato probably had mentioned his name. But I remember very distinctly that I just picked up the issue of *Critique* which had the early version of *Grammatologie*, started reading it, and thought it was wonderful – just as I'd thought that Poulet was wonderful. There obviously were reasons for that. It was at that moment that I was prepared to go back to where I was at the beginning. It seemed very personally motivated, as a solution to problems in my own work.

The attraction of Poulet for me, in part, was that I thought that the New-Critical method – even the Burkean or Empsonian one – was not all that effective as a way to deal with the works that I had been hired to teach, namely Victorian ones. Poulet allowed me to write essays on, say, Matthew Arnold. "Dover Beach" is not all that great a poem, from the point of view of Brooks and Warren. But Matthew Arnold, *pace* Harold Bloom, strikes me as a very interesting author, especially in those late religious books. He's open both to a Pouletian and to a deconstructive reading, which is why he gets back into *The Linguistic Moment*.

IS: Let's terminate this backward movement with *Poets of Reality* where, as I say, the big question is nihilism, and where you say that "If there is to be a God in the new world it must be a presence within things and not beyond them" (p. 10): it must be an immanence, rather than a transcendence. I would use this point as a way of merging into your biography, and asking you about your religious upbringing. To what extent was your attachment to the criticism-of-consciousness school, in those early years, tied up with the theological question that is so central in your early books?

JHM: Very little, in any explicit way, because I'd long since stopped going to church. My specific American upbringing was certainly different from any of the others of your interviewees. It was rural, and southern. Both of my parents came from Virginia. My father was an ordained southern Baptist minister who later became a university president. I've a brother who is a Presbyterian minister. I've a grandfather who taught men's Bible class in a small country church in Virginia for forty years, and knew the Bible backwards and forwards. Although I went to Sunday School until I was a senior in high school, one of my resentments about American Protestantism is that you don't get taught anything. I can find Habakkuk in the Bible, and I know how to make soap models of houses in Palestine, and that's about what I learned in twelve years of going to Sunday School. There was very little real teaching about what's going on in the Bible, and that's an interesting fact. So, in one sense I had a religious upbringing, and in another sense I didn't. But what I *was* taught was a rigorous respect for truth, and some kind of vague assumption that the truth might be dark, ominous, not at all reassuring.

I was pretty much on my own in college, and later on, but I

think that some sense of a connection between the study of
literature and philosophical or religious concerns has been with me
all along. I remember Paul de Man saying that religious questions
are the most important ones, and I'm prepared to agree with that.
No matter how negative your conclusions about them might be,
those are important questions, and to detach the study of literature
from them seems to me a mistake.

IS: In *Poets of Reality*, nihilism is cured by rejecting transcendence,
and merging mind with world, where something spiritual and
saving is still to be discovered. What about now? What is the
theology of deconstruction? Hasn't one, in fact, moved back to a
transcendence? If language thinks us, rather than us thinking
language, then who made language?

JHM: Well, what are we, from this point of view, but language, or
a locus of language? The opposition that I was working on back
then was between transcendence – in the sense of some kind of
Platonic never-never land – and immanence, and you might say
that the development since then has been in the direction of seeing
that immanence as a linguistic one. This involves seeing literature
not as the naming of some kind of presence in the physical world
– as in the reading that I gave of Stevens or Williams in *Poets of
Reality* – but rather as the exploration of some kind of otherness
that is located within language itself: another kind of immanence.
It's no less a rejection of any kind of transcendence. Particularly
if you define language as something that is within me, when I read
the poem, because I become the locus where the poem is read,
interpreted and so on – rather than thinking of language as
something that's out there, beyond me, somewhere else.

IS: I guess that the question that Bloom might ask here would be:
then what gets meaning started in the first place? What gets
language started? How do you avoid some kind of transcendental
account of how meaning originates?

JHM: You can stay within language on that. That's the very point,
I take it, of Derrida's notion of *différance* or trace: that language,
from any conceivable human point of view, is something that is
always already there; and that the lure of getting before it is an
impossible lure. All you do is get further and further back towards
a place where language is already there. That doesn't make it
transcendent; it means that we are, for better or for worse, within
language from the beginning, and can't get outside it.

IS: We come now to Stevens. (But have we ever been outside him?)
The one thing I don't have to justify in this series of interviews is
having chosen a Stevens poem as an example. It is extraordinary
how many of my interviewees have been formed by Stevens. And,

in fact, he has accompanied you every step of your way. In *Poets of Reality*, it's Stevens who helped you out of nihilism, by showing how the confrontation with nothing can be a supreme victory, since nothing is something: Being (pp. 278–9). And he's also there in every step of your path through deconstruction. From being the poet of grounding in reality, he accompanies you into the vertigo of language, and becomes the poet of ungrounding, of groundless-ness, of *mise-en-abyme* and abyss. Here, at the end of this series, I want to ask you what I asked Frye at the beginning: what is the quality in Stevens that makes him a companion of so many theoretical critics?

JHM: Not de Man. I remember him saying that he'd never been able to figure out Stevens. He obviously didn't like him very much.

IS: Neither does Said.

JHM: Neither does Said, and though Said and de Man are different kinds of non-Americans, that may be the explanation. That wouldn't explain Kermode, although I think that part of Kermode's problem with Stevens has followed from the fact that he's from the Isle of Man. He talks about Larkin, in his interview, and I think he's right to say that Larkin is hard for a non-Englishman to read. I admire Larkin, but I don't have an immediate rapport with it.

For many of us Americans, the obvious fact about Stevens is that here is a twentieth-century American poet who didn't sell out to England and become an English citizen, or do the worse thing that Ezra Pound – who is clearly part of world literature – did. Stevens is very provincial. You read it, and it's terrific: it's like Paul Valéry or Goethe or something, but he worked in Hartford, Connecticut. Therefore, with an easy conscience, I can do two things at once: I can read a local poet, who writes about the thin men of Haddam – which is right up that road, across the Connec-ticut River – and at the same time know I'm doing something that isn't less important than reading Plato. That may be part of it.

Also, it's clear that he's especially open to academic criticism. My fascination with and admiration for William Carlos Williams is exactly the reverse: that Williams is so resistant to intellectualiz-ing. He is a very great poet, but difficult for somebody trained in abstractions. I can deal with ideas, and the thing itself, and so on – no problem – but what do you say about "The Red Wheel-barrow" or about a poem that just describes a sycamore tree?

IS: This particular poem isn't one that you've ever given an exten-sive reading to, although, interestingly, in *Poets of Reality*, you use it as a kind of motto for the criticism-of-consciousness approach:

"The poem is 'not ideas about the thing but the thing itself,' part of the world and not about it" (p. 9). What would you do with the poem now if, for some reason, you *had* to produce an essay on it?

JHM: Since I knew that you were going to ask me this, I've read it a little, which means that if I really gave you an answer it would take another hour and a half. I can perhaps differentiate, a little bit, the reading I would give from the reading that your other distinguished interviewees have given. It struck me as interesting, some of the things that they didn't talk about. One would be the weirdness of the title – a weirdness that I was prepared, in *Poets of Reality*, not to worry too much about: I just appropriated the phrase, and did what I wanted with it.

What is it? It's not a complete sentence, and just sort of hangs there: "Not Ideas about the Thing but the Thing Itself." It's the label for the poem. Does it name the poem? Is the poem not ideas about the thing, but the thing itself? And what would that mean? Or does it name the experience that the poem records, which would be rather different? Or does it simply say: "I wish I could have access to, or write a poem that was, not ideas about the thing but the thing itself"? Is it a kind of wish, or a hypothesis? There's obviously no way to know. The poem doesn't give you any support.

Secondly, I would say at this point that the word "thing" is a pretty pregnant word here. Again, it's a little hard to know what he means by "the thing." Does he mean, by "thing," the sun? Does he mean the scrawny cry? In what sense is a scrawny cry a thing? Either to call the sun a thing, or to call the scrawny cry a thing, doesn't quite seem right. The sun is not something that one normally thinks of as a thing. I would be inclined to move in the direction of emphasizing that word "it," which occurs over and over again, and which has a clear referent: the scrawny cry. "He knew that he heard *it*,/A bird's cry . . ." But then it keeps coming back: "*It* was not from the vast ventriloquism/Of sleep's faded papier-mâché . . . *it* was a chorister . . . *it* was like . . ." By the time you've got to the end of those "its," the "it" has detached itself from that cry, and has become a kind of name for "the thing itself." I would think that, in fact, "it" could be demonstrated that he's using that word "thing" in its full etymological and historical complexity, as a name for that which is manifested by the rising of the sun.

None of the other interviewees has said that this is a poem about the appearance of something out of hiddenness, out of occultation: the sun; the cry; spring; the earliest ending of winter; and the poet waking up out of sleep, coming into consciousness. Those are all, metaphorically, said to be like one another, and I take it that they're all forms of appearance which are related to the thing itself, whatever that is: some kind of "it." A "thing," in the sense of a gathering together, as in a medieval assemblage of people; a "thing" in the sense of some substratum which is hidden and never appears.

I also found it interesting that nobody took note of another fact about the poem, which is the synaesthesia: the way in which a visual thing is expressed in terms of a sound thing. The bird's cry announces the rising of the sun, so that there's a lateral metaphor which says "a chorus," a great lot of people singing a great Bach chorus, the "B Minor Mass," "is like" the appearance of the sun. This will allow me to get in a lick at Harold Bloom: that reminds me not of "our father Walt Whitman," but of Goethe, and that great opening of the second part of *Faust* where the sun rises as a great racket, as a loud noise. There is precisely the same displacement from sight to sound, and it clearly has something to do with the un-nameability, in literal language, of the appearance of the sun. You can't look the sun in the eye, and you can't name it as such, so instead of naming that you name this great chorus. Said, with all his knowledge of music, missed what I take the "chorister whose c preceded the choir" to be: that little pitch-pipe noise that you hear in an acappella choir; the muted, soft, scrawny "c" you hear before the whole noise begins. That figure here is the bird's cry, which announces the appearance of the sun, which is blinding and deafening. That mixture of senses is fundamental to the poem, because it is a lateral displacement that is an expression of the other one, the displacement from this hidden "thing" or "it" to any manifestations or metaphors of it. Hostile as Said is to Stevens, he's got hold of something with that notion of what he calls "tinkliness": so many of Stevens's poems are fragile, evanescent. This is a poem about thresholds, and it says in effect that "it" – the cry that has become all these other things – is a new knowledge of reality just at that threshold moment before the sun rises. That's when you really learn something about reality. Once the sun has risen above the horizon, and the chorus is singing full blast, you're in the ordinary world, where you have only ideas about the thing. The thing itself takes place at that point: the earliest ending of winter.

Also, nobody worried about "panache." I can tell you what a panache is, if you don't know. It's very specific: it means a tuft of feathers, as on a helmet. It's from the Italian *pennacchio*, which is from the Latin *penna*: a feather. Quoth the dictionary. Only secondly does it mean flamboyant or flagrant behavior. So that when he says that "The sun is rising at six,/No longer a battered panache above snow," he must have been reading the dictionary. He must mean the sun rising as if it were that tuft of feathers on a helmet. So there is a latent personification of the sun as though it were that giant on the horizon that he talks about in "Primitive Like an Orb." The seeing of the sun as a person is another version of that displacement from sight to sound, in the sense that it's both a revelation – something we can understand – and another covering-over, in the sense that prosopopoeia is an inadequate figure. The references that people made to "The Snow Man" seem to me appropriate, because if the "battered panache above snow" is a helmet with a tuft of feathers on it, it's a displacement of that famous snowman. That's all I have to say. You've made me interested in the poem: maybe I'll write about it.

IS: Your discussion was so clear that I didn't even feel the need to interrupt. Lastly, a couple of biographical questions. Where did you spend your childhood?

JHM: I was born in Virginia. Then, my father was a graduate student at Columbia, and I lived a whole winter on Riverside Drive. I was an academic child, in the sense that I was born while my parents were in graduate school, which put an end to my mother's graduate career. My wife was born in New Haven while her father was a graduate student here, which put an end to *her* mother's career. (As would not necessarily happen now, which is an interesting historical fact.) *Our* first child was born when I was at Harvard, so there's a tradition of that.

I lived first in Lewisburg, Pennsylvania: at Bucknell, where my father was Dean of Men. He got a Ph.D. in Psychology under John Dewey. His dissertation was on "The Practice of Public Prayer": it was a pragmatic, Deweyan interpretation of prayer which said that if it works, socially, it's good: never mind whether God answers the prayer. Then I lived in upstate New York, which is where I was really in the boondocks. It was a town of fifty families, and I went to a one-room school. Then high school outside Albany, New York, and on to college at Oberlin, in Ohio.

IS: Isn't that where Barbara Johnson went?

JHM: Somewhat later.

IS: A couple of minutes after.

JHM: Then to Harvard for graduate work, where I learned mostly from the other students. And then my real education began at Johns Hopkins, as a teacher: that was where I was really formed, by Poulet and Wasserman. For all practical purposes, I am still a Hopkins man: my idea of what you do, in our profession, is a Hopkins one, not a Yale or Harvard one.

IS: It is a good thing that an Australian is doing these interviews, because it is necessary to be quite without tact, and Australians are naturally gifted in this regard. When I first met you – which was, as it happens, in Australia – I noticed that you do not have the complete use of both arms. The reason I ask you what is the source of that is that it may well have had a determining effect upon making you more bookish as a child.

JHM: Unfortunately for your hypothesis, it was later. I was 21 years old, and it was polio: one of the last epidemics. I was married, at graduate school, and was in Maine, staying in my wife's family's summer place there. There was a small disease going around the neighborhood, which was polio. I was the only person who got any paralysis from it. I was very lucky that it was only the one arm.

It certainly had an effect on my life. My wife was a tremendous help. She prodded me in the direction I would have gone already, which was an absolute determination to work hard and get ahead in the world. It was something I already had, but it reinforced the feeling that, whatever you do, you ought to do it with your whole heart. You should take it as far as you can go, and be damned to the consequences for your ambition.

Really interesting work, in any field, involves crossing frontiers, and in a way defying authority. The serious illness at that stage of my life reinforced that. The dissertation I wrote at Harvard was completely un-Harvard. My director, Douglas Bush, detested Burke, primarily because he has a bad style and uses the editorial ''we,'' but also because he was theoretical. I was tolerated there, but writing the dissertation was in no way reinforced by the department which I found myself in. That's also been a feature of my time here at Yale. The thing that frightens me about Yale is that it has institutionalized and accommodated me so well. Everybody has been so nice to me!

IS: That brings up my last biographical question. Apart from an obvious desire to be nearer to Australia, what are the *intellectual* reasons for your decision to move to California?

JHM: The primary motive was intellectual, or professional. It's hard to define both in ways that would be fair to Yale, and how it's been to me, and at the same time be not *too* nice about Yale. I wouldn't be leaving Yale if I were entirely happy here. One way to define this might be to say that, although the sort of thing I do has been very cordially received here, I have the feeling that we've gone just about as far as we can go at Yale, with deconstruction. It might, in fact, fare better here if these older people were gone. I'm 58, and what I feared about staying was that I would be in a Yale which, over the next twelve years, would be less and less intellectually stimulating for me. Whereas the risks involved in going out to California are unpredictable. I can't tell where my work is going to go, and I feared that staying here it would go on being the same. I have the feeling that if I came back to Yale in ten, twenty, or thirty years it would still be here, and still be essentially the same. There's a massive intellectual inertia here that makes it a wonderful university, but which also makes it hard to do anything with. Whereas Irvine – ten, or twenty, or thirty years from now – is going to be different. Twenty years ago it was just a cow-pasture; twenty years from now it may be a cow-pasture again. Let's hope that that won't happen: but you see what I'm saying. I also have the feeling that there has already been some displacement of intellectual action to the West Coast.

IS: This is the end of a journey for me, indeed of an education. Where better to wash up – after a series that has been so concerned with questions of professionalism and the university – than at the feet of the President of the Modern Language Association of America? Who better to award the ribbons to the major prize-winners, to say nothing of the pen-and-ruler sets for the runners-up?

JHM: I would say two things about the interviews as a whole. Your enterprise is a political one or a social one, and one of the dangers of the assemblage that you have and some of the things that are said – including by you – would be to give Frye a little too much centrality, as our father. All honor to Frye, but there would be something conservative about that, and about saying that everything in American criticism derives from Frye. I don't think that's the case, at least in the sense of saying that Frye's own work now – I'm agreeing with Kermode here – is broadly effective. It has diffused itself. I like Frye as a practical critic, but the grand synthetic stuff, in the *Anatomy of Criticism*, is something I've never been able to read. I like Frye, for example, on Dickens, or on Wallace Stevens. But, at least for me, Frye has not had that importance.

The second thing to say, thinking of Bloom, is that, in so far as Bloom's own interview would lend reinforcement to that picture which your interviews tend to give, it is the most amazing piece of misunderstanding. The real precursor for Bloom is T. S. Eliot: anybody can see that. It's not Frye at all. Part of the strategy of his interview is to name it as Frye, because that's an easy person to be obligated to. The real person he was obsessed with at the beginning, and continues to be obsessed with, is the man he calls "the abominable Eliot." That's a much more interesting history. For all of us, when we were going to graduate school, the really looming figure was T. S. Eliot. If you wanted to make your way, you had to do something different from Eliot. And if you were Bloom, at Yale, how did you do this? You wrote your dissertation on Shelley. A more gentle way of putting this is to say that it's another example of heterogeneity. The actual course of the development of American, English (Kermode) and Canadian (Frye) literary criticism is, in fact, more complicated than a simple scheme that would say, "Here was Northrop Frye, who initiated something, and everybody is a tributary to him."

The final thing to say is that these interviews are already historical, in the sense that the people you've interviewed – including the younger ones, like Barbara Johnson and Frank Lentricchia – are already well established. What interests me, on the other hand, is the young trees that are growing up underneath the established ones. And that's a little less predictable. What's really interesting is the question of what's going to happen next: who those people are, where they are, and what they will use out of all this. I don't see any clear indications about that, beyond the sense that there surely is tremendous strength in that New Historicism, *and* tremendous strength in deconstruction.

IS: The emphasis on Frye may be to some degree a result of my own obsession – but, then, in your company there is no need to apologize for imposing one's little, marginal obsession on the world. Actually, if there's a peculiarity in your work in the 1960s, I find – from the point of view of this obsession – that you are straining not to quote from Frye. What's that all about?

JHM: I've given you one answer to it, which is that I didn't find the paradigmatic side of Frye attractive, so I resisted it, for better or for worse, much more than I would have resisted Eliot. I don't know why that is.

I think that the interview with Frye is a wonderful interview. Others have pointed to the wit and the irony. We were together in the abortive enterprise of trying to produce a rival to the *Norton Anthology* for a number of years, so I would see Frye fairly often. He was absolutely wonderful. I remember he looked down at his shoes at one point, and said: "Yes, we'll really sell *big* in Texas!"

As for my resistance to Frye: I needed to make space for something else. One of the reasons for my reservations was in no way Frye's fault. I have been for a long time an editor of *ELH*, and there was a period during the tremendous influence of Frye when every manuscript that I opened up said, "You will notice that I am using the categories of Northrop Frye." I'm sure that Norrie was not all that happy about it either, this feeling that you got a long way just by adopting that seasonal pattern and the various generic categories. That side of Frye didn't seem to me to facilitate reading of the quality that Frye himself performs.

Unlike Kermode, I would say that, if somebody said "You must spend the next month reading Northrop Frye," I would be much more interested in reading the books which simply work out the implications for *actual* readings – of Shakespeare or whomever – of the presuppositions that came in the great revelation. The insights in these readings are related to Frye the systematizer, but not predictably. That has always seemed to me a good example of an important disjunction. You can read Georges Poulet, and figure out what it is that you're supposed to talk about and look for, but that is not going to make it possible to write an essay anything like as good as any of Poulet's. You can read Derrida from one end to the other: but try to do what he does! What either critic sees in the works they read is not predictable from the schemas that you would work out on the basis of asking "What's archetypal criticism?" or "What's deconstruction?" That's one of the reasons that it's a mistake to try to do criticism on the basis of answers to such questions.

IS: Well, I'm glad that a series of interviews in which Frye has been overemphasized has ended with a long discussion of Frye.

Selected bibliography

Jacques Derrida

Speech and Phenomena, translated by David B. Allison, Evanston, Northwestern University Press, 1973.

Glas, Paris, Editions Galilee, 1974

Of Grammatology, translated by Gayatri Chakravorty Spivak, Baltimore, Johns Hopkins University Press, 1976.

Edmund Husserl's "The Origin of Geometry": An Introduction, translated by John P. Leavey, Stony Brook, N. Hays, 1977.

Writing and Difference, translated by Alan Bass, Chicago, University of Chicago Press, 1978.

Spurs: Nietzsche's Styles, translated by Barbara Harlow, Chicago, University of Chicago Press, 1979.

La Carte postale de Socrate à Freud et au-delà, Paris, Flammarion, 1980.

Dissemination, translated by Barbara Johnson, Chicago, University of Chicago Press, 1981.

Positions, translated by Alan Bass, Chicago, University of Chicago Press, 1981.

Margins of Philosophy, translated by Alan Bass, Chicago, University of Chicago Press, 1982.

"The Principle of Reason: The University in the Eyes of its Pupils," *Diacritics*, 13, no. 3 (1983), 3–20.

"No Apocalypse, Not Now," *Diacritics*, 14, no. 2 (1984), 20–31.

"Of an Apocalyptic Tone Recently Adopted in Philosophy," *Oxford Literary Review*, 6, no. 2 (1984), 3–37.

Signéponge = *Signsponge*, translated by Richard Rand, New York, Columbia University Press, 1984.

Northrop Frye

Fearful Symmetry: A Study of William Blake, Princeton, Princeton University Press, (1947) 1970.

Anatomy of Criticism: Four Essays, Princeton, Princeton University Press, (1957) 1973.

The Educated Imagination, Bloomington, Indiana University Press, (1963) 1964.

T. S. Eliot, London, Oliver & Boyd, 1963.
Fables of Identity: Studies in Poetic Mythology, New York, Harcourt, Brace & World, 1963.
The Well-Tempered Critic, Bloomington, Indiana University Press, (1963) 1977.
Five Essays on Milton's Epics, London, Routledge & Kegan Paul, (1965) 1966.
A Natural Perspective: The Development of Shakespearean Comedy and Romance, New York, Columbia University Press, (1965) 1967.
Fools of Time: Studies in Shakespearean Tragedy, Toronto, University of Toronto Press, (1967) 1977.
The Modern Century, New York, Oxford University Press, (1967) 1969.
A Study of English Romanticism, New York, Random House, 1968.
The Stubborn Structure: Essays on Criticism and Society, London, Methuen, 1970.
The Critical Path: An Essay on the Social Context of Literary Criticism, Bloomington, Indiana University Press, (1971) 1973.
"The Definition of a University," in Bruce Rusk (ed.), *Alternatives in Education*, London, University of London Press, 1972, pp. 41-59.
The Secular Scripture: A Study of the Structure of Romance, Cambridge, Mass., Harvard University Press, (1976) 1978.
Spiritus Mundi: Essays on Literature, Myth and Society, Bloomington, Indiana University Press, 1976.
"Presidential Address 1976," *PMLA*, 92 (1977), 385-91.
The Great Code: The Bible and Literature, Toronto, Academic Press, 1982.

Harold Bloom

"A New Poetics," review of *Anatomy of Criticism* by Northrop Frye, *Yale Review*, 47 (1957), 130-3.
Shelley's Mythmaking, New Haven, Yale University Press, 1959.
The Visionary Company: A Reading of English Romantic Poetry, London, Faber & Faber, (1961) 1962.
Blake's Apocalypse: A Study in Poetic Argument, London, Gollancz, 1963.
Yeats, New York, Oxford University Press, 1970.
The Ringers in the Tower: Studies in Romantic Tradition, Chicago, University of Chicago Press, (1971) 1973.
The Anxiety of Influence: A Theory of Poetry, New York, Oxford University Press, (1973) 1978.
A Map of Misreading, New York, Oxford University Press, 1975.
Kabbalah and Criticism, New York, Seabury Press, 1975.
Figures of Capable Imagination, New York, Seabury Press, 1976.
Poetry and Repression: Revisionism from Blake to Stevens, New Haven, Yale University Press, 1976.
Wallace Stevens: The Poems of Our Climate, Ithaca, Cornell University Press, 1977.
"The Breaking of Form," in *Deconstruction and Criticism*, New York/London, Seabury Press/Routledge & Kegan Paul, 1979, pp. 1-37.
Agon: Towards a Theory of Revisionism, New York, Oxford University Press, 1982.
The Breaking of the Vessels, Chicago, University of Chicago Press, 1982.

Geoffrey Hartman

The Unmediated Vision: An Interpretation of Wordsworth, Hopkins, Rilke, and Valéry, New York, Harcourt, Brace & World, (1954) 1966.
André Malraux, London, Bowes & Bowes, 1960.
Wordsworth's Poetry, 1787-1814, New Haven, Yale University Press, (1964) 1971.

Beyond Formalism: Literary Essays, 1958-1970, New Haven, Yale University Press, 1970.
The Fate of Reading and Other Essays, Chicago, University of Chicago Press, 1975.
Criticism in the Wilderness: The Study of Literature Today, New Haven, Yale University Press, 1980.
Saving the Text: Literature, Derrida, Philosophy, Baltimore, Johns Hopkins University Press, 1981.
Easy Pieces, New York, Columbia University Press, 1985.

Frank Kermode

Romantic Image, London, Routledge & Kegan Paul, 1957.
Wallace Stevens, London, Oliver & Boyd, 1960.
Puzzles and Epiphanies, London, Routledge & Kegan Paul, 1962.
The Sense of an Ending: Studies in the Theory of Fiction, New York, Oxford University Press, 1967.
Continuities, London, Routledge & Kegan Paul, 1968.
Modern Essays, London, Collins, 1971.
Shakespeare, Spenser, Donne: Renaissance Essays, London, Routledge & Kegan Paul, 1971.
D. H. Lawrence, New York, Viking, 1973.
The Classic: Literary Images of Permanence and Change, Cambridge, Mass., Harvard University Press, (1975) 1983.
The Genesis of Secrecy, Cambridge, Mass., Harvard University Press, 1979.
The Art of Telling: Essays on Fiction, Cambridge, Mass., Harvard University Press, 1983.
"The Decline of the Man of Letters," *Partisan Review*, 52 (1985), 195-209.
Forms of Attention, Chicago, University of Chicago Press, 1985.

Edward Said

Joseph Conrad and the Fiction of Autobiography, Cambridge, Mass., Harvard University Press, 1966.
Beginnings: Intention and Method, New York, Basic Books, 1975.
Orientalism, New York, Pantheon Books, 1978.
The Question of Palestine, New York, Vintage Books, (1979) 1980.
Covering Islam: How the Media and the Experts Determine How We See the Rest of the World, London, Routledge & Kegan Paul, 1981.
The World, the Text, and the Critic, London, Faber & Faber, (1983) 1984.

Barbara Johnson

Défigurations du Langage Poétique: La Seconde Révolution Baudelairienne, Paris, Flammarion, 1979.
The Critical Difference: Essays in the Contemporary Rhetoric of Reading, Baltimore, Johns Hopkins University Press, (1980) 1985.
"Editor's Preface: Teaching as a Literary Genre," *Yale French Studies*, no. 63 (1982), iii-vii.
"Teaching Ignorance: *L'Ecole des Femmes*," *Yale French Studies*, no. 63 (1982), 165-82.
"Gender Theory and the Yale School," in Robert Con Davis and Ronald Schleifer (eds), *Rhetoric and Form: Deconstruction at Yale*, Norman, University of Oklahoma Press, 1985, pp. 101-12.

"Rigorous Unreliability," *Yale French Studies*, no. 69 (1985), 73–80.

Frank Lentricchia

The Gaiety of Language: An Essay on the Radical Poetics of W. B. Yeats and Wallace Stevens, Berkeley, University of California Press, 1968.
Robert Frost: Modern Poetics and the Landscapes of Self, Durham, NC, Duke University Press, 1975.
After the New Criticism, Chicago, University of Chicago Press, 1980.
"Reading Foucault," *Raritan*, 1 (1982), no. 4, 5–32; 2 (1982), no. 1, 41–70.
Criticism and Social Change, Chicago, University of Chicago Press, 1983.
"On Behalf of Theory," in Gerald Graff and Reginald Gibbons (eds), *Criticism in the University*, Evanston, Northwestern University Press, 1985, pp. 105–10.

J. Hillis Miller

The Disappearance of God: Five Nineteenth-Century Writers, Cambridge, Mass., Harvard University Press, 1963.
Charles Dickens: The World of His Novels, Cambridge, Mass., Harvard University Press, 1965.
Poets of Reality: Six Twentieth-Century Writers, Cambridge, Mass., Harvard University Press, 1965.
The Form of Victorian Fiction, Notre Dame, University of Notre Dame Press, 1968.
Thomas Hardy: Distance and Desire, Cambridge, Mass., Harvard University Press, 1970.
"Georges Poulet's 'Criticism of Identification'," in O. B. Hardison (ed.), *The Quest for Imagination*, Cleveland, Case Western Reserve University Press, 1971, pp. 191–224.
"The Critic as Host," in *Deconstruction and Criticism*, New York/London, Seabury Press/Routledge & Kegan Paul, 1979, pp. 217–53.
"Theory and Practice: Response to Vincent Leitch," *Critical Inquiry*, 6 (1980), 609–14.
Fiction and Repetition: Seven English Novels, Cambridge, Mass., Harvard University Press, 1982.
The Linguistic Moment: From Wordsworth to Stevens, Princeton, Princeton University Press, 1985.
"President's Column: Responsibility and the Joy of Reading," *MLA Newsletter*, 18 (1986), no. 1, 2.